PRAISE FOR *REIMAGINING OPERATIONAL EXCELLENCE*

"This breakthrough book introduces a new genre of entrepreneurship marketing that uses operational excellence to drive efficiencies and value propositions and allows businesses to adapt to emerging threats and opportunities—a guideline for businesses on dealing with market dynamics. Vivid role models from the best practices throughout Asia show how."

> —David Aaker, vice chair, Prophet; author, *The Future of Purpose-Driven Branding*; called by Phil Kotler "the father of modern branding"

"This book, by three exceptional authors, is an excellent treatise on the importance of operations and, more tellingly, how to approach that responsibility. There is a lot in here for seasoned executives who are open to being challenged with new viewpoints and just as much for those new to management. I urge everyone to set aside time to read this book. The case studies are excellent and highly instructive."

> —Gerald Zaltman, Joseph C. Wilson Professor Emeritus, Harvard Business School; cofounding partner, Olson Zaltman

"Drawing from a rich tapestry of case studies and experiences across Asia, this book reshapes our understanding of operational excellence. It provides fresh perspectives that are both inspiring and pragmatically instructive—an invaluable resource for leaders and professionals looking to harness the pioneering spirit of Asian business practices."

> —Professor Dr. Marc Oliver Opresnik, Distinguished Professor of Marketing, Lübeck University of Applied Sciences, Germany

"*Reimagining Operational Excellence* not only offers a playbook for exceptional performance, it does so by sharing brilliance from across Asia. Every executive aspiring to global excellence should prioritize this book."

> —Robert C. Wolcott, PhD, venture investor, advisor, and author of *Proximity*; adjunct professor of innovation, University of Chicago and Northwestern University

"Customer centricity, speed, flexibility, and execution are the keys to success in this fast-paced world. *Reimagining Operational Excellence* will show you how companies can better orchestrate strategic business functions and position themselves stronger in a fierce competition to win in the digital economy."

—**José Salibi Neto, founder, HSM; coauthor, *Disruptive Leadership: Transformative Skills and Competencies to Lead in a Technology-Driven World***

REIMAGINING OPERATIONAL EXCELLENCE

PHILIP KOTLER
HERMAWAN KARTAJAYA
JACKY MUSSRY

REIMAGINING OPERATIONAL EXCELLENCE

INSPIRATIONS FROM ASIA

WILEY

Published by John Wiley & Sons, Inc., Hoboken, New Jersey.
Published simultaneously in Canada.

For general information on our other products and services or for technical support, please contact our Customer Care Department within the United States at (800) 762-2974, outside the United States at (317) 572-3993 or fax (317) 572-4002.

Wiley also publishes its books in a variety of electronic formats. Some content that appears in print may not be available in electronic formats. For more information about Wiley products, visit our web site at **www.wiley.com**.

Library of Congress Cataloging-in-Publication Data is available:

ISBN 9781394239245 (Cloth)
ISBN 9781394239252 (epub)
ISBN 9781394239269 (epdf)

Cover Image and Design: © M Corp
SKY10078110_062124

Here is the best guide to our future marketers for achieving operational excellence and job success.

—Philip Kotler

To the Asia Marketing Federation (AMF) with its 18 countries/ economic regions that support the "Asia to the World!" spirit.

—Hermawan Kartajaya

To my late parents, Charles and Djoewati.

—Jacky Mussry

Contents

Foreword

In the ever-changing business world, where adaptability is the key to success and innovation is the lifeblood of progress, the book *Reimagining Operational Excellence: Inspirations from Asia* couldn't be more timely. The book is a sequel to *Entrepreneurial Marketing: Beyond Professionalism to Creativity, Leadership, and Creativity* and dives even deeper into the intricacies of modern marketing, illuminating the path to operational excellence in an era characterized by dynamic change and heightened expectations.

Building on the foundations laid in the previous book, the authors turn our attention to operations, the core of the holistic omnihouse model. Here, operations emerge as the lynchpin that connects the seemingly disparate realms of entrepreneurship and professionalism. Through careful analysis and insightful commentary, the book shows how the symbiotic relationship between these two areas of expertise forms the pillars of quality, cost, delivery, and service (QCDS), culminating in the achievement of operational excellence.

What makes this book special is that it draws on real-life examples from the vibrant Asian business landscape. Asia is rightly seen as the rising model. The case studies from South Korea, India, Japan, Singapore, and China illustrate that cultural and organizational contexts manifest themselves in outstanding capabilities. From the surprising Korean wave to the meticulous productivity of Japan, each case study is a testament to the profound impact of entrepreneurial and professional capabilities on QCDS metrics and, by extension, operational excellence.

The book's narrative goes beyond a purely academic discourse; it serves as a pragmatic guide for individuals and organizations alike. Whether you are a student seeking to understand the nuances of modern marketing paradigms, an entrepreneur navigating the turbulent waters of a startup, or a seasoned practitioner seeking sustainable growth, this book will provide invaluable insight to help you move forward.

As we stand on the cusp of the environmental, social, and governance era, where such considerations are paramount, the lessons set out in these pages are all the more relevant. They serve as a guide for companies of all sizes, challenging them to embrace innovation, cultivate leadership, and promote a culture of sustainability.

Philip Kotler, Hermawan Kartajaya, and Jacky Mussry invite us on a transformative journey that crosses boundaries, defies convention, and charts a path to a future where operational excellence is not just a goal but a reality.

—Professor Hermann Simon
Bonn/Germany, summer 2024

Preface: The Next-Level Operations in the Next Curve

The world is indeed very dynamic and unpredictable. The COVID-19 pandemic has subsided, and everything is back in full swing, but we are all still exposed to various classic problems such as climate issues, geopolitical tensions (which have led to conflicts and even wars in different parts of the world), various social and humanitarian issues, and the vulnerable economic conditions. The continuing acceleration of technological developments in multiple fields also keeps shaking up the world and bringing humankind into an increasingly complex landscape of never-imagined challenges.

Regardless of these dynamics, business must continue, with an even stronger focus on environment, social, and governance (ESG) factors. Our book *Entrepreneurial Marketing: Beyond Professionalism to Creativity, Leadership, and Sustainability* (Wiley, 2023) explains that conventional or procedural approaches are insufficient and will no longer be able to provide adequate results. To survive and develop in these challenging conditions, a business organization must apply an expanded marketing approach by integrating various dichotomous capabilities to increase its agility, flexibility, and resiliency.

The concept of this holistic approach is summarized in the *omnihouse model*, where the core component that can facilitate an organization's success is the operations aspect. Operations become an essential bridge between various dichotomous elements in the model. Operations can understand what the marketing department wants to achieve and, at the same time, help fulfill the finance department's primary goals. Operations can ensure that the use of advanced technology is genuinely humanity-oriented. Operations also become a bridge between two dichotomous clusters, namely, entrepreneurial and professionalism capabilities.

These two clusters of entrepreneurship and professionalism can influence operational excellence through quality, cost, delivery, and service (QCDS).[1] Business organizations need a higher level of operational excellence to continue on the next curve toward 2025 and their journey to 2030 and beyond. In the next curve, operational excellence will be one of the critical determinants of whether our company will grow, stagnate, or even decline. Therefore, we must leverage all the momentum available with all our capabilities.

It is difficult for companies to have all the capabilities contained in the omnihouse model. However, limited capabilities do not mean the company cannot influence the QCDS aspect and ultimately achieve solid operational excellence.

This book attempts to present examples from various Asian countries that have gone through different processes on their respective journeys to nurture the formation of multiple capabilities, which became the foundation for many companies in each country to become competitive global players.

Why Asia? When the International Monetary Fund (IMF) predicted the performance of the world economy in 2023, with a total global gross domestic product (GDP) of US$105 trillion, Asia's GDP was expected to reach US$35.8 trillion, or the equivalent of 34% of the worldwide GDP. This portion exceeded North and Central America's total GDP of US$31.3 trillion (equivalent to 29.7% of global GDP), making Asia the world's largest economy.[2] The dominance of Asia's economy, with China as the leading player, is expected to continue, which, according to Goldman Sachs projections, will reach a total GDP of US$90.6 trillion, or almost 40% of the total global GDP of US$227.9 trillion.[3]

Apart from that, we can be inspired by some Asian countries that have succeeded in overcoming various tough challenges so that they can compete and stand on an equal footing with Western countries that have advanced far, even when these Asian countries were still starting to build their capabilities from scratch or even did not have any capabilities at all. We can see it from the long and arduous journey of various Asian countries becoming countries with a solid industrial base and, in turn, able to stand on the global stage.

We can concisely understand this long journey from the various backgrounds of some countries and how they eventually became very competitive globally. However, it should be noted that there is no guarantee that the countries referenced in this book will remain competitive in the long run. Everything depends on so many factors, including how the government and society in each country take advantage of the existing momentum and how committed they are to developing relevant capabilities and competencies from time to time. Furthermore, individuals, companies, and even countries must collaborate with others to face a world that is often hostile. Collaboration can positively affect individuals, communities, companies, industries, and even a country.

This book will briefly review the concept of operational excellence and examine how the various elements of the entrepreneurship and professionalism clusters affect QCDS. Converging these two clusters is an essential foundation for forming a company's adaptive capabilities in the long term.

In line with the increasingly complex nature of defining quality, we will explore how the new quality perspective is closely related to sustainability or ESG aspects, encouraging companies to continue strengthening their stakeholder-centric orientation to affect society. Cost elements can no longer rely merely on a cost-cutting approach but must align with social values that refer to humanity. An environmental-related cost reduction, for example, will be able to provide a very relevant social contribution.

In line with the growing importance of ESG aspects, technology-based product delivery (reflected by the rapid growth of e-commerce) will cause a significant shift from *on-estimate* to *on-conscience* delivery methods to provide optimal customer experience. Likewise, the supporting services required will shift from standard to transformational service. Service will also take an essential role in line with various social changes through transformative service.

After understanding operational excellence and QCDS, we will see many stories from various Asian countries, each capable of influencing operational excellence. South Korea is powerful in creativity and innovation capabilities, ultimately creating a *hallyu* effect and bringing multiple companies and brands from that country to become world-class solid players. Samsung, for example, has succeeded in building extraordinary operational excellence based on robust creativity and innovation capabilities.

In addition, we will look at India, which has succeeded in building strong entrepreneurship and leadership capabilities shaped by its unique social, cultural, economic, and environmental backgrounds. It is no longer strange to hear that many large world-class companies worldwide are now led by made-in-India leaders.

Japan—an icon for its productivity and improvement capabilities—is where the post–World War II concept of Kaizen originated, making it synonymous with productivity and continuous improvement. Even though it has often been discussed in various literature, it would feel incomplete if we did not highlight the journey of how Toyota became one of the most outstanding automotive companies in the world despite the decline in Toyota's share price at the end of 2023 due to scandals in several Toyota's subsidiaries, among others: safety-test scandal at Daihatsu, emission scandal at Hino Motors, and data scandal in several diesel engines including for the Land Cruiser 300 and Hilux. However, until early 2024, Toyota could remain the world's number one player in the car market.[4]

We will also learn from a small country with extraordinary capabilities that have made it one of the leading countries in the world: Singapore. We will examine how professionalism and managerial capabilities are ingrained in Singaporean society and have led to extraordinary achievements in various institutions, both government and corporations. At least these two capabilities have made Singapore a global hub. It is an outstanding achievement for a small island country that covers an area of about 730 square kilometers, slightly bigger than the city of Jakarta. All of Singapore's accomplishments were initiated with hard work and discipline since the era of Singapore's founding father, Lee Kuan Yew. Who doesn't know Singapore Airlines? Did you know that one of the universities from Singapore is included in the top 10 ranking of the world's best universities?[5]

As a finale, we will explore China, one of the global economic powerhouses that has successfully built its omni capabilities, which has significantly affected its ability to create operational excellence through robust execution. China's path to achieve what it has achieved today is a long journey from various eras of leadership with different revolutionary focuses: the cultural revolution under Mao Zedong, the economic revolution under Deng Xiaoping, and the social revolution under Xi Jinping. China has successfully converged and balanced its entrepreneurial capabilities with those of its professional capabilities (a combination of creativity and productivity, innovation and improvement, entrepreneurship and professionalism, and leadership and management), making China a supreme global player.

By understanding the concepts of operational excellence, QCDS, and various entrepreneurial and professional capabilities, which are a subset of the new genre of entrepreneurial marketing, it is hoped that we can make business organizations more competitive and even have a more robust existence in the long term. We can learn valuable lessons from the various examples presented in this book. Suppose we can apply this next level of operational excellence in our company. In that case, we will have more significant opportunities to use all the potential of our company, which in turn can ensure our company participates, survives, and even becomes an important player on the world stage, now and in the next curve.

So, happy reading. Be inspired!

Acknowledgments

The authors are grateful for the invaluable support and encouragement from the entire management team of M Corp, especially the leadership team: Michael Hermawan, Taufik, Vivie Jericho, Iwan Setiawan, Ence, Estania Rimadini, and Yosanova Savitry.

A special thank-you and highest appreciation to Victoria Savanh, who managed and directed the writing process of this book from the beginning until its publication. The authors would like to thank the editorial team at Wiley for their fantastic attention and collaboration at every stage of the writing process for this book: Deborah Schindlar, Michael Joseph Das, Susan Geraghty, Thandapani Sudhagaran, and Kim Wimpsett.

We would also like to thank and give a thumbs up to the MarkPlus Institute team, who has worked tirelessly for almost one year to help conduct research, brainstorm with authors, and prepare many valuable materials. Special thanks to colleagues who have devoted their energy, time, and thoughts and involved deeply in the preparation and writing process of several chapters: Taufik (Chapters 2, 4, and 6), Yosanova Savitry (Chapters 10 and 11), Ardhi Ridwansyah (Chapters 7, 8, and 9), and Giovanni Panudju (Appendixes B, C, and D).

Special thanks and appreciation to Raditya Yusril, who has helped with excellent coordination and played a significant role in the research and writing process, as well as in organizing meetings and brainstorming. Appreciation also goes to Felix Rahardja and his team, who helped design the cover of this book, and also to Nabilah Ainurrahmah, who prepared various figures for each chapter in this book.

With deep appreciation, we also wish to acknowledge the support from the member organizations of the Asia Marketing Federation and the Asia Committee for Small Business.

CHAPTER 1

Operations as the Center of Gravity

The Omnihouse Model

If you picked up this book, you are probably familiar with the term *entrepreneurial marketing*—not the mainstream one but the new genre that essentially attempts to converge various dichotomous elements (i.e., entrepreneurial and professional mindsets) in a business organization. This holistic approach enables companies to be agile, flexible, and resilient in facing the fast-paced, ever-changing, and uncertain business landscape. But when we review the model, namely, the omnihouse model, it is not the marketing element that is the center of the model; it is operations (see Figure 1.1).

> **Note**
>
> Appendix A provides the details of the omnihouse model for those not familiar with it. We also recommend our book *Entrepreneurial Marketing: Beyond Professionalism to Creativity, Leadership, and Sustainability* to learn more about the model.

In this book, we will explore this aspect of operations by looking at how the various elements of the entrepreneurship cluster and the professionalism cluster have an impact on quality, cost, and delivery

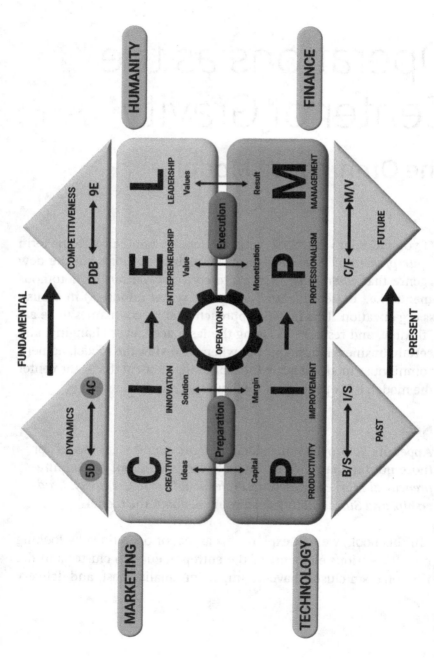

FIGURE 1.1 The omnihouse model

(according to the concept developed by Masaaki Imai) plus service (QCDS). In Figure 1.1, you can note the following:

- The entrepreneurship cluster is sandwiched between marketing and humanity and consists of creativity, innovation, entrepreneurship, and leadership (CI-EL).
- The professionalism cluster sits between technology and finance and consists of productivity, improvement, professionalism, and management (PI-PM).

We will use examples from companies in various Asian countries and other parts of the world in line with Asia's increasingly significant role in the world economy in recent decades. At least five Asian countries (China, India, Indonesia, Japan, and South Korea) are now members of the G20.

Introducing a New Model of Entrepreneurial Marketing

The concept of a new genre of entrepreneurial marketing discussed in this book was developed because of our experience from the crisis triggered by the COVID-19 pandemic: a company cannot survive if it relies only on a professional management approach. The business is constantly changing; hence, management needs to change accordingly. Competitive companies constantly adapt, either incrementally or radically.

DuPont is one example of how gradually adapting can become a company's foundation and even make it more competitive. DuPont started as a producer of gunpowder and explosives needed during the Civil War. Over time, DuPont gradually adapted and eventually developed a wide range of products that are part of our daily lives, such as synthetic rubber, polyester, nylon, and Teflon—which also entered into a diverse set of fields: health care, electronics, and nutrition. That expansion was also made possible through the company's exceptional commitment to R&D.[1]

Something similar happened in the case of PPG Industries, Inc., which produced only plate glass when it was founded in 1883. Now, it has diversified with various products covering all types of glass, chemicals, paints, optical materials, and biomedical systems.[2]

Some companies' small but high-speed adaptive capabilities during the COVID-19 pandemic saved their future. CareSignal, a remote patient monitoring platform, created a new service line to provide COVID-19 education when they realized the pandemic would significantly affect their business. It took the CareSignal team only a few days to set up and launch the new service, which was called COVID Companion and was designed to monitor health care workers exposed to or infected with COVID-19 and low-risk patients who could manage their illness at home. It provided a dedicated platform for remote monitoring and helped health care system manage the surge in cases and ensure the safety of both patients and staff.[3] Chemical producer BASF also made a gradual transformation to improve competitiveness and secure long-term growth several years ago. Various acquisition and divestment efforts are expected to generate significant cumulative transformation and impact.[4]

Some other companies have opted for radical transformations. Let's look at Apple's journey. It started out by making computers and software but then quickly expanded to offer various products, from music streaming and AI-powered personal assistants to wearables. Likewise, Netflix started as a DVD rental service but underwent an extraordinary revamp and eventually became a major player in streaming entertainment, including creating content.[5] After Netflix made changes to its business model and in line with technological developments, in 2015 the Netflix streaming business (domestic and international) contributed nearly 90% to the company's revenue.

German steel maker ThyssenKrupp also demonstrated a radical approach. Faced with pressure from competitors from low-cost producers in Asia, ThyssenKrupp took a drastic step: leaving the business of making and selling steel. In 2012, the company began investing in industrial solutions, providing capital equipment, software, and services to manufacturers, including refineries and automakers, which then grew very fast and now contribute almost half of the company's total revenue.[6]

With examples like these, we can understand a new type of entrepreneurial marketing that helps business organizations become highly adaptive and avoid marketing blind spots, such as ignoring changes in the macroenvironment, misalignment of marketing and finance, disharmonious marketing and sales relationships, weak integration of online and offline marketing, overlooking human capital, and lacking humanity in marketing. Marketing blind spots are a condition in which a company has carried out various marketing management processes properly but does not realize there are still many unconnected elements that hinder the company and ultimately cause it to lose its ability to compete.

The essence of the new genre of entrepreneurial marketing is about converging the various dichotomies within the organization itself. Learning from the phenomenon of marketing blind spots, a business organization must be able to converge elements of marketing and finance, technology and humanity, as well as the two main clusters in the omnihouse model that have so far been considered opposites, namely, the "entrepreneurship" cluster (which consists of components of creativity, innovation, entrepreneurship, and leadership) and the "professionalism" cluster (which includes productivity, improvement, professionalism, and management). This convergence process—let alone combining two opposing mindsets—as a holistic approach to the new genre of entrepreneurial marketing is not easy, especially if an organization has significant rigidity and inertia.

Forming an interconnected, flexible, and results-driven organization will put immense pressure on the operational aspect, because it must balance rigidity and flexibility to remain relevant in a dynamic business environment, increase organizational survivability in various turmoils, and be sustainable in the long term.

Reviewing Operational Excellence

In the past, certain companies wielded operational excellence as a crucial element in their competitive advantage, providing new insights regarding operational excellence that we often refer to today.[7] Examples include the following companies:

- Ford introduced the conveyor belt assembly line, which is the cornerstone of modern mass production processes.
- Toyota put forward the concept of continuous improvement and a production system "just in time."
- Amazon is a digital era icon that combines process orchestration with digital technology support that can integrate online virtual worlds with the real world.

When achieved, operational excellence can optimize business processes to increase efficiency and productivity, affecting the company's operating margin, net profit, employee turnover, and customer satisfaction. Additionally, the engagement of workers with their companies will increase and can positively affect companies' profitability and employee turnover. Finally, business organizations that achieve operational excellence will become agile and flexible and have a sustainable competitive advantage. In short, operational excellence is a long-term strategic role for the company.[8]

Operational excellence is strategic for companies because it has several essential characteristics:

- **Focus on value creation.** Operations are the fulcrum of various organizational departments that form an integrated value chain within a company. Operations is an intermediary between marketing, which usually focuses on the top line, and finance, which prioritizes the bottom line in the income statement.
- **Maximize efficiency.** Operational excellence significantly affects a business organization's efficiency (and, in turn, productivity) through various cost/expenditure savings, which significantly increase operating margins and net profitability.
- **Support innovation.** Operational excellence enables companies to have sensitivity, adaptive ability, and flexibility to deal with various changes in the business environment, see new problems and challenges, and immediately respond in the form of innovations.
- **Nurture improvement.** Operational excellence encourages everyone involved to have a good understanding of what is going on in the company, what is going well and what is not, so that

everyone can make the necessary improvements in various value-creation processes on a day-to-day basis.

- **Improve competitiveness.** Having better operational excellence than competitors will improve a company's competitive position in an industry and business competition in general and provide an opportunity to be more sustainable than its competitors.
- **Focus on people.** Operational excellence can be achieved only with strong employee engagement. Therefore, it is a consequence for the company to provide the best for its employees so that they also offer the best for the company in all processes, from production, distribution, and sales to services.
- **Put customers first.** The best of operational excellence is offering customers the highest quality products and services that can be delivered according to customer expectations at the most optimal costs to provide reasonable prices.
- **Implement sustainability.** Through various improvements and innovations, companies can develop operational excellence oriented toward sustainability and, even more broadly, on the environmental, social, and governance (ESG) aspects through implementing cleaner/greener processes, reducing waste, implementing a circular economy, and so on.

These strategic aspects are why the operations element is central to the omnihouse model of entrepreneurial marketing.

Moving Toward Flexible Operations

The new entrepreneurial marketing concept of operations as the center of gravity emphasizes that companies must be able to converge professional and entrepreneurial capabilities to advance toward a successful future. Hence, companies must possess strategic flexibility because managing rigidity and flexibility is critical.[9]

Companies can no longer be fixated on improving business by pursuing only efficiency improvements, which will later be reflected in various financial ratios such as return on sales, asset turnover, return on assets, return on equity, and so on. So, high flexibility in the operational aspect required to deal with the ever-changing market becomes increasingly crucial in the current and future complex business environment.[10]

The business environment is becoming increasingly complex, aligning with the involvement of companies in the business ecosystem (both conventional and digital). This ecosystem provides a substantial entry barrier, solutions for more extensive problems, and versatile platforms. As companies become more integrated, operations must be able to execute various value creation and objectives from multiple functions, including marketing and finance. Additionally, operations must realize the idea of technology for humanity.[11]

Stretching the Flexibility Frontier

The active involvement of companies in a business ecosystem requires a more advanced form of operational excellence. Hence, operations must rely on more than just the company's internal resources and capabilities due to dynamic interactions with multiple parties in a business ecosystem increasingly influencing them. The company's flexibility will be significantly affected by several characteristics that form the company's new operational excellence (see Figure 1.2), namely, the following:[12]

- **Seamless interdependency.** The integration of a company depends on the number of parties that cooperate with it in the same business ecosystem, the extent of interdependence, and the seamlessness of the relationship. The more parties that collaborate, the higher the interdependence, and the more seamless the relationship, the higher the integration is formed.

- **Flawless compatibility.** Companies must examine the compatibility of technology used in their operational activities with other organizations in the same ecosystem. Additionally, organizations must employ a similar process, methodology, protocol, governance references, and culture. The more perfect the compatibility with other organizations in terms of process, methodology,

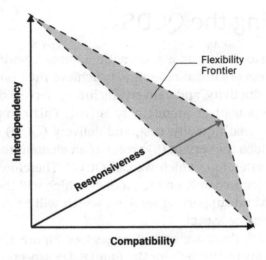

FIGURE 1.2   Stretching the flexibility frontier

protocol (including IT protocol), governance references, organizational structure/flow/bureaucracy, vision, mission, and culture in a business ecosystem, the more it shows the character of operational excellence.

- **Immediate responsiveness.** Companies can use a business ecosystem to remain relevant in an ever-changing business environment, responding quickly to changes even if they show discontinuous trajectories. The faster the operational responsiveness of the company supported by its ecosystem, the stronger the indication that the company is performing operational excellence.

Suppose companies have increasingly seamless interdependencies, have flawless compatibility, and can respond to changes in the business environment, including various changes in the market or industry. In that case, companies can push the flexibility frontier further to gain capabilities beyond the operational excellence we have known.[13] Every company needs a post-operational excellence capability that enables it to create a competitive advantage (through operational competitive advantage), which is essential for fast organizational learning processes and making changes accordingly.[14]

Stretching the QCDS

Operational excellence, as a systematic approach widely applied in various business organizations, aims to achieve the best performance in quality, productivity, and delivery, including service delivery.[15] One reference component of productivity is cost. This component aligns with Masaaki Imai's quality, cost, and delivery (QCD) concept.[16] We add to Imai's idea the service (S) aspect as an element that needs to be given greater attention, which we call QCDS. Therefore, the delivery aspect will be focused only on the product, which will then be complemented by several supporting services, which will be discussed separately in the service aspect.

If simplified, there are several stages (see Figure 1.3) that a company will usually go through for the four QCDS aspects.

Stage 1: Divisional-Centric QCDS

At this stage, quality is still determined by the input. The company seeks to find the best inputs (from various suppliers) at the lowest possible prices, which will later be used in the production process. Therefore, the purchasing or procurement department/division role is very central. The company's financial orientation is still on cutting costs as much as possible—especially when input prices cannot be reduced to become cheaper—without overthinking the indirect impact. Most important, costs must be kept as low as possible to lower production, primarily to increase profitability.

The delivery of products (goods and services) depends on the company's readiness or other reasons, such as meeting a minimum quantity or economies of scale. Therefore, companies can often provide only an estimate to their customers regarding when their products can be delivered (and received). The support services offered are standard (with rigid procedures) and apply equally to all customers.

Stage 2: Company-Centric QCDS

The company's value chain has been prioritized to focus on producing the best quality product from inputs and production processes. The company's financial direction is more on cost reduction, namely,

Extension →

ELEMENT (Expansion ↓)	STAGE: S1 Divisional-Centric	S2 Company-Centric	S3 Customer-Centric	S4 Stakeholder-Centric
Quality	Input	Output	Outcome	Impact
Cost	Cost cutting	Cost reduction	Customer value optimization	Social values contribution
Delivery	On estimate	On schedule	On demand	On conscience
Service	Standardization	Personalization	Customization	Transformation

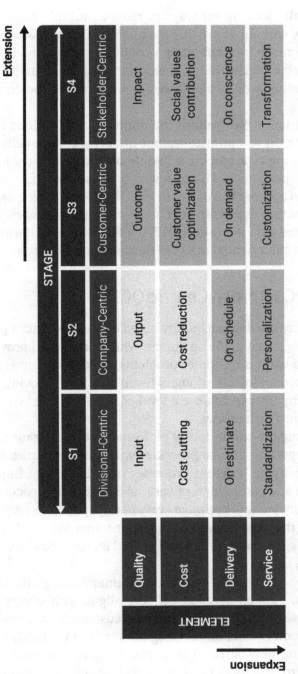

FIGURE 1.3 Stages of QCDS

systematically looking for ways to reduce multiple costs to increase profitability without sacrificing the quality of its products. Cost reduction can be made by eliminating various wastes, improving efficiency (which affects productivity), ensuring consistent quality control to lower repetitions of work processes or scrap, reducing downtime, and so on.

The company has realized the importance of various elements in the value chain to optimize output quality. Product delivery can be done according to a specific schedule with different choices to meet customer expectations. The company has also started applying a personalization approach to a certain level for its customers, especially for the segment that significantly contributes to its total sales. The role of enterprise resource planning (ERP) is vital. However, this input-output approach is still oriented solely to the company's interests.

Stage 3: Customer-Centric QCDS

The company has defined quality based on the customer's perspective, and this is reflected in the outcomes, which can indeed provide diverse solutions to various customer problems, making customers feel satisfied and become loyal customers (even willing to provide advocacy), and the company can achieve a level of sales that can be immediately converted into cash inflow.

The company continuously performs cost optimization, for example, by integrating diverse processes with various parties in a supply chain, simplifying different processes or bureaucracy, implementing digitization and automation of various operational aspects, and so on. The company seeks to optimize every penny spent for everything it can get and, at the same time, maximize customer value. This effort will reduce costs, improve output quality, and increase business value (and profitability).

Delivery can already be done on-demand according to customer preferences. This on-demand delivery aligns with efforts to provide supportive services that can already be customized according to individual customer preferences. Integration with the supply chain (both upstream and downstream) is crucial in optimizing customer value. In this regard, the role of customer relationship management as part of ERP is becoming increasingly important, and, likewise, the role of supply chain management is also critical to achieving seamless integration with the supply chain.

Stage 4: Stakeholder-Centric QCDS

The company has defined the quality of its products based on their impact on the broader community, including those related to the environment. Various considerations of costs are no longer purely monetary but take into account different social costs. The company already has a systematic approach to eliminate various outputs that harm society. The company has placed social values as a reference in setting quality standards, such as providing high-quality products through a green process, enforcing a low (or even no) carbon footprint policy, using recycled materials, implementing a strict circular economy regimen, and many other results. The ESG criteria, which are sustainability benchmarks considering various impacts on stakeholders, have been implemented.

Delivery also provides a broader choice, not only on demand but also by implementing a delivery system with a less harmful impact on the environment, for example, by using an environmentally friendly transportation mode with low carbon emissions, using packaging that is also environmentally friendly or made of recycled materials, and so on. All refer to a collective conscience to do the best for the broader community and the environment.

Various supporting services are transformative by educating customers to also become more environmentally conscious, for example, implementing a paperless system, involving local communities as part of the service process, implementing the 3R principles (reduce, reuse, and recycle), and so on. Corporate responsibilities are becoming increasingly complex, so not all matters can often be handled by the company alone. Therefore, companies should be part of the business ecosystem to collaborate with various other parties and harness the ecosystem advantages, including streamlining the product development process and supporting services.

Becoming part of an ecosystem will provide companies with broader opportunities to access new sales channels as an alternative or complement existing ones, expand capabilities, strengthen interactions (and even engagement) with customers, and take advantage of various possibilities for developing new products and supporting services.[17]

Looking at the Impact of CI-EL and PI-PM on QCDS

The criteria for quality elements (input and output) and cost (cutting and reduction) in stages 1 and 2 are standard practices in various companies. Therefore, as we embark into the post-operational excellence era, companies must be able to expand the "benefit" approach solely based on quality and cost of delivery and service. In addition, we must also be able to extend from divisional-centric and company-centric to customer-centric and even to stakeholder-centric stages.

It should also be noted that the CI-EL and PI-PM components also influence the operations element as the centerpiece of the omnihouse model (see Figure 1.4).

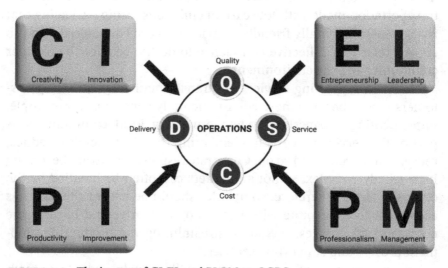

FIGURE 1.4 The impact of CI-EL and PI-PM on QCDS

Creativity and QCDS

According to Enriko Ceko from Canadian University College, creativity and quality management are subjects that have recently attracted the attention of various groups worldwide. His studies show strong evidence of a link between creativity and quality management.[18] The process of creative thinking will encourage the implementation of quality management.[19]

In his article "Quality and Creativity: Enemies or Allies?" Paul Sloane asked a provocative question: Can quality and creativity be on the same side, or are the two opposite? Quality is usually achieved by eliminating unwanted variations, setting strict standards, and eliminating waste and errors. Meanwhile, creativity (and innovation) is concerned with exploring radical, unorthodox ideas, deliberately deviating from existing standards, and often experimenting. It may seem like two opposing philosophies, but both can and should coexist. Every organization must find out how the paradox of creativity and quality will lead to successful innovation.[20]

We need creativity to reduce the company's various costs, especially in times of crisis. We need to be creative in reducing multiple expenses while maintaining the value of the money spent by the company and ensuring that the company's operations continue to run smoothly.[21]

Companies must be creative to reduce costs, especially with increasingly cost-conscious customers. So, companies must think differently, not just how to run the same business more cheaply, but how to do business differently. In short, companies need to run more cheaply and do business differently.[22]

Creativity is essential for product delivery. As many restaurants lost their primary way of delivering food due to the pandemic, they changed the delivery method by sending food orders directly to homes through customer orders, and some even pivoted their business into selling frozen food. This creativity can save a company from bankruptcy.

Creativity is essential for overcoming complex problems due to significant volume problems in handling orders, receiving calls, and answering emails. Creative solutions like chatbots can help maintain service quality, especially during first contact. Creativity drives the team to be more adaptive and brings the company to excellence.[23]

Innovation and QCDS

Marina Artunes, professor at Lisbon Accounting and Business School of the Lisbon Polytechnic Institute, and her colleagues tried to find the connection between innovation and total quality management (TQM). One of the findings is that companies that adopt innovation as their strategy in various processes promote adopting TQM practices. Statistically, there is a significant relationship between product innovation and implementing TQM practices.[24]

Cost innovation aims to increase the value of a business by making various improvements in managing multiple costs. This innovation can be pursued, for example, by automation, which can increase the speed of the production process and improve quality; dematerialization—using less material without compromising the value; using various tools to increase employee productivity; mass customization; and many more.[25]

Various innovations in delivery have enabled us to use autonomous delivery vehicles, which significantly speed up delivery times and reduce labor costs. Warehouse automation is becoming a mainstay for retailers to streamline their supply chains, and using robotics technology with minimal human involvement results in a fast and error-free delivery process. This method can also reduce labor costs, making delivery costs cheaper.[26]

In the service aspect, we also see the role of innovation in making significant changes aimed at simplifying the service process for customers through more accessible and faster ways.[27] Through service innovations in various industrial sectors in different parts of the world, companies can provide more value to customers and, at the same time, increase company revenue since customers are willing to spend more and even give referrals to others.[28]

Entrepreneurship and QCDS

An entrepreneurial mindset encourages people to be creative and innovative to create quality products, improve existing ones, look for opportunities and solutions to society's problems, and enable them to be creative and innovative.[29] Entrepreneurship is driven by individuals with the vision to improve product and life quality for many people worldwide.[30] Entrepreneurship is essential to achieve fast and sustainable economic growth.[31] In a study by Saumyaranjan Sahoo and Sudhir Yadav on hundreds of SMEs in India, it was found that entrepreneurial orientation indirectly affects the firm performance of manufacturing SMEs, which is mediated by TQM.[32]

Researchers in Malaysia proved that entrepreneurial capability has a mediating role between cost management practices and the competitiveness of the strategic priorities of SMEs.[33] Entrepreneurs—in the context of business owners—are responsible for managing production factors and risk to achieve profitability, so they are concerned about reducing costs to attain commensurate margins.[34] This type of professional needs to be able to think, behave, and act like a true entrepreneur while managing a company's business by not only managing production factors but also taking risks. We call these people entrepreneurial professionals.

Leadership and QCDS

Only a little research has been done on the direct effect of leadership on quality. Still, for a long time, the Malcolm Baldrige National Quality Award has included leadership criteria—among several others—to evaluate the quality improvement of various companies in the United States. Quality experts such as Edwards Deming and Joseph Juran have argued that the leadership role of top-level management is crucial in successfully implementing quality management. Their argument is supported by the research conducted by Paul Hirtz and colleagues that show that the type of transformational leadership determines the successful implementation of quality management in the administrative/service domain.[35]

Leaders and their leadership styles affect employee retention. A research study published in early 2020 on employees of manufacturing SMEs in a province in Mainland China shows that a transformational leadership style (moderated by organizational citizenship behavior) affects employee retention. Transformational leadership style can enhance organizational citizenship behavior and employee retention.[36] Good leadership is significant in attracting new talents and maintaining high-quality existing employees.[37] Employee retention needs serious attention because the costs are also high if employee turnover is high. It can reach 1.5 to 2 times the amount of the exiting employee's salary, not to mention several hidden costs, such as advertising costs for recruitment, new employee training, and costs to recover lost productivity.[38] In short, leadership will have an impact on costs.

One of the critical roles of leadership is maintaining values, including brand values. Strong leadership will ensure the company can deliver all its value propositions to customers based on predetermined brand values. Showing what has been promised by a brand is the responsibility of all parties in an organization.[39] Therefore, strong leadership is needed to unify various management functions and direct everyone to the same goal with the same values. Strong leadership can help create a customer-focused environment within a company, positively affecting how it treats its customers in the various services provided.[40]

Research on service quality at a higher education institution found a significant influence of leadership style on faculty service quality: the more substantial the leadership style, the higher the impact.[41] In another survey conducted in dozens of hotels involving more than 200 frontliners, it was found that participative leadership positively influenced the commitment of frontliners to provide quality customer service.[42]

Productivity and QCDS

There is a concern that efforts to increase productivity can worsen quality; in fact, quality can improve accordingly with increased productivity.[43] High productivity demands require companies to create product output with quality according to predetermined specifications, avoiding unnecessary costs such as scrap due to low quality. An intense productivity regimen will lead to high-quality processes and production results.[44]

A strong productivity orientation will reduce costs for each unit of product produced. Higher productivity can be achieved by using materials without waste and creating products that meet specifications. Additionally, labor can be reduced by increasing output with the same number of laborers. A strong productivity orientation will reduce costs for each unit of product produced.

The most critical detail is that a company must pay attention to the production and product delivery processes to increase productivity. So, companies must ensure high accuracy and deliver products that meet customer specifications and can be received or consumed at the agreed time.

Likewise, with service, a company focusing on productivity will put significant effort into delivering quality service efficiently and simultaneously, ensuring a good customer experience.[45] Therefore, companies must continuously identify and eliminate various irrelevant customer services, especially high-cost ones.

Improvement and QCDS

Improvements to product quality and various supporting services are essential in shaping customer satisfaction and loyalty, which will affect the company's business growth (as reflected in improved margins). Furthermore, improvements in the company's various business processes can reduce costs, improving operating margins and net income. Advances in multiple processes so that the quality can improve will affect efficiency and, at the same time, meet the customers' expectations, which are increasingly demanding and challenging to satisfy.[46]

The delivery process, especially in this digital era, is very much determined by the process the first time customers make contact through various digital-based platforms, starting from searching for information, ordering, sending, receiving, and using products to after-sales service, which must be able to provide optimal user experience (UX) overall. Website platforms, for example, must pay attention to design, functionality, content, and usability to meet these UX goals.[47]

Improvement in the service aspect, especially in this digital era, needs to focus on several ways to strengthen digital customer service strategy, which can be summarized into three stages: understanding customer journeys (including their needs), using appropriate technology, and measuring success rates.[48] Digital literacy and technology that mimics human characters are essential for successful service delivery through omnichannels. Companies must be able to determine the proportion of service mix provided conventionally and digitally.

Professionalism and QCDS

Professionalism will strongly affect the quality of the products offered to customers. Every production process—from sourcing various input factors, preparation, and manufacture to the finished product delivered to customers—will determine the overall quality. Professionalism provides consistency in the application of the best procedures in various value-creation processes that result in the production of quality products.

By following obvious procedures, a company avoids various non-value-creating activities to save time, effort, and other resources that avoid cost overruns. Professionalism prevents companies from being inefficient in this manner.

If carried out professionally, delivery will provide certainty to customers because they can clearly understand what is happening, avoiding suspicion and frustration due to various uncertainties. Professionalism will form more robust integrity in the company, essential for creating trust for customers.

Support services that are also delivered professionally will ensure that the company's quality of services are maintained. Professionalism also means consistently monitoring all service touch points, immediately making adjustments if there are discrepancies in service standards, minimizing or even eliminating frustration points, and anticipating failures before they occur.

Management and QCDS

Management of quality, also known as quality management, is a framework used by many companies to ensure constant improvement so that companies can continue to produce the best products and services. Quality management will affect the company's competitive advantage by increasing customer satisfaction and loyalty.[49] In addition, it also increases company productivity through efficient value-creation processes and effective use of company assets. Quality management is one of the essential pillars because it aims to maintain quality in all aspects of the business so that the company always stays true relative to competitors in a particular market domain.[50]

Cost management is associated with planning and controlling a company's budget, making projections of future budget use to increase efficiency and effectiveness and avoid overrunning costs.[51] Cost management enables companies to monitor their financial health and obtain critical information to make strategic or tactical decisions to create sustainable growth. This productivity can be seen in reduced costs, increased profit margins, favorable return rates, and opening investment opportunities.[52]

The development of digital technology provides new challenges for companies to manage their point of delivery more efficiently, both in-store and online, so that they can meet customers' purchase delivery demands more conveniently whenever and wherever they are. The in-store delivery experience also increasingly relies on various digital technologies to enhance customers' shopping experience. Therefore, delivery management becomes even more crucial because it must optimize the omnichannel experience for customers.[53]

Delivery management is essential for companies to ensure the successful delivery of products (tangible and intangible) and services to customers. Better delivery management can increase the number of purchases from existing customers and increase the possibility of getting new customers, leading to increased revenue and profitability.[54]

Service management is a discipline aimed at providing relevant quality service to customers. Without service support, customers' interest in buying products can be reduced. Interaction with customers through multiple services is one way to maintain a long-term relationship and create customer loyalty. Consistently making customers happy through various quality support services will build customer loyalty.[55]

Key Takeaways

In this chapter, we reviewed operational excellence and explored how the various elements of the entrepreneurship cluster and the professionalism cluster affect quality, cost, delivery, and service. Following are the key takeaways from this chapter:

- Companies can exist long term only if they continue to adapt to the changing environment.

- The essence of the concept of entrepreneurial marketing is how an organization can converge various dichotomies within the organization.
- Operational excellence has a very strategic role for the company because it is the core of value creation, the foundation for maximizing efficiency, supporting innovation, nurturing improvement, increasing competitiveness, focusing on people and customers, and is oriented toward sustainability. That is why the operations aspect is placed at the center of the omnihouse model.
- Flexibility, including in operations, is essential for the company to succeed in the future.
- There are four stages in stretching the QCDS: divisional-centric QCDS (stage 1), company-centric QCDS (stage 2), customer-centric QCDS (stage 3), and stakeholder-centric QCDS (stage 4).
- Every element of CI-EL and PI-PM influences QCDS.

CHAPTER 2

Competing with the West

Asia as the Rising Model

In the Preface you learned that Asia's role in the world economy is becoming increasingly significant. The journey of some Asian countries aligning themselves with Western countries has been a long and challenging process. We will briefly describe the rise of Asia in this chapter as background to understand the various examples in the following chapters.

Asia in the 1960s: A Good Student

In the early 1960s, Asian countries were not on the same economic performance level as the Western countries. On September 30, 1960, at the UN Assembly meeting, Indonesian President Soekarno made a speech titled "To Build the World Anew." In his remarks, he told the world leaders about creating a world without colonialism and imperialism.[1]

When Soekarno made that speech, today's economic phenoms, such as Qatar, Singapore, and the United Arab Emirates (UAE), were not even independent countries. Singapore became independent in 1965 after Malaysia rejected Singapore's reunion proposal. Both Qatar and the United Arab Emirates declared their independence from British rule in 1971.

Although several Asian countries vied to become independent countries, the United States, known as the Western world leader, set out to dream big. On September 12, 1962, John F. Kennedy, the president of the United States at that time, gave his "We Choose to Go to the Moon" speech at Rice University in Houston.[2] By the end of the 1960s, the United States would send an astronaut to the moon.

For several Asian countries, such as China, India, Japan, and the UAE, the target set by Kennedy at that time was beyond their wildest dreams. For example, China, known as the contributor to world civilization through inventions of papermaking, printing, gunpowder, and the compass in ancient times, was in soul-searching mode during the 1960s Cultural Revolution. However, Japan, while on the verge of becoming a prosperous industrial country in the 1960s by launching the Shinkansen bullet train, was busy preparing to host the Olympics in 1964.

The contrasting positions of Asian countries and Western countries in the 1960s can be likened to the relationship between student and teacher. In fact, several Asian countries were good students in the 1960s. They studied the best Asian student, Japan, which succeeded in building high-standard operational capability at the same level as Western countries.[3] After watching the launch of the bullet train, other Asian countries implemented the industrial development approach taken by Japan by starting from a low-tech industry and slowly but surely moving up to a higher technology industry sector over time.

Competing with the West: The Flying Geese Model

In the 1960s, in addition to campaigning for independent countries in Asia and Africa, Soekarno encouraged countries not to take sides between the Western Bloc led by the United States and the Eastern Bloc led by the USSR.[4] However, South Korea, Taiwan, Singapore, and Hong Kong, afraid of communism, had no choice but to lean toward the Western Bloc. Therefore, they received Western assistance to follow in the footsteps of Japan in applying the flying geese model.[5]

The flying geese model is often used to explain the phenomenon when some Asian countries began to grow their economies rapidly in the 1980s. At that time, Japan was considered the leading power, followed by several other countries in the Asian region. Based on each country's comparative advantage, this "following" phenomenon formed a geese flying pattern, hence, the model's name.

Leader of the Geese: Japan

Unlike the other Asian countries, in the 1960s Japan was on track to advance at the same rate as Western countries. Its automotive industry at the time created car products with the objective of fuel efficiency. In doing so, Japanese car companies produced small cars supported by small engines.

That decision enabled Japanese automotive companies to build their market, especially domestically. Moreover, that market helped the companies improve operational excellence in their manufacturing facilities and product performance. Slowly but surely, Japanese automotive companies became strong contenders to Western players with brands in particular segments.

In the early to mid-1970s, when the world experienced the oil crisis, Japan started to show its ability to compete with the West and win market share. Its relatively small cars rode the oil crisis momentum by highlighting their efficiency. In addition to vehicles, many other Japanese products started to prove Japan's competitive advantage against Western products in various categories, such as TVs, radio/tape players, cameras, or other household products.

In the 1970s, the world started to recognize Japanese brands as being associated with good quality and efficient production. This achievement was a long process through Kaizen, or a quality improvement paradigm.

That's when the flying geese model started to take effect. The world started to welcome Japan as an "advanced" country, and South Korea, Taiwan, Hong Kong, and Singapore were ready to follow in its footsteps.

From Low-Tech to High-Tech Industries: South Korea, Taiwan, Hong Kong, and Singapore

In the 1960s, after seeing Japan's success, the leaders of South Korea, Taiwan, Hong Kong, and Singapore created industrial development policies and environments that were favorable for business growth.[6] For instance, in addition to promoting companies that were participating in the industrial development process, the leaders set guidelines for funding the industrialization process and selling products in domestic and international markets. Those policies helped companies in these four countries to focus on building operational excellence.

This ability attracted the attention of Western countries. As a result, the West started to help South Korea, Taiwan, Hong Kong, and Singapore function as original equipment manufacturers (OEMs).[7]

These four countries proved excellent as OEMs not only in low-tech industries such as textiles but eventually in higher-tech industries as well. As a result, the four countries decided to prepare their workforce to be able to operate in higher-level industries, for example, high-tech companies. Through this approach, the four countries started producing various industrial products that met the criteria of the brand owners and end customers.

The journey of South Korea, Taiwan, Hong Kong, and Singapore to become industrialized economies provides an important lesson: start in a low-tech industry to build operational excellence; then, once you succeed at that level, acquire the knowledge, skill, and technology needed for operational excellence in a higher-tech industry.

We'll talk more about how these countries achieved this change in the "The First Generation of Flying Geese" section of the chapter.

The Next Industrialized Countries: Indonesia, Thailand, Malaysia, and the Philippines

The successful application of the flying geese model encouraged Japan to expand it to other Asian countries such as Indonesia, Thailand, Malaysia, and the Philippines. These four Asian countries wanted to follow in the footsteps of Singapore. In addition to pursuing the OEM path, these countries wanted to become the next newly industrialized countries by taking advantage of their natural resources and large populations.

The flying geese model differed from country to country, and the creativity, innovations, and entrepreneurship of the different leaders produced different industrialized outcomes.

In fact, these countries were ignored by Western experts such as Paul Krugman, who said in 1994 that Asian industrialization was marked by perspiration, not inspiration.[8] Maybe Krugman had that opinion after struggling to find Asian brands other than Japanese ones.

Krugman's claim received attention again when Indonesia and Thailand were hard hit by the Asian crisis of 1997–1998, triggered by the fall in the exchange rates of these countries so that they could not pay their US dollar debts, which suddenly increased. In 1998, Philip Kotler and Hermawan Kartajaya coauthored *Repositioning Asia: From Bubble to Sustainable Economy*. They believed the creativity, innovation, and entrepreneurship used to evolve into industrialized countries, combined with quality improvement paradigms, would help Asian countries improve their economies.

Today, 25 years later, Asian countries are not only in a better position—including bargaining positions—but also produce many brands, such as Samsung, Hyundai, and others, that not only compete but win the competition against Western brands, including in Western markets. As a result, brands from several Asian countries have started to become inspirations for many aspiring global brands.

We'll talk more about these countries in the "The Second Generation of Flying Geese" section of the chapter.

Key Moments of Competing with the West

Figure 2.1 shows a timeline of key moments of US, Japan, and other Asian companies since 1960. You can see that Japan was an early leader among Asian countries, and others followed by the flying geese model. Many Asian companies such as Toyota, Samsung, and TikTok are now direct competitors to comparable US companies.

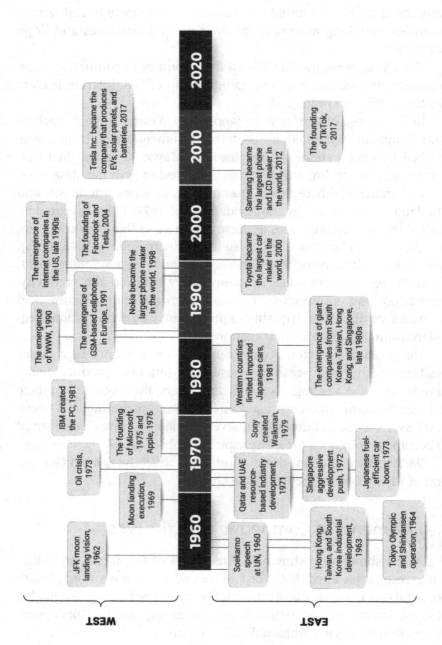

FIGURE 2.1 Key moments of competing with the West

Timeline content:

WEST
- JFK moon vision, 1962
- Moon landing execution, 1969
- Oil crisis, 1973
- The founding of Microsoft, 1975 and Apple, 1976
- IBM created the PC, 1981
- The emergence of WWW, 1990
- The emergence of internet companies in the US, late 1990s
- The founding of Facebook and Tesla, 2004
- Tesla Inc. became the company that produces EVs, solar panels, and batteries, 2017

EAST
- Soekarno speech at UN, 1960
- Hong Kong, Taiwan, and South Korea industrial development, 1963
- Tokyo Olympic and Shinkansen operation, 1964
- Qatar and UAE resource-based industry development, 1971
- Singapore aggressive development push, 1972
- Japanese fuel-efficient car boom, 1973
- Sony created Walkman, 1979
- Western countries limited imported Japanese cars, 1981
- The emergence of giant companies from South Korea, Taiwan, Hong Kong, and Singapore, late 1980s
- The emergence of GSM-based cellphone in Europe, 1991
- Nokia became the largest phone maker in the world, 1998
- Toyota became the largest car maker in the world, 2000
- Samsung became the largest phone and LCD maker in the world, 2012
- The founding of TikTok, 2017

The Outstanding Middle Eastern Countries: The UAE and Qatar

Countries in East Asia witnessed Japan's journey to becoming a developed country with excellent operational ability, which encouraged them to follow suit. But there is another approach to competing with the West. Specifically, the UAE[9] and Qatar[10] in West Asia used their natural resources of oil and gas as the basis of their industrial development. However, due to the type of technology used in resources-based industrial development, the two countries (with small numbers of citizens) are currently at different stages of industrial development.

Unlike countries in East Asia, which started with low-tech industries and moved to higher-tech ones over time, the UAE and Qatar jumped into the industry sector with high-tech industries, which required a huge capital expenditure. Moreover, because of the nature of oil and gas as precious resources, the two countries and other Middle East countries, such as Saudi Arabia, Kuwait, Oman, and Bahrain, invited big multinational companies with technology and capital, including from Japan, to help develop their resources-based industries. Still, the UAE and Qatar created development funds early in their respective countries.

The two countries accumulated money from exporting oil and gas to invest in the downstream oil and gas products, such as petrochemicals. Through this kind of investment, the two countries minimized the impact of revenue volatility tied to oil prices in the market. They followed the same investment strategy in the professional sports industry, where money enriched operational capability building through the recruitment of high-level professionals and workers from other countries.

Because both of these countries have a small number of citizens, their leaders needed to make bold decisions by inviting big corporations and also luring professionals and workers from elsewhere. The success of industrial development in these two countries encouraged more professionals and workers to come, which, in effect, encouraged the emergence of various supporting industries, such as transportation and housing. This triggered one of the leaders of the UAE to think big.

The Shift to Services

Knowing the limitation of its oil reserves, Rashid bin Saeed (1958–1990), the ruler of Dubai, a member of the UAE Federation, decided to transform the territory into the new trading and travel hub in the West region of Asia. In doing so, Rashid bin Saeed created many tourist attractions and developed the Emirates airline. In addition, different types of professionals and workers from foreign countries came to Dubai to help build the operational capabilities in the service-related industry.

Slowly but surely, Dubai has become one of the world's busiest travel and trading hubs. Qatar, which had accumulated even more money than Dubai, decided to follow in the steps of Dubai in all processes of travel and trading hub transformation. In addition, both countries decided to send their best students to study in foreign countries to prepare them to be critical executives to ensure operational excellence in various industries within their countries.

The airlines of Dubai (Emirates) and Qatar (Qatar Airways) have become essential tools for transforming the travel hubs. Emirates and Qatar Airways are among the few airlines worldwide that can serve significant numbers of flight routes globally with aggressive promotions. Emirates and Qatar Airways have built excellent global airline operations, making them strong competitors of Western airlines.

In fact, many Western airlines are afraid to compete with the airlines of the western part of Asia, as ultimately their shareholders will do anything to make them have operational excellence at competitive prices. However, it is about more than money, because the two airlines assemble professionals and workers from various countries to serve international travelers across the globe. It is a challenging process because it requires different cultures and disciplines to achieve operational service excellence.

East Versus West: A Non-Zero-Sum Game

Since the Enlightenment in the 17th and 18th centuries, companies from Europe and the United States have set a high bar in terms of operational excellence from product to market. For example, during its heyday, Nokia of Finland produced various cell phones, from low end to high end, and commanded a 51% global market share. It was a rare phenomenon for a company from a small country to produce and market globally.

Microsoft is another good benchmark. It succeeded in helping build the PC market and has become a dominant player in the global market since. In addition, the company is a gold standard for having long-term operational excellence from the production stage, including product improvement and innovation and delivery, to the market stage in the global market.

Japan, which championed Asian countries and succeeded in creating several global market leaders, does not have a company that has performed as well as Nokia did in its heyday, let alone Microsoft. Nokia was a dominant handphone maker in the world in the early 2000s, and Microsoft has dominated personal and office software in the world since the 1980s. No Japanese brands, including Sony, have achieved the same position as Nokia and Microsoft. However, Japanese companies might not need to follow in these footsteps because they face a more competitive environment due to the easier accessibility of acquiring technology or going to market. After all, Japanese companies have already achieved Emperor Meiji's 1868 vision of having equal standing with Western countries.

So competing with the West, championed by Japan in the 1960s, is not a zero-sum game. Instead, it is similar to a teacher-student interaction. A student may acquire knowledge and skills and eventually become better than the teacher.

In today's era, when continuous learning has become a critical success factor for professionals and workers to survive in the competency market, Asian companies have a mindset that they need to compete against the West, and they use that thought as the driver for making better products through more efficient operations. As a result, several Western companies, which were great players in a particular era, might eventually fade away. Even Japanese companies, which used to be the inspiration for other Asian companies, are facing the impact of this mindset. For some Asian countries, Japan has been regarded as advanced as Western countries, even being the only Asian country included in the G8. But some Asian countries, like South Korea and China, also "attack" Japan in a similar way to how the Japanese acted toward Western brands from 1970 to 1980. Japanese consumer electronics brands, which used to dominate the industry, are slowly but surely being replaced by South Korean and Chinese brands.

Pathways to Competing with the West

The leadership of Japan in the Meiji Era understood that they had no choice but to copy the success of Western countries, mainly European countries. During the Meiji Restoration, beginning in 1868, in addition to political changes inspired by the French Revolution, Japan made scientific-based economic and social changes. Those changes laid the foundation for creating industrialization in Japan. Japan continually built up the capabilities and capacities to eventually be able to compete with Western countries, becoming the first Asian country to do so.

Through industrialization, Japan had the grand ambition to have equal standing with Western countries and colonizers in many parts of the world and then gain their respect. That ambition drove Japan to industrialize its military. As a result, in the years leading to World War II, Japan succeeded in producing military products that could compete with Western products, colonizing many Asian countries, and started World War II in the East by attacking Pearl Harbor.

Japan's excellent military industry was a result of Japan merging the Western model with its own system. Therefore, the Japanese modernization process is a combination of the Western approach and the Japanese tradition, including in the powerful role of the emperor, who is considered a guiding mentor to move the country forward with a clear focus.

Although other Asian countries in pre–World War II also had powerful emperors or kings, they didn't have national leaders who had visions of being competitive on the world stage. The Japanese emperors had a vision and drove the government to implement a road map and set milestones. Japanese industrialization was not only about having manufacturing facilities but also about becoming a believer in planning, organizing, directing, and controlling, which are the critical characteristics of operational excellence.

What makes the Japanese version of planning, organizing, directing, and controlling remarkable is the influence of Japanese culture on maintaining harmony through consensus. In the late 1940s after World War II, Toyota introduced the Kaizen method, which became the critical success factor for Japanese operational excellence.

The Japanese journey to become an industrialized nation relied on leadership and entrepreneurship and creativity and innovation. The invention of Japanese management methods influenced by Japanese

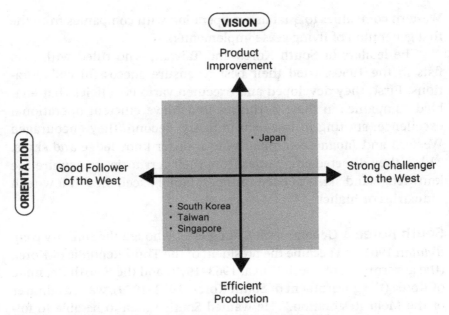

FIGURE 2.2 Industrial development matrix of countries in Asia

traditions has made many other Asian countries quick to follow Japan, including those that Japan once occupied, through the flying geese phenomenon.

Since the end of the 20th century, Japan has carried out industrialization and encouraged companies to build operational excellence to be in equal standing with Western countries. However, the first generation of flying geese implementers had no ambition to compete with Japan, let alone the West (see Figure 2.2).

Instead, the first generation of flying geese implementers wanted to follow Japan and the West to improve and innovate, not compete.

The First Generation of Flying Geese

The first generation of flying geese implementers tried to be efficient, good followers. Such positioning would later make them some of the world's best OEM groups. That is why, when in the context of the Cold War the West wanted to maintain its influence in Asia, the ability to perform efficient operational excellence became the *raison d'etre* for

Western companies to establish cooperation with companies from the first generation of flying geese implementers.

The leaders of South Korea and Taiwan, who ruled with iron fists in the 1960s, tried their best to ensure successful collaborations. First, they developed and executed various policies that enabled companies in their territories to achieve efficient operational excellence, starting in low-tech industry. Second, they encouraged Western and Japanese companies to transfer knowledge and skills. Third, they directed companies from their territories to acquire the knowledge and skills needed for operational excellence in low-tech industries or higher.

South Korea   General Park Chung Hee, who led the military *coup d'etat* in 1961 and became the president of the Third Republic of Korea (the government of South Korea, 1963–1972) and the Fourth Republic of Korea (the government of South Korea, 1972–1979), was an admirer of the Meiji Restoration.[11] He wanted South Korea to be able to follow the Japanese journey to become an industrialized country, but in a short time. Unlike Japanese leaders who set the policy and managed the industrialization process, the government of General Park directly controlled the industrialization process.

The government selected several family-owned businesses to develop low-tech industries such as textiles and footwear and sell the products internationally. Furthermore, the government encouraged established family-owned businesses to accumulate knowledge and skills to achieve operational excellence quickly in the low-tech industry. As a result, the family-owned businesses met Park Chung Hee's government target.

The success of South Korea's low-tech industry in building operational excellence in a short time encouraged the government of Park Chung Hee to help family-owned businesses make operational excellence in higher-tech industries. The family-owned companies, which at that time already operated in various industries, welcomed the direction of the government. However, higher-tech sectors like electronics and telecommunications require high capital, so the family-owned businesses transformed into big conglomerates locally known as *chaebol*.

Under the government's guidance, the chaebols kept building operational excellence in various industries, from low-tech to higher-tech, in less than two decades, transforming South Korea from an underdeveloped nation in 1961 into a prosperous, industrialized country. In a relatively short time, the chaebols became known as the drivers of South Korean industrial development.

In the post–Park Chung Hee era, the chaebols continued to acquire knowledge and skills in high-tech industries such as chips and liquid crystal displays (LCDs), previously the domain of Western or Japanese companies. In the 1990s, the Korean company Samsung became a strong global contender in chips and LCDs. At the turn of the century, Samsung became the worldwide chip and LCD leader.

While it has yet to succeed on the scale of Samsung, Hyundai is another chaebol phenomenon. Today, Hyundai is one of the top 10 car companies, representing the established car companies that can offer fossil fuel and electric vehicles. These two types of products showcase how Hyundai builds complicated operational excellence.

Taiwan   If General Park Chung Hee led the industrial development of South Korea from 1963 to 1979, which paved the way for the chaebols to build operational excellence from low-tech to high-tech industries, General Chiang Kai Shek led the industrial development of Taiwan. In doing so, General Chiang was guided by Sun Yat Sen's doctrine of maintaining a harmonious relationship between capital owners and workers. Unlike the government of Park, which prioritized selected family-owned businesses for industrial development, General Chiang encouraged more diverse participation of industry players.

In addition to big family-owned businesses and state-owned companies, Taiwan involved the participation of small and medium enterprises (SMEs).[12] This decision was made based on the success of Taiwan's SMEs in transforming Taiwan's agriculture sector and rural areas. In addition, Taiwan's SMEs built operational excellence in low-tech and even higher-tech industries.

Taiwan's SMEs helped the industrial development process of the country. It was an exciting phenomenon, given that many of Taiwan's SMEs employed fewer than 100 workers and many more employed fewer than 10. Moreover, Taiwan's SMEs leveraged the legacy of small-scale operation during the Japanese colonization to serve the surrounding community as an industrial culture that enabled them to adopt the demand for operational excellence needed in many types of industrial development.

So, the brand owners who wanted to outsource their production process in Taiwan had various alternatives to OEMs, from SMEs to big family-owned businesses. Moreover, if the demand for their products increased, they could easily find options, including decreasing production costs. The SMEs inspired other countries to believe that SMEs could become one of the actors in the industrial development process.

Hong Kong and Singapore Hong Kong also had SMEs that participated in the industrialization process.[13] Driven by the immigrants who moved from Mainland China, the SMEs helped transform Hong Kong from an *entrepôt* to a critical manufacturing actor in Asia. Starting with low-tech industries, the manufacturing sector players, including its SMEs, slowly but surely transformed Hong Kong as one of the positive alternatives for OEMs in Asia.

Along the way, Hong Kong could build operational excellence in the manufacturing sector and the vast array of service sectors. As one of the gateways to Mainland China, Hong Kong made operational capabilities to handle large flows of goods and people quickly and efficiently. As a result, it became one of the benchmarks of operational excellence in service industries worldwide.

When Singapore became an independent country in 1965, its leader, Lee Kuan Yew, decided to have a strong connection with the Western world. Similar to leaders in South Korea, Taiwan, and Hong Kong, Lee Kuan Yew invited companies from the Western World and Japan to build factories in his country. To convince companies from those countries, he didn't rely only on Singapore's position as a trading hub in Southeast Asia but also on a favorable legal system for foreign companies.

Due to good responses from American and Japanese companies, Singapore became an industrialized country less than a decade after becoming independent. It exported textiles, garments, and basic electronics to various countries worldwide. Lee Kuan Yew persuaded foreign companies in Singapore to train Singapore's workforce to have skills and knowledge at higher levels in the manufacturing and service sectors, such as hospitality and health care.

Through that approach, Singapore quickly followed in the footsteps of South Korea, Taiwan, and Hong Kong. With the ability to transform its manufacturing sectors to a higher level, within 25 years after independence, Singapore became one of the newly industrialized countries.

The unique situation of Hong Kong and Singapore in the 1960s was supported by the ideal strategic position of their ports, making them the new trading hubs of that decade. The growing trading volume that moved through their docks slowly helped them have excellent port operations.

The emergence of the new trading hubs in Asia in the 1960s encouraged people to travel to visit. Over time, their airports became traveling hubs with many passengers. Similar to their ports, the two countries developed excellent airport operations.

Due to implementing operational excellence efficiently in a disciplined manner and for a long time, the companies of the first generation of flying geese implementers finally had branded operational excellence. Remarkably, this was done in the manufacturing process and service industries. In addition, Hong Kong and Singapore demonstrated branded operational excellence in the service industry through their ability to build the world's busiest ports, which have become the key to success in developing international trade from Asia, and airports, which have become international aviation hubs in Asia.

Hong Kong and Singapore succeeded in creating airline companies that branded operational service excellence and hospitality, a hallmark of Asian business. Even though they did not set high targets at the start, in the end, Singapore and Hong Kong became two of the best in the world for branded operational service excellence.

South Korea and Taiwan, which were under the control of a military regime for several years, chose a different path than Hong Kong and Singapore. Apart from trying to become one of the best OEMs in the world, they aimed to produce successful product brands by positioning quality products at affordable prices or differentiated products. Stan Shih, founder of Acer, one of the pioneers of Taiwanese technology companies, describes this positioning in his company motto, "Me Too Is Not My Style."

Achieving Operational Excellence The first generation of flying geese implementers became good followers in a disciplined way because they didn't have that many choices. They don't have abundant natural resources, and apart from South Korea, they have a small population as a domestic market base. In addition, they face threats from other countries, which makes them choose to be closer to Western countries and receive many benefits, such as being business partners with Western companies.

It is what made the first generation of flying geese implementers the best example of the disciplined market leaders in operational excellence—product leadership and customer intimacy—a concept introduced by Michael Treacy and Fred Wiersema in 1995. Although operational excellence can be achieved through discipline and focus, external factors were needed for these countries to succeed. Such efforts have been applied for years and have finally become embedded into a new culture that has increased these countries' competitive advantage.

The Second Generation of Flying Geese

The second generation of flying geese implementers—Indonesia, Thailand, Malaysia, and the Philippines—have many natural resources and a large population. But, they feel they have no outside threats. These countries have huge market (due to their large population) and significant natural resources. Therefore, they tend to be complacent, and there is no strong incentive to focus immediately on building operational excellence capabilities. Therefore, having the discipline and focus to build operational excellence is not in their main agenda.

This second generation still has produced world-class players, partly because each country can leverage its own unique characteristics. For example, Thailand, which has superior agriculture, is trying to become the kitchen of the world. By contrast, Indonesia, renowned as the world's fourth most populous country, has the world's largest microfinance industry. Meanwhile, Malaysia is trying to be an alternative to Singapore by taking advantage of having a large area and leveraging its larger population.

The path taken by the second generation of flying geese implementers has inspired other Asian countries. China and India rely on a much larger population than Indonesia, a long tradition of knowledge, and their being independent nations. That is why, although they started to build operational excellence later than the first and second generations of flying geese implementers, they are catching up faster and have more companies that have achieved operational excellence.

Competing with the West with the New Rules

Even though Asian companies have succeeded in competing with or even beating Western companies, that does not mean that Western companies have lost. With the lifestyle standards of its citizens, Western companies can no longer compete with Asian companies' efficient operational excellence. Even so, they have quickly changed the game's new rules by incorporating sustainable development goals (SDGs).

Sustainable Development Goals

The World Economic Forum collaborated with Deloitte, EY, KPMG, and PwC to publish the white paper "Measuring Stakeholder Capitalism," which aims to define standard metrics for sustainable value creation, which, in essence, tries to align corporate values and strategies with the UN's Sustainable Development Goals (SDGs) to serve society better. In the value-creation process, a company must refer to four pillars: governance, planet, people, and prosperity (4Ps). These four pillars accommodate SDGs as shown in Figure 2.3.[14]

There is also a categorization of SDGs into five sustainability principles or pillars consisting of people, planet, prosperity, peace, and partnership, as shown in Figure 2.4.[15]

Sustainable Development Goals (SDGs)	The Four Pillars (4P)			
	Principles of Governance	Planet	People	Prosperity
1. No poverty				✓
2. Zero hunger			✓	
3. Good health and well-being			✓	
4. Quality education			✓	
5. Gender equality			✓	
6. Clean water and sanitation	✓			
7. Affordable and clean energy	✓			
8. Decent work and economic growth			✓	✓
9. Industry, innovation, and infrastructure				✓
10. Reduced inequalities			✓	✓
11. Sustainable cities and communities				✓
12. Responsible consumption and production	✓	✓		
13. Climate action		✓		
14. Life below water		✓		
15. Life on land		✓		
16. Peace, justice, and strong institutions	✓			
17. Partnerships for the goals	✓			

FIGURE 2.3 Four pillars and the SDGs

Environmental, Social, and Governance Goals

ESG needs to be fully standardized because every agency that conducts scoring or ratings still seems to interpret the three ESG components based on their perspective. Many companies already use ESG as part of their contribution reports to stakeholders in addition to standard/conventional reports, which show the achievement of profits and returns usually intended for shareholders. A comprehensive assessment using ESG criteria is critical for investors to assess a company so they can direct their capital to investments that align with sustainability and the values the investors hold.[16]

There are several ESG scores and rating agencies that various companies, such as Bloomberg, MSCI, RepRisk, and Sustainalytics, widely use. Referring to the article published by Armanino, of the four mentioned, RepRisk is currently the most used by all public and private companies in all industries (see Figure 2.5).[17]

Sustainable Development Goals (SDGs)	The Five Ps				
	People	Planet	Prosperity	Peace	Partnership
1. No poverty	✓				
2. Zero hunger	✓				
3. Good health and well-being	✓				
4. Quality education	✓				
5. Gender equality	✓				
6. Clean water and sanitation		✓			
7. Affordable and clean energy			✓		
8. Decent work and economic growth			✓		
9. Industry, innovation, and infrastructure			✓		
10. Reduced inequalities			✓		
11. Sustainable cities and communities			✓		
12. Responsible consumption and production		✓			
13. Climate action		✓			
14. Life below water		✓			
15. Life on land		✓			
16. Peace, justice, and strong institutions				✓	
17. Partnerships for the goals					✓

FIGURE 2.4   The 5Ps and SDGs

Agency	Scoring	Number of Companies
Bloomberg	100 to 0	11,800+
CDP	A to D−	9,600+
FTSE	A to D−	7,200+
ISS	A to D−	7,300+
MSCI	AAA to CCC	14,000+
Refinitiv	100 to 0	9,000+
RepRisk	AAA to D	200,700+
S&P Global Ratings	100 to 0	10,000+
Sustainalytics	0 to 40+	13,000+

FIGURE 2.5   ESG scoring and rating agencies comparison

RepRisk states that it uses a collectively exhaustive framework that complies with various ESG standards, regulatory frameworks, and the 17 SDGs mapped out in more than 100 RepRisk risk facts.[18]

It is essential to note that most countries and companies are aware of (and even actively participate in) the SDG movement, but the SDG achievements are still not as expected. Yet, the deadline of 2030 is only a short time away. This is why we must initiate the sustainability movement independently. Hence, there exists an organization known as Inner Development Goals, which has formulated 23 essential skills (see Appendix B) aimed at assisting both countries and companies to attain their goals.

Favorable New Conditions for SDGs

These goals are complex challenges increasingly demanded by global consumers, especially after the COVID-19 pandemic. Awareness of SDGs among Western consumers is higher than in Asia; therefore, they demand that Western companies contribute as much as possible to achieve the SDGs. This is a challenge for Asian companies, which don't have external pressures like in the West that are driving the achievement of these SDGs. But, external factors partly have triggered the success of building efficient operational excellence in Asia.

Asian companies operating in the West have external factors driving the implementation of the SDGs. However, because Asia is getting more prosperous, these companies might prefer to prioritize the Asian market, which does not have SDG demands as strict as in the West. So that raises the question, can Asian companies become strong challengers in implementing the SDGs?

When we started to write our first book in 1998, *Repositioning Asia: From Bubble to Sustainable Economy* (Wiley), we believed that sustainability was a term that Asian companies would become familiar with. At that time, sustainability was more related to a company's going business concerns. Many Asian companies later became SDG implementers and successfully ensured the company's sustainability. In our book *Marketing 3.0: From Products to Customers to the Human Spirit* (Wiley, 2010), we introduced the need for companies to build awareness that to have considerable profits they as well need to care about people and the planet. Incidentally, the book was published before a global agreement in 2015 to achieve the SDGs by 2030. So, what we campaigned for in that book seems more straightforward than the 17 interlinked objectives of SDGs.

But as has been shown by several generations of flying geese implementers, starting with a simple target can produce many achievements over time. It is also tricky in the West to find great companies that adhere to all the UN's 17 SDGs. They also choose how many goals they can achieve in the short term.

Interestingly, the European Union (EU) is an external factor that can force many companies to meet the SDG targets. They use rules and incentives, such as carbon taxes, that encourage companies to comply or ease exports to Europe. Several Asian companies that have entered and will enter the European market are also interested in following EU standards for SDGs.

Those companies are expected to become SDGs brand endorsers, what we (Philip Kotler, Hermawan Kartajaya, and Iwan Setiawan) wrote in *Marketing 4.0: Moving from Traditional to Digital* (Wiley, 2017). This decision will be a differentiator in future competition, especially among Gen Z workers and consumers. Gen Z in Asia can force companies to have a fear of missing out, resulting in external factors that cause Asian companies to be disciplined in achieving the SDGs so they can compete with other companies in the new rules of the game.

Regarding SDG-oriented technologies, economies, and markets, there are many similarities between Western countries (especially European countries) and Asia. But in Europe, it is the powerful EU that can set SDG regulations, whereas there is no such bloc in Asia (see Figure 2.6).

In addition to regulations, companies that want to win in the European SDG-oriented market must win customers' hearts by, among other things, caring for the well-being of people and the planet.

Without regulation of the regional bloc in Asia, companies that want to win the substantial Asian SDG-oriented market must win the heart of Gen Z. This generation is trying to leverage its colossal number and digital fluency to force companies to care for the well-being of people and the planet.

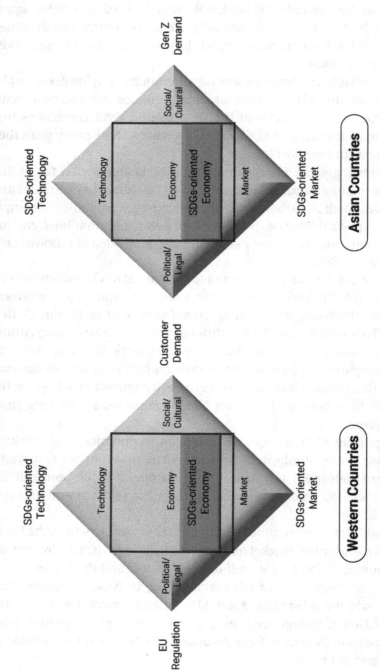

FIGURE 2.6 Comparison of SDG-oriented markets in the West and Asia

Key Takeaways

In this chapter, we talked about the long journey of how Asian countries built their capabilities from scratch to the point where they could start to compete with Western countries. Following are the key takeaways from this chapter:

- While Western countries were very advanced in the 1960s, many Asian countries were still underdeveloped, even trapped by various difficulties, such as armed conflicts with the communist parties. Some countries had just become independent in the early 1970s.

- In the 1960s, Asian countries were often regarded as good students who learned much from Western countries to develop their land. Japan was the best student then and became an example for many other Asian countries of extraordinary operational excellence capabilities. This process became known as the formation of the flying geese model.

- There are two generations of flying geese. The first generation consisted of Taiwan and South Korea, followed by Hong Kong and Singapore. The second generation of flying geese were Indonesia, Thailand, Malaysia, and the Philippines, which have many natural resources and large populations.

- Industrialization in Hong Kong, South Korea, and Taiwan was supported by policies that can create a favorable business environment. These policies, in turn, fostered low-tech industries and then gradually shifted to high-tech industries.

- The UAE and Qatar are two countries that are very competitive in the Middle East region. They extensively use their natural resources, namely, oil and gas, from exporting to petrochemical development. Realizing the limitations of their oil reserves, they further shifted to the service sector.

- The journey of competing with the West spearheaded by Japan in the 1960s was not a zero-sum game in which the mindset of Asian companies competing with the West encouraged them to make a better product through more efficient operations.

- In the 2010s, Western countries brought competition to a higher level with the acknowledged need to fulfill the UN's SDGs. This achievement is a challenge for companies in Asia, especially for countries that have yet to implement strict regulations based on SDGs.
- Sustainable value creation, which aligns with the UN's SDGs, aims to encourage various companies to serve a better society. Companies will be evaluated to determine whether they have complied with a number of ESG criteria that refer to the SDGs. Countries and companies must be aware and understand this, considering that the deadline of 2030 is only a short time away.

CHAPTER 3

The New Perspective of Quality

From Input to Impact

A lmost every product people want to buy now offers customization options. Dell, for example, has long offered customizable PCs. Customers can order PCs in various configurations by choosing from multiple options, starting with the system's main components to other add-ons, for example, processors, graphic cards, memory methods, storage types, and displays.[1] They can even get their PC in different colors like chartreuse and pink.

Starbucks has long since allowed its customers to customize the various coffee drinks they want, including the type of milk, the coffee content, the sugar content, which determines the level of sweetness, and even specific temperature preferences from cold to extra hot. Customers can customize orders beyond the standard existing menu.[2] Customizable menus generate high margins for Starbucks's revenue, reaching US$1 billion annually, as said by Sara Trilling, president of Starbucks North America, to investors on November 3, 2022.[3] That's twice than in 2019.[4]

IKEA does not want to be outdone; it offers the IKEA Pax System, a wardrobe and storage solution designed to suit each customer's needs and preferences.[5] Customers can customize many things, including the wardrobe's interior layout and the internal components of the configuration to accommodate various clothing and accessories.[6] IKEA provides this Pax System Planning on its website, where buyers can start a design from scratch on a blank canvas or modify something that has been designed before.[7]

LEGO has long given its customers the freedom to choose every LEGO piece in various shapes, sizes, and colors. LEGO Pick a Brick allows customers to find the most appropriate LEGO components to suit their unique creations. This feature simultaneously encourages creativity and provides flexibility because each customer can have their needs met to complete their specific projects called "My Own Creations" (MOC), which standard LEGO sets cannot fulfill.[8]

Customization Effects on Quality

With all of these modern customization options, how does a company retain its product quality? Several decades ago, it was easy to answer this question because quality was often associated with a product's specifications and various supporting services with static requirements or standards.

The specifications are usually simple, especially for many familiar tangible products (both perishable and nonperishable), from cars and clothes to food. Cars, for example, determine their quality based on the engine's reliability, comfort when the vehicle travels along the road surface, safety factors, and so on. An automotive company can produce cars according to generally accepted standards. If the company can exceed these standards, it is said that its vehicles are of high quality.

The question of quality is more interesting now that the customer's bargaining position is becoming more robust and the degree of conformance no longer refers to static standards or specifications set by the producer. The definition of quality is becoming increasingly complex and depends on what context or perspective is used as a reference. The notion of quality is increasingly shifting to the customer and is different between one customer and another. In short, defining quality has now become dynamic.

This dynamic definition of quality, in turn, also influences how we measure customer satisfaction levels. The more similar the standard of a product, the easier it is to compare the level of satisfaction between one customer and another. However, it is increasingly difficult to make these comparisons because, in line with the increasing influence of personalization and customization, the level of satisfaction is now relative. Further, the greater the customer's freedom to customize, the greater the possibility that customer satisfaction will increase.

Nike By You or NikeiD is an excellent example of how its customers can customize various Nike products, including footwear and clothing, by choosing different colors and materials. Customers can easily create designs from multiple color choices, images, templates, and many more options. Offering this level of customization alone can increase customer satisfaction. Matthew Friend, EVP and CFO of Nike, said that customer engagement with Nike products increased by 27%, and repeat buyers surged by 50% in 2021 compared to the prior year.[9]

Subaru also does something similar by allowing its customers in the United States to customize the cars they buy with various features, colors, and even interior trim based on their tastes.[10] A 2023 study conducted by JD Power shows that Subaru has the highest customer satisfaction rating among all car brands. The study places the Subaru Forester as one of the top three models in the compact SUV segment.[11] In fact, according to *Consumer Reports*, the 2023 Subaru Forester is the best SUV for less than US$30,000.[12]

Likewise, Ray-Ban glasses allow buyers to customize eyewear products according to personal preferences, including the model, lenses, frame, temple tips, engraving, and even the casing of the glasses. Options like this are much more than sufficient than what buyers expect.[13] Ray-Ban's interface for product visualization and customization is playful, colorful, fun, and provides a high-quality product visualization.[14] A net promoter score tracks whether a company's customers would recommend its products to others. It ranges between −100 to 100. Unsurprisingly, Ray-Ban's net promoter score reached 34 in January 2024, with 57% promoters, 20% passives, and 23% detractors, placing Ray-Ban first among its competitors.[15]

Quality Versus Sustainability

Usually, the higher the quality desired, the more money the buyer pays. However, the concept of sustainability, which emphasizes the importance of environmentally and socially conscious business, is becoming just as important as quality. The increased public awareness of environmental protection and social interests means companies must reflect a commitment to sustainability in the various products they offer to the public. Not doing so could be detrimental to a company, as Forever 21 experienced.

The fashion retailer Forever 21 was seen as not being a sustainable brand despite being considered luxurious in some emerging economies. Forever 21's supply chain practices were criticized because it was accused of sweatshop-like conditions and labor violations at its supplier factories. Forever 21's production process was also negatively viewed because it contributed significantly to environmental impacts such as water pollution, textile waste, and carbon emissions. In addition, the disposable fashion culture promoted by Forever 21 encouraged excessive customer consumption, thereby increasing the contribution of waste, which can damage the environment.[16]

What are the consequences? Forever 21 filed for bankruptcy in late 2019. Several factors triggered this failure, and one of them was not considering sustainability aspects amid tight competition and ignoring dynamic consumer expectations that started to expect eco-friendly fashion.[17]

Nestlé also faced a lot of pressure and was the target of a boycott campaign triggered by the controversy over baby formula products. Nestlé was accused of giving the impression that the formula milk products they market are almost as good as birth mother's milk. This false impression was seen as unethical and raised various issues, especially in less economically developed countries with low-income populations.[18]

In 2019, Nestlé was also said to be one of the biggest plastic polluters in the world (after PepsiCo and Coca-Cola). Based on a worldwide survey published by the Break Free From Plastic organization, Nestlé is expected to remain a major polluter unless it makes significant policy changes.[19]

It gets worse. Nestlé is suspected of siphoning tens of millions of gallons of pure water from rivers, packaging it, and branding it as Arrowhead Water. Forestry officials highlighted that this activity caused severe disruption to Strawberry Creek, where the water was sourced.[20] On the other side of the world, the same thing is causing problems for a small Pakistani community in the village of Bhati Dalwan, which is experiencing a water crisis triggered by the construction of a Nestlé bottling facility.[21] The company is also accused of destroying rainforests because it has released millions of tons of carbon into the atmosphere, killing hundreds of species already on the verge of extinction.[22]

Apart from several companies previously mentioned, according to the annual report of Break Free From Plastic regarding top plastic-polluting corporations of 2022, there are also many other companies on this list, including Mondelēz International, Unilever, Procter & Gamble, Mars, Inc., Philip Morris International, Danone, and Colgate-Palmolive.[23] These corporations are not the only ones hurting the environment, but they were recently in the news with documented troubles.

Reliability Is a Must

Even if a product meets specifications that follow the customer's wishes and can be obtained and enjoyed at the time the customer desires, it still has to fulfill other significant obligations, namely, reliability and durability.

The Tesla Model X offers customization options that can be accessed through its website, where customers can choose various color options, interiors, wheel size, and other adjustments.[24] This freedom given to potential buyers is an excellent way to increase customer satisfaction. Unfortunately, a promising start turned out to be hampered by various problems.

Many people complain that the manufacturing quality of the Tesla Model X is poor, along with inconsistent quality control. The battery also often has problems, including charging, which results in inconvenience and decreased mileage. Falcon-wing doors look fantastic but often frustrate many owners because they frequently malfunction. The door is often jammed, so it can open or close only halfway. The 2022 Tesla Model X has often been recalled due to various safety-related problems, from side airbags that improperly deploy, seat belt chimes that don't work, automatic emergency braking that doesn't work correctly, and failing to stop at a stop sign.[25]

The Tesla Model X also has several problems with its suspension, so you often hear creaking, clunking, or squeaking sounds when the car is maneuvered or running on poor or inconsistent road surfaces. In addition, the Tesla Model X reportedly had problems with its high-voltage battery coolant heater unit. If a fault occurs in the high-voltage system, the warning alert often works too late, resulting in damage that should not happen.[26] So, whatever extent of customization can be done by customers, in the end, the reliability or durability of a product is also important.

Understanding and Managing Customer Expectations

The combination of customization, incorporating sustainability as part of quality, and ensuring reliability will determine whether the value proposition offered by a brand or product is commensurate with the amount of money it costs (and also whether it satisfies different nonmonetary needs, such as convenience and providing positive emotions).

Even though it was a long time ago, the case of Starbucks in Australia shows the kind of challenges a company can face: after accumulating losses of US$105 million in the first seven years of its presence in Australia Starbucks ultimately closed more than two-thirds of its outlets in 2008. Why was that? Australian society has long had a coffee culture in line with the arrival of immigrants from Italy and Greece in the mid-1900s who introduced Australians to espresso. Australians are also used to special coffee items, such as a flat white or an Australian macchiato.[27]

With its own coffee culture, Australians prefer to buy coffee from local coffee shops. The coffee shop is a place for them to meet their friends to get to know each other and even the local barista. This holistic definition of quality is the basis for Australians assessing coffee. If seen from a coffee perspective alone, Starbucks has a weak point of differentiation but offers its products at higher prices. The coffee choices provided by Starbucks tends to be more sugary, when Australians are used to coffee without sugar or only a little sugar. A quality package like this might be successful in several other countries in the Asia-Pacific region, but it does not conform to the Australian vision of coffee consumption.[28]

As you can see, the definition of quality depends on the eye of the stakeholder. A good understanding of the definition of quality in customers' eyes is fundamental and determines business success. However, producers are also obliged to educate their customers or at least manage their expectations.

Apple, for example, tries to manage customer expectations with the "Apple Marketing Philosophy," which consists of three aspects:

- First is empathy, where Apple tries to explore the emotional aspects of customers in such a way that it can understand customer needs (and build an intimate connection with customer's feeling) much better than similar companies.
- Second is focus, namely, by executing as well as possible all the decisions that have been made and by ignoring other opportunities that are not important.
- Third is impute, namely, by presenting the best Apple products in a way that is equivalent to the product's goodness so that it will meet customer expectations.[29]

Apple is well aware that its customers want simplicity and have embedded that concept in its brand strategy. The design company Siegel+Gale (originator of the Simplicity Index) states that simplicity drives loyalty, growth, and sales. Sixty-four percent of consumers will tend to recommend a brand when interacting with it. Since 2009, a stock portfolio of the simplest publicly traded brands has shown a market advantage of 686%. And 55% of consumers say they will pay extra to avoid complicated experiences.[30]

Moving Toward Stakeholder Centricity

In Chapter 1, we discussed that the stages of QCDS consist of various levels, from the divisional-, company-, and customer- to the stakeholder-centric. You also learned that the input and output approach is inadequate. Even referring to outcomes is no longer sufficient; we must expand and move to the impact level.

Quality Factor Input Alone Is Insufficient

We can't rely on quality input alone because even the best input in the production process will not significantly affect the results if the production process is terrible. For example, one of Samsung's most sophisticated smartphones is the Galaxy Note 7. This smartphone is equipped with various outstanding features such as a high-quality screen, stylus, and excellent design, as well as a high-capacity battery with the ability to charge in a short time, which at the launch was seen as one of the advantages of this product.[31]

Only a short time after its initial launch, various issues occurred. Many customers reported problems. The smartphone would suddenly shut down, overheat, and even catch fire. An investigation found defects in the battery due to imperfections in the production process. This imperfection was because the factory that made smartphone batteries did not implement adequate quality control standards.[32]

As a result of these various problems, Samsung had to recall more than 3 million smartphones that had been sold, with an estimated cost of more than US$6 billion. Not only that, but Samsung also stopped production and scraped all the remaining Galaxy Note 7 products. Samsung's brand image wavered significantly and affected customer trust as well.[33] In conclusion, even though the input is good, if there is a problem at just one point in the production process, it can produce terrible final results.

A Good Product Quality Is Not Enough

If a quality input has gone through various production processes that run very well, have strict quality control, and have succeeded in producing a quality product output, it may not produce the expected outcome.

Quality products that previously received a warm welcome from the public are now becoming more mediocre and even less popular, with various new players competing fiercely to offer more attractive value propositions.

IBM (US) laptops are gone, and now Lenovo (China) is winning. Nokia (Finland) smartphones are no longer heard of, and now the Samsung (South Korea) and Oppo (China) brands are winning.

In the United States, the combination of General Motors and Ford Motor Company, which previously dominated the market, now has a market share of about 31% combined. If you include Tesla's electric cars in the market share, the total is only about 35% for the former two car giants. The rest of the car market is dominated by automotive products from Japan (such as Toyota, Honda, Nissan, Subaru, and Mazda), South Korea (Hyundai), and Germany (Volkswagen).[34]

Previously, only Japan and some other European industrial countries could provide excellent products. Still, with the increasing strength of South Korea and China, Japan now has to compete neck-to-neck with various products made in South Korea and China.

Display Market: Japan Versus South Korea   We can also learn from the digital display market (screens widely used in various devices such as smartphones, laptops, televisions, wearables, and so on, with different sizes and technologies). Four countries are the leading players in the display market: Japan, South Korea, China, and Taiwan. In 2020, South Korea was the number one leader in the display market (overall at 36.9%), and this has been the case for almost two consecutive decades. Meanwhile, China was slightly below South Korea with a market share of 36.2%, followed by Taiwan with a market share of 22.6%, and Japan only got a small percentage of 3.6% (see Figure 3.1).[35]

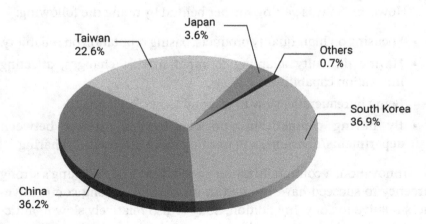

FIGURE 3.1   Market share of display (overall)

The industry led by two South Korean technology giants, namely, Samsung and LG, is determined to widen the gap with its closest competitor, China, by committing to investing more than KRW56 trillion to increase its global market share to reach 50% by 2027. South Korea will achieve that by widening the technology gap five years ahead with its closest competitors and raising its self-sufficiency ratio in materials, parts, and equipment to 80% from 65% as of 2022.[36]

Television Market: Japan Versus South Korea   What about the television market? Sony, which once dominated the global television market share, now has to recognize the leadership of Samsung, which managed to achieve a market share of almost 20% in 2022.[37] Combined with LG and TCL (from China), these three companies may already control more than 40% of the world television market share.

What makes South Korea such a strong player in the electronics industry? For simplicity's sake, let's compare Sony (Japan) and Samsung (South Korea) based on research results that Choong Lee and colleagues have published.[38] Samsung has experienced extraordinary growth and increasingly rapid market capitalization by adopting a strategy that assumes commoditization in the electronic market. Samsung is also very bold in making massive investments in innovation. These choices have succeeded in pushing Samsung to become a significant player.

However, Sony is getting further behind by doing the following:

- Focusing on high-quality products, basing reputation on reliability.
- Having difficulty adapting to rapid market changes, affecting innovation capabilities.
- Being bureaucratic, slow to respond to market demands.
- By having competition and conflicts of interest between departments/divisions, and needing more information sharing.

Innovation, a commoditization perspective, and Samsung's strong urgency to succeed have resulted in increasingly strong competitiveness relative to Sony. In addition, Sony is also relatively slow to anticipate market changes even though its products are high quality and reliable. Sony still needs to restructure its organization, while Samsung is getting more potent as a brand.

Simply relying on quality as the main strength is no longer sufficient for Sony to win the competition in a dynamic market. As Samsung has exemplified, remaining competitive requires agility, vigorous innovation, and sharpness in anticipating market dynamics.[39] Perhaps it is time for Japan, which believes that product quality is everything and can sell itself, to change its conservative view. Quality becomes generic, and we must consider many other things beyond the conventional definition.

Automotive Market: Japan Versus China   Japan has also received quite a heavy blow from China. If we look at the automotive industry, especially the electric vehicle (EV), carmakers from Japan cannot ignore that China's auto industry is now on the rise. The strengthening consumer interest in EVs has increased the EV market share globally.

Japanese automakers (including Toyota), which tend to be slow to develop and penetrate the market, might lose ground in several of their main markets to competitors from China.[40] It is even strongly predicted that China will surpass Japan regarding the number of passenger cars exported (see Figure 3.2). As history repeats itself, EVs are helping China do to Japan what Japan did to the United States in the 1970s.[41]

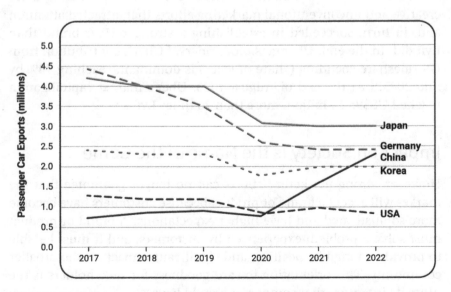

FIGURE 3.2   Passenger car exports [42] / with permission of Richard Katz

China is on its way to take over the world automotive market and now has become the second largest exporter of passenger vehicles, surpassing the United States and South Korea. This will create new tensions among its trading partners and competitors.[43] China is increasingly narrowing the gap with Japan after successfully surpassing car exports from Germany in 2022.[44] On top of that, in mid-2022, giant Chinese automaker BYD overtook Tesla as the largest EV manufacturer in the world and competed fiercely in the European market.[45]

A Robust Marketing Strategy Is Still Necessary

The quality of a product is not enough to determine market success. The marketing efforts need to be intense to ensure its success. We can learn from the competition between Uber and Lyft, two successful ride-hailing companies. Uber has been operating since 2009 and is more successful than Lyft, which began competing in 2012. One of the factors for Uber's success is its more aggressive marketing strategy. Uber uses various marketing communications channels, including digital-based ones (online advertising and social media), and leverages word-of-mouth in its multiple promotions.[46]

Uber was more daring in experimenting, thus encouraging more creative and unconventional marketing efforts that attracted attention and, in turn, succeeded in establishing a stronger Uber brand than Lyft did. In the end, Uber gets more riders.[47] Uber's contribution from US rideshare spending (share of sales) is dominant, reaching 74% by mid-2023.[48] At the end of August 2023, Uber's market capitalization reached US$95.34 billion, more than 20 times Lyft's.[49]

Impact on Society Is the Name of the Game

However, strong marketing efforts can no longer guarantee that the market will accept a brand or product because customers have become more sophisticated and have higher expectations. A brand or product must solve a problem experienced by customers, and it must be able to provide a tangible, positive, and significant impact on the broader community. This orientation toward goodness for stakeholders is the ultimate intention that companies should have.

The NYU Stern Center for Sustainable Business and Rockefeller Asset Management collaborated to examine the relationship between environmental, social, and governance (ESG) and financial performance by studying more than 1,000 research papers published between 2015 and 2020. ESG performance is an essential reference for assessing whether a company is considered by investors as conscious of environmental issues, social issues, and corporate governance in their decision-making process to invest or not in a particular company.

The results of this study indicate that the longer the company has been engaged in ESG practices, the more positive the effect on financial performance. Sustainability-related initiatives in companies also seem to encourage better financial performance mediated by improved risk management and more innovation. A company with low carbon output can enhance financial performance. The implementation of the ESG framework must be tangible, not just limited to ESG report disclosures, which do not necessarily relate to financial performance.[50]

Indeed, currently, many companies still define quality by looking at outcomes. But companies have begun to look at the impact of their products as part of their new definition of quality.

Now, we will step beyond customer-centricity and talk about implications for society, from input to impact (see Figure 3.3).

The increasingly relevant orientation toward impact is also shown by the increase in the number of S&P companies that disclose some information related to ESG. In 2020, it was found that 93% of S&P companies revealed ESG reports, which then increased to 99% of S&P companies at the end of 2021. This number increased by 30 companies compared to the previous year.[51]

The increasing relevance of ESG indexes can no longer be discounted. The Benchmark Survey found that globally ESG indices rose from 2019 to 2020 by 40.2%; in 2021, they grew even higher,

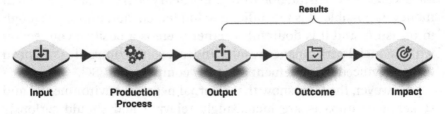

FIGURE 3.3 From input to output adapted from [52]

43.2% compared to 2020—a significant growth in line with increasing investor demand.[53]

Measuring Impact

ESG evaluation doesn't assess a business solely by profitability or returns aimed only at shareholders. ESG evaluations should be made auditable, for instance, by implementing the IFRS (International Financial Reporting Standards) S1 (financial disclosure related to sustainability) and IFRS S2 (financial disclosure related to climate change). Hence, it should be embedded into the business model, not just relying on "voluntary" (and even "one-sided") ESG reporting, which is not embedded in the business model and can't be audited in a widely accepted standards. They also provide essential information for customers who want to make more-informed purchasing decisions.[54]

ESG performance reporting is a mechanism that can show that a company's operational processes align with sustainability, an essential foundation for companies to remain stable and resilient when facing various emerging issues.[55] For investors, it can help find investments whose performance is sustainability-related. For the government, ESG performance reporting can be used to guide policies, which aim to provide services related to sustainability to support its constituents. For company management, the ESG framework is the basis for company operations to achieve various financial and nonfinancial targets, especially sustainability-related ones.[56]

Recent studies have found that a company can outperform the market and produce good long-term value if it has a high ESG score or rating.[57]

However, ESG has been criticized by those who say it is not desirable because it is a distraction from the primary goal of making as much money as possible, it is too difficult to implement and fulfill, it is tough to measure, and it is doubtful whether there is a positive connection with financial performance results. Indeed, some companies still need to be convinced to implement and fully comply with ESG.

However, the facts show that external negative environmental and stakeholder impacts are increasingly relevant and should seriously concern companies. There has been quite a lot of research showing that companies can achieve remarkable financial performance but, at the same time, also have high compliance with ESG.[58] We will use the ESG framework in the following discussion because it simultaneously accommodates the 4Ps, 5Ps, and SDGs we discussed in Chapter 2.

Shifting from Company-Centric to Stakeholder-Centric

Where a company falls on the company-centric to stakeholder-centric continuum will have consequences on different ESG aspects. The more stakeholder-centric, the stronger the compliance with ESG aspects, so the exposure to environmental, social, and governance risk is minor (see Figure 3.4).

Likewise, the role of quality assurance is also in line with a company's level of ESG compliance. At stage 1, quality assurance focuses only on various production factors that will be used in the production process, and therefore, management devotes a lot of attention to sourcing management.

At stage 2, quality assurance is focused on ensuring that production results meet various standards set by the company. Companies will devote much attention on the production process to the inventory to assess this stage. Therefore, companies must be able to implement good production, inventory, and product management on top of sourcing management.

At stage 3, quality assurance refers to assessing whether the results of various production processes and various supporting services are at least equal to or even exceed industry standards and meet customer expectations. In this regard, management tasks become more numerous and complex because they have to ensure a flawless distribution, customer, and brand management process.

At stage 4, quality assurance must ensure that quality is holistic from input, output, and outcome to a positive and significant impact on the broader community. In line with that, in addition to all the scope of management work that must be in place from stages 1 to 3, we must carry out one additional task, namely, stakeholder management.

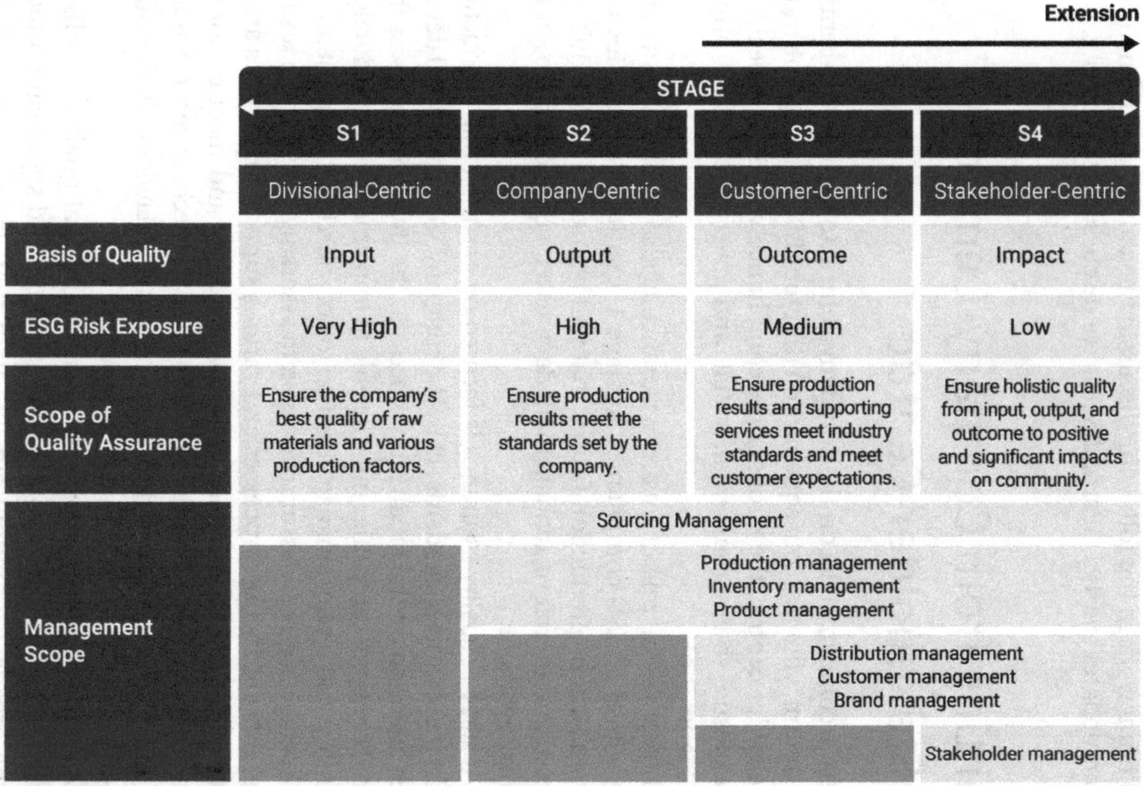

	S1	S2	S3	S4
	Divisional-Centric	Company-Centric	Customer-Centric	Stakeholder-Centric
Basis of Quality	Input	Output	Outcome	Impact
ESG Risk Exposure	Very High	High	Medium	Low
Scope of Quality Assurance	Ensure the company's best quality of raw materials and various production factors.	Ensure production results meet the standards set by the company.	Ensure production results and supporting services meet industry standards and meet customer expectations.	Ensure holistic quality from input, output, and outcome to positive and significant impacts on community.
Management Scope	Sourcing Management		Production management / Inventory management / Product management	Distribution management / Customer management / Brand management / Stakeholder management

STAGE → Extension

FIGURE 3.4 Shifting from company-centric to stakeholder-centric (quality)

Roles of Leadership and Management

In the omnihouse model, we see that the function of leadership is to protect values. At the same time, management ensures that the company can achieve results that meet the interests of shareholders and also comply with ESG aspects as expected. Therefore, leadership and management are dichotomies that must be converged (see Figure 3.5).

To ensure that the implementation of leadership will also accommodate ESG aspects, we should consider the following leadership roles:

- **Reviewing corporate values.** See whether existing corporate values are still relevant to externalities. Corporate values should be adjusted so ESG can be increasingly embedded in the company's strategy and daily operations.

- **Strengthening leadership commitment.** It is essential to ensure that all top-level management can set an example and that values will become part of the company's culture. This can be done through various outreach and training programs.

- **Overseeing ESG-based decisions.** Leaders must ensure that the management team's strategic and tactical choices have accommodated all considerations supporting ESG goals.

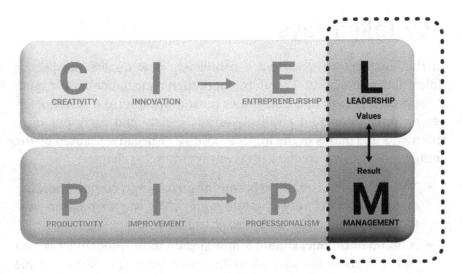

FIGURE 3.5   Convergence between leadership and management

So that the convergence between leadership and management can be consistent, several management roles must mirror those of leadership in supporting compliance with ESG aspects. Management needs to pay attention to the following:

- **Goals and measurements setting.** The scope of profitability and ESG targets must be realistic, executable, and measurably transparent so that compliance checks, continuous improvement, and adaptation to various feedback and changes in stakeholder demands can be carried out.
- **Collaborate with ESG-based partners.** Management needs to ensure that not only the company's value chain is ESG-oriented but also the company engages with the supply chain and even the business ecosystem, which also complies with the ESG framework.
- **Engage with stakeholders.** It is essential to build long-term trust from customers, employees, investors, and regulatory bodies. Strong confidence from stakeholders will have a positive impact on financial performance.

Clarifying leadership and management roles can significantly increase the company's market value.

Key Takeaways

In this chapter, we discussed a completely new quality perspective linked to sustainability. Therefore, more than a customer-centric quality approach is required. Companies must move toward a stakeholder-centric orientation that positively affects society and carry out measurements and audits of the impact (positive or negative) caused by the company. Following are the key takeaways from this chapter:

- The definition of quality is becoming increasingly complex because quality refers to a very dynamic context. The way we measure customer satisfaction levels is also changing.
- A brand or product should follow sustainability guidelines as well as being good quality and, at the same time, should be reliable and durable.

- Customers seek the product's functional or emotional benefits or a combination of both. Companies need to understand and manage customers' expectations to ensure that the quality level of their products and services conforms to the benefits customers seek.
- We can no longer rely on the conservative view that product quality is everything. We must consider a holistic definition of quality.
- Companies can no longer provide solutions to their customers only through various brands and products but must also show environmental and social responsibility. A company's impact on the environment and society is important.
- Focus on ESG is increasingly relevant, and the shift to becoming a stakeholder-centric company has consequences related to the scope of quality assurance and management.
- Leadership roles include reviewing corporate values, strengthening leadership commitment, and overseeing ESG-based decisions.
- Management must focus on setting goals and measurements, collaborating with ESG-based partners, and engaging with stakeholders.

CHAPTER 4

The New Perspective of Cost

From Cost-Cutting to Social Contributions

Japanese automaker Toyota is not in the top 10 list of global companies in terms of profit, sales, or market capitalization as of September 2023 (see Figure 4.1).[1] Even in the automotive category, it doesn't rank first in any of those categories (see Figure 4.2).[2] Nonetheless, Toyota is a world-class company that is unrivaled in its contribution to teaching operational excellence related to cost, which has had an impact on many companies from various industries.[3]

In addition to being an inspiration for implementing Kaizen, or continuous improvement, Toyota's car production process has become a benchmark for operational excellence in controlling costs for manufacturing companies worldwide. Remarkably, Toyota opened its various production facilities to other companies that wanted to lower production costs so they could learn about the Toyota Production System in the field.[4] Those who visit a Toyota facility can see how quality, cost, delivery, and process improvement have become a culture, even when those involved in the production process are neither nonpermanent staff members nor Japanese citizens.

Company	Country	When first passed			Record Value Date	Record value (US$ billion)	
		US$1 trillion	US$2 trillion	US$3 trillion		Unadjusted	Inflation-adjusted
Apple	US	2 August 2018	19 August 2020	3 January 2022	30 June 2023	3,062	3,062
Microsoft	US	7 June 2019	22 June 2021	–	18 July 2023	2,670	2,670
Saudi Aramco	Saudi Arabia	11 December 2019	12 December 2019	–	10 May 2022	2,450	2,450
Alphabet	US	16 January 2020	8 November 2021	–	18 November 2021	2,000	2,160
PetroChina	China	5 November 2007	–	–	5 November 2007	1,200	1,533
Amazon	US	4 September 2018	–	–	13 July 2021	1,900	2,052
Meta	US	28 June 2021	–	–	7 September 2021	1,078	1,164
Tesla	US	25 October 2021	–	–	1 November 2021	1,235	1,334
Nvidia	US	30 May 2023	–	–	23 August 2023	1,200	1,200

FIGURE 4.1 Largest companies in the world by market capitalization as of September 2023

No	Automotive Company (Country)	Revenue (US$ billion)	Net Income (US$ billion)	Market Cap (US$ billion)
1	Volkswagen AG (Germany)	284.34	19.76	81.0
2	Toyota Motor Corp. (Japan)	270.58	20.39	189.4
3	Stellantis (Netherland)	181.58	16.97	45.2
4	Mercedes-Benz AG (Germany)	156.23	25.64	70.2
5	Ford Motor Co. (US)	151.74	9.01	46.1
6	General Motors (US)	147.21	9.68	50.0
7	Honda Motor Co. Ltd. (Japan)	126.17	5.29	39.8
8	Tesla Motors (US)	74.86	11.19	435.1
9	Nissan (Japan)	73.73	0.9	12.7
10	BYD Co. Ltd. (China)	51.37	1.48	74.7

FIGURE 4.2 Largest automotive companies in the world based on revenue as of June 2023

Cost Management with Humanity

One of the highlights for those studying at Toyota's manufacturing facilities is seeing their effort to control costs. Toyota ensures there are no interruptions in the production process in order to meet the planned cost targets; in addition, many Toyota manufacturing facilities display cost reduction target charts that are easy for everyone to see. This chart rallies the joint efforts of all those in the manufacturing facility to achieve low costs over time.[5]

PI-PM Concept in Action

Efforts to control costs at the Toyota manufacturing facilities are a form of applying the productivity-improvement and professional-management (or PI-PM) concept of the omnihouse model, which is one of the most essential aspects of operational excellence, namely, the cost aspect. The management team and professionals in the manufacturing facility continuously make improvements to control costs and strive to increase worker productivity in the manufacturing facility. Through increasing worker productivity, management at the manufacturing facility can still maintain low costs even if they don't do layoffs, whether on a small or large scale.

For the improvement process to be seen as an effort to reduce costs, like it or not, the management team and professionals in the manufacturing facility are expected to have strong leadership in contributing to achieving operational excellence. The management team and professionals in the manufacturing facility must have the leadership skills to achieve cost reduction targets over time. As a result, they look to creativity and innovation to create a series of low-cost production processes from time to time, as shown in Figure 4.3.

In 1950, Toyota sent cost control initiators to various manufacturing facilities in the United States to conduct a comparative study with the aim of better understanding how best to control costs.[6] The team assigned to do a comparative study then shared their knowledge with other departments. A workshop was held based on the results of the comparative study.

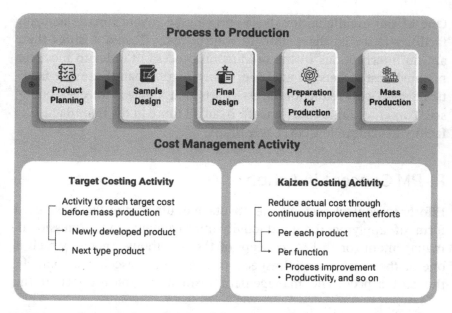

FIGURE 4.3   Target costing and Kaizen [7] / with permission of Institute of Management Accountants.

This was followed by implementation in some Toyota production units. Even though the impact was relatively small, it fostered enthusiasm that Toyota was going in the right direction. Toyota employees in production units were engaged in the process and became increasingly eager to seek various improvements to the production process to obtain low production costs.

The small success achieved by several production units that implemented improvements based on the results of comparative studies has encouraged other departments to make the same changes. The improvement efforts now have been systematized and structured, but by extending these changes to various other units, they increase the total impact.

Toyota's management has also created significant initiatives based on these production units in cost planning, mass planning, and standardization of parts. These changes are not one-time initiatives but are part of applying a Kaizen culture and process improvement.

Operational Excellence and Humanity

Many people do not realize that focusing on operational excellence to realize low costs can have a positive impact on people, especially employees, which in turn can affect society at large.

The measures aim to have everyone involved in minimizing or eliminating waste and increasing productivity. For example, cost-reduction efforts do not end in layoffs. Further, the measures can get everyone involved to minimize or eliminate waste and increase productivity. Labor costs do not have to be cut or reduced but are still maintained because the labor can be assigned to do other work, whether to increase product yield or improve product quality.

Everyone from workers to management in Toyota's production units are excited about creativity, innovation, and continuous improvement processes because they are critical components of achieving operational excellence in costs. Everyone is seen as individuals who will contribute to the production process and not just burden the company's finances. Therefore, employees don't mind doing additional jobs, so their wage allocation contributes to eliminating waste or increasing product quality.

Because employees have an entrepreneurial spirit and even leadership skills, they are also willing to work individually or jointly toward low-cost management over time. Implementing improvements and innovations is not an assignment from a higher management level but a desire to make a significant contribution from time to time. Under these conditions, employees are not easily complacent but will try to break the record for efforts to reduce costs achieved in previous years.

In other words, cost management with humanity is not only seen from the presence or absence of layoffs or the size of layoffs. Still, it encourages workers' continuous participation in cost control, as shown in Figure 4.4. This perspective also aligns with the Philip Kotler, Hermawan Kartajaya, and Iwan Setiawan book *Marketing 3.0: From Products to Customers to the Human Spirit* (Wiley, 2010), which shows how companies can pursue maximum profit while also being concerned for people and the planet. Concern for people certainly includes those involved in the production process. Employees do not become complacent but will try to break records for efforts to reduce costs achieved in previous years.

After all, even though technological progress, including AI technology, can improve processes, it is the entrepreneurial spirit, leadership skills, and professional attitudes that create great companies. Therefore, efforts to achieve operational excellence to produce low costs within the framework of the creativity-innovation and entrepreneurship-leadership (CI-EL) and productivity-improvement and professionalism-management (PI-PM) models are a way of managing costs with people.

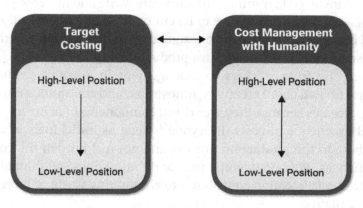

FIGURE 4.4 Two-way cost management [8] / with permission of Taufik

Entrepreneurial Cost-Cutting

Toyota, the world's benchmark in cost management, has developed a culture of cost-cutting and continues to improve efforts to reduce costs, creating situations that minimize the impact of cost-cutting. Even though cost-cutting is the most popular cost-management technique and is occasionally applied by companies of all sizes and industries, its implementation is often due to compulsion. Rarely is it done voluntarily.

Voluntary Cost-Cutting

Voluntary cost-cutting is part of the mindset of many workers and professionals usually at a managerial level in various Toyota manufacturing units, often by finding creative and innovative ways to lower production costs from time to time, especially when facing tough business conditions. Volunteering to cut costs happens more often than in traditional companies because there is transparency in cost management, including the target of low production costs to be achieved in awful business conditions. Collaboration for cost-cutting occurs not only in planning but also in implementation.

Not all companies are as lucky as Toyota because workers and management can voluntarily plan and implement cost-cutting. Moreover, planning and implementation are carried out continuously because they understand that the ultimate goal to be achieved is operational excellence at low cost as a mainstay to help restore a better financial condition.

Although only a few companies have a culture like Toyota, other companies still do voluntary cost-cutting. The worldwide COVID-19 pandemic in March 2020 created opportunities for many companies to cut costs. As a result of the sudden implementation of lockdowns and work from home (WFH) around the world, business activities came to a sudden halt.

Business activities such as sales, which are the company's source of income, stopped, but many companies already had costs that could not be contained, such as direct and indirect costs related to the production process. The trouble was that these costs were related to contracts or agreements with outside parties, many of which were long term and part of negotiations to obtain lower costs.

However, due to the sudden lockdown and WFH implementation, cost management data was not readily available to make decisions about cost-cutting efforts. Most had to rely on general data on various monthly costs. Still, more data was needed about the relationship between costs allocated to a production factor and its eventual performance. This lack of data about cost cuts made it difficult to know what areas to cut costs were to be prioritized and would have minimal impact on the company's business activities in the medium and long term.

Indeed, when it comes to cost-cutting, the rule of thumb has been to minimize medium- and long-term impacts. The problem is that efforts to reduce the implications are complex because production factor performance data is often not readily available. The other problem is the short time to make such cost-cutting decisions.

The impact seen in the short term is often prioritized in the form of reduced costs that can be saved. Acting on considerations like this, especially in an atmosphere of lockdown and WFH, companies felt forced to lay off employees and close production facilities that would end up affecting operational excellence in the medium and long term.

Examples from Leaders Matter

Despite facing an extreme situation as brought on by the COVID-19 pandemic, several company leaders chose a different way to handle cost-cutting, for example, by announcing that they would drastically cut their salaries first. This action encouraged voluntary efforts from other professionals and workers in the company to follow in the footsteps of the company's leaders in voluntary cost-cutting.

These professionals, responsible for managing the company, showed entrepreneurial leadership. In addition to showing the importance of voluntary cost-cutting, they also showed their commitment to togetherness in carrying out cost-cutting. So even though it's not as practiced by Toyota through a culture and process of continuous improvement in efforts to reduce costs, companies whose leaders implement salary cuts for their positions first get support from their employees in further cutting costs.

Because the forms and types of cost-cutting often carried out are well known to everyone in the company, widespread support for cost-cutting simplifies the implementation process—without going through a complicated negotiation process—and simultaneously minimizes the impact. At the same time, it also minimizes work process disruptions that often occur after cost-cutting is carried out. Even those affected by layoffs can accept it because the company has no choice but to maintain business continuity amidst a problematic situation. During the COVID-19 pandemic, leaders in many companies enhanced momentum to continue building a culture of realizing low production costs to enhance operational excellence in the future, no matter the circumstances.

Even with this, the uncertain situation triggered by the COVID-19 pandemic makes one or two cost-cutting practices inadequate. However, because there is an initiative to set an example in cost-cutting, the turmoil and disturbance that arise when implementing cost-cutting can be minimized.

In other words, even if it is done once and when business or financial conditions are bad, cost-cutting can be part of realizing operational excellence in the form of low costs and, at the same time, building a company's corporate culture. If, in a period, you carry out massive cost-cutting, and once the dire situation has passed, then you incur unnecessary costs again. It does not indicate a change in corporate culture triggered by cost-cutting.

Building a Cost-Cutting Culture

Building a corporate culture willing to cut costs takes much work. Sometimes, the best way to do so is to spend more time as a team, such as eating together at the company's cafeteria, which does not seem to directly relate to the production process. Because it is done daily, workers see management as cost-conscious people with integrity regarding cost-cutting, resulting in the workers also believing that cost-cutting efforts are carried out even in any field and by anyone in the company.

Of course, setting an example is not enough. Management's transparency in production cost targets and profit margins will help employees feel like they are part of the process.

Apart from that, it is necessary to give individual appreciation to those who have good performance but are affected by cost-cutting not only to those who achieved sales targets or targets for creating new products. By extending these positive emotions to those who have succeeded in reducing costs, even though they are no longer working in the company, the company will engender good will among all who work there. After all, large profits are obtained because of the significant sales figures and low production and nonproduction costs.

It must be admitted that cost-cutting becomes simpler when companies try to restore sound financial conditions in the face of tough competition or situations such as the COVID-19 pandemic. In such a business landscape, the operational interruption of cost-cutting is minor.

Cost-Cutting Driven By Business Landscape Changes

Cost-cutting becomes different when companies face changes in the business landscape triggered by technology, political-legal, and cultural, economy, and market. These changes are different from incremental cost-cutting efforts. Scenario planning must be developed based on a good understanding of the macro environment that can also see the impact on various elements in the microenvironment. Likewise, if someone understands the microenvironment well, they must be able to see the relationship with multiple factors in the macro environment.

We can conduct this analysis using the 4Cs framework. In the context of cost management, a company must understand the cost structure of its competitors so that it can develop various products with lower costs. However, a company that has succeeded in reducing its costs must still be able to provide the best solutions to its customers through various products (and supporting services) to its customers with higher value than its competitors.

Cost Reduction–Oriented Leadership

Implementing cost-cutting followed by a new cultural change is a good way to start down the path of cost reduction. Usually, cost-cutting is done only once and during terrible business conditions. However, cost reduction can be made at any time and even during good business conditions. Implementing cost reduction will be more straightforward if a new culture is oriented toward creating operational excellence via low costs.

Toyota provides an excellent example of how to implement continuous cost-reduction initiatives. The company started the initiative by conducting benchmarking by visiting several manufacturing facilities in the United States in the 1950s. After returning to Japan, the team moved toward for benchmarking and conducted various workshops to explore the possibility of lowering production costs. After successfully reducing costs for a very long time, Toyota decided to allow other companies to visit its manufacturing facilities and learn about how Toyota implemented benchmarking, including offering workshops, to reduce the cost.

Future Challenges for Cost Reduction

A new culture related to cost management will be easier to implement if various workshops are provided to explain what is happening. Workshops can start by discussing multiple scenarios of changing business landscapes faced by companies. The workshops should explain not only the anticipated changes and their implications for competition and customer preferences but also what must be done so that the company can survive and win the competition through low costs.

Identifying exact production costs today is difficult. In addition to standard expenses such as electricity, buildings, or labor, which may differ from country to country, there are also inputs for the production process.

That makes many of the world's leading companies today, including those from China, open themselves up to visits from other companies, especially in the production process department. Of course, they will not open in detail. But at least it will show what the automation process has done and the type of roles of humans in the production process.

Studying various industries around the world will reveal that the product cost structure per unit is increasingly complex. The additional costs arising from utilizing the latest technology to produce better products, including shorter time to market, contribute to lower total costs in the medium and long term. A cost reduction effort takes work.

Cost Reduction Through Technology and Outsourcing

Another workshop aimed toward cost reduction could look at current outsourcing practices, whether they involve nonproduction or production aspects. Are cost savings obtained through outsourcing to retain the quality standard of the input materials in the production process? Are costs incurred to ensure the quality of input materials made through outsourcing?

Nowadays, many companies choose two cost reduction initiatives, which at first cost a lot but in the long run can be cost effective. Under the Industry 4.0 scheme in Germany, many large companies cooperate with small and medium enterprises that have passed qualifications to become partners with large companies. The process of selecting and searching for existing production capacity is carried out quickly, followed by a fast production process that supports technology-based cost reduction initiatives.

Leaders of companies that reduce costs by relying on technology and outsourcing have a solid long-term vision, the second cost-cutting initiative. They don't want to do small cost reductions with only a short-term orientation but rather look for changes that will result in cheaper long-term cost advantages. In other words, the existence of cost reduction that has a long-term impact depends on the presence of visionary leaders and the impact of the initiatives undertaken.

The courage of several Japanese company leaders to take the flying geese approach is a well-known example of long-term cost reduction efforts.[9] The increasing cost of living and welfare in Japan, which affects labor costs, clearly requires higher sales volumes to overcome this increase. Relying solely on the Japanese market is only possible in the short run.

Moving the production base or outsourcing to other countries' markets, which do not yet have good purchasing power, is considered a bold investment in the short term. It is not certain that these markets will absorb products made in factories in countries with a low purchasing power.

But the decision by the leaders of Japanese companies to move factories offshore was the right one. Apart from finally being able to meet their cost reduction goals, they were also able to expand their market and sell more products.

The Acceleration of Digital Transformation

Visionary leaders regarding cost reduction apply the flying geese approach that is also carried out by many companies worldwide. During the COVID-19 pandemic, visionary leaders accelerated digital transformation to continue running their businesses amid the lockdown and the WFH implementation.

Although digital improvements will save costs in the medium and long term, additional costs where sales are small or nonexistent at first glance do not appear to be a cost reduction.

Reducing the number of offices provides immediate cost savings. However, accelerating digital transformation, on top of additional investments in technology, incurs additional costs in training and customer education to handling customer complaints and ensuring that the acceleration of digital transformation can run as planned. Fortunately, many visionary leaders considered medium- and long-term views during the COVID-19 pandemic.

Although there were some disturbances, including a limited internet network in terms of coverage and speed that was not within the company's control, slowly but surely the internet providers increased coverage and improved speed, and corporate leaders could see an increase in employee activity, which could be used to support employees. During the COVID-19 lockdown and WFH, employees could work longer hours, including during usual holidays. This additional time was used for digital transformation training, customer education, and complaint handling.

Because they were at home, many employees felt they had additional time to support company activities to adapt to the new business landscape. They also didn't charge for working overtime or for doing extra work. This provided an unplanned cost reduction and an increase in productivity.

Once employees and customers adapt to the accelerated digital transformation, they can begin to increase the number and reach of their customers. Even though many customers experienced a decrease in their purchasing power due to the COVID-19 pandemic, they could see that there is better productivity. So, once there was a vaccination process and economic recovery efforts during the COVID-19 pandemic, they saw a rapid increase in sales.

Adaptive Cost Management for Customer Value Optimization

Humane cost management requires the involvement of the workforce in the cost-reduction process and providing high value to customers. It isn't easy because efforts to create value can be an additional cost if you do not base them on good strategies and tactics, creating value as a reason for customers to buy products or services. Continuously providing high value to customers will be easier if all units owned by the company are managed as a value-creation chain, even though initially, all units have different goals.

Providing Value to Customer

The value in the eyes of customers and potential customers is seen from the amount of the total get compared to the total given. Total get includes functional and emotional benefits, and total give includes costs and other expenses.

Functional benefits will be seen from the level of product quality based on various relevant technical measures. In that case, emotional benefits can appear in recognition or have their status symbol. Both of them will oversee the image formation process so that the target market believes that the product to be purchased and consumed has high technical performance and is recognized by many people as having a high status. It is what, for example, has been done by luxury car manufacturers such as Mercedes-Benz and BMW.

Of course, they also educate about technical performance and build the image that those who value high technical performance are successful and have excess money. So they don't hesitate to say they get a high total gain, either because of high technical performance or the associations arising from being a luxury product user. A high total gain is far more significant in value than the total given in costs and other expenses for buying an expensive product.

Companies can use the value chain model introduced by Michael Porter in 1985 through his book, *Competitive Advantage: Creating and Sustaining Superior Performance* (Free Press, 1985). In this model, company activities are grouped into two parts: primary and secondary. Primary activities are those directly involved in value creation, from acquiring raw materials to after-sales service. Secondary activities can support the efficiency and effectiveness of primary activities.

The model Michael Porter introduced can help provide a macro overview of costs to provide value to customers. The company's activities have expanded and become more complex since Porter introduced his value chain model, which means this model has been combined with other models and concepts to make it relevant to changing times. Many cost management experts have creatively developed cost management concepts and techniques that can describe all costs to create value so that they are recorded and reported in full.[10]

The Implementation of Activity-Based Management

An example is introducing the concept of activity-based costing and activity-based management (ABM). According to ABM, as with the value chain model, activities in the company are divided into two kinds: those that provide added value and those that do not. However, the emergence of cost concepts such as ABM still requires recording the activities carried out to provide unique value and deserve high customer appreciation, which may be considered secondary or non-value-added activities in specific periods. Still, with changing times, it can change as the primary activity or value-added activity.

In 1970, BMW pioneered what is now known as connected mobility, long before the internet or even mobile communication. It was not yet a critical secondary or non-value-added activity at that time. But when it started introducing the integrated navigation system in 1994 or even BMW Telematics in 1998, BMW began to have secondary activities or non-value-added activities that could provide high value to customers. The connected mobility initiative, which was started in 1970 and continues to experience various value improvements that can be delivered to customers, now allows BMW to have a source of income other than traditional sources such as car sales, spare parts, or service in workshops, namely digital services.[11]

A primary or value-added activity makes it easy to manage costs up to profitability. BMW achieved this through painstakingly introducing products and educating customers so that they believed in the products' high value. Therefore, when BMW charges customers for various connected mobility products, BMW also has the option of charging based on integrated packages or based on actual use by customers, either in new cars or used cars.

Through BMW's creativity and innovation ahead of the times, and by continuing to make improvements, what was originally a nice-to-have value offering has become an expected value and even a point of a differentiation. The investment or costs incurred have not only been recovered but have even increased the company's profit. In other words, occasional customer value optimization can enable the emergence of adaptive cost management.

Differentiated Social Values Contribution

BMW management's vision of pioneering connected mobility in the 1970s was not the only example of creativity and innovation ahead of that time. Entrepreneur activist Anita Roddick and her partner

Gordon Roddick pioneered what is now known as *ethical capitalism*. Through a unique cosmetics business from England, The Body Shop, Anita Roddick introduced ways of applying ethical capitalism through ethically sourced, cruelty-free, and natural cosmetic ingredients.[12]

The Dawn of Ethical Capitalism

In running an ethically sourced business, Anita purchased directly from manufacturers of cosmetic raw materials not tested on animals. Anita believed that natural ingredients were safer to use and that no products should be tested on animals. But Anita's principle of ethical capitalism was not only limited to the product manufacturing value chain but also other ethical principles.

Such a value proposition attracted many people in the UK and Europe. That's why when Gordon suggested Anita develop a business through a franchise, many welcomed it. So the pioneered cosmetic shops appeared everywhere, and many customers bought their products.

At that time, it was difficult to imagine that ethically sourced and cruelty-free products could become a profitable business, creating a surprising situation when The Body Shop's valuation soared when it was finally listed on the London Stock Exchange in 1984. With a rapidly increasing valuation, Anita could carry out ethical capitalism in other arenas.

Coincidentally, before Anita started the cosmetics business in 1976, in the United States in 1970, Peggy Short and Jane Saunders set up a cosmetics shop whose products were self-made and also happened to use the name The Body Shop. But this US company was limited in size, and Anita Roddick wanted to expand her network in America. To avoid copyright issues, Anita Roddick paid Peggy Short and Jane Saunders for the copyright to use the name The Body Shop in the United States. It turned out to be the right step because the media in the United States helped increase its popularity, and even Harvard Business School made a case study related to ethical capitalism introduced by Anita Roddick in 1991.

Anita Roddick's actions became a pioneer for many companies who wanted to make social contributions and create attractive value for customers. Even though awareness of the environment and animal protection was not widely known in the 1970s or 1980s, it turns out that many people liked the ethical capitalism introduced by Anita Roddick. Not only do they choose The Body Shop's products but they also refill their original containers, which besides saving production costs is also environmentally friendly.

It turns out that the number of people interested in the social values contribution introduced by The Body Shop was quite large. Since its introduction in 1976 until 2000, The Body Shop became a profitable business with ample margins. It turned out that social values contribution was a value appreciated by customers.

Many other businesses wanted to emulate Roddick's model. What was interesting is that regulators were also interested in ethical capitalism. Regulators made regulations based on ethical capitalism, such as prohibiting cosmetic companies from conducting animal testing.

Eventually, The Body Shop's uniqueness diminished. But what distinguished The Body Shop were the players who first actively campaigned, practiced, and consistently implemented its framework, enabling the brand association of The Body Shop with ethical capitalism to continue.

Of course, different eras can contribute to increasing awareness of social values. Interestingly, similar to The Body Shop, companies that have become pioneers of corporate social responsibility or the 2030 Sustainable Development Goals, and consistently do so over a long period, have created value in their customers' eyes. Through such activities these companies can not only recover various costs incurred by such social values contributions through a premium selling price but also gain other sources of income.

Tesla is an example. As a pioneer of non–fossil fuel vehicles, Tesla not only has strong differentiation but also benefited when regulations regarding carbon taxes emerged. Until 2020, Tesla's revenue from carbon tax was even greater than its operational profit (although carmakers from China are getting stronger and starting to overshadow Tesla in the EV market).[13]

With more and more electric vehicle manufacturers, the income generated through carbon credits has decreased; however, this also means that there is a decrease in the differentiation of social values contribution offered by regulators. Therefore companies need to think about operational excellence in social values contribution.

If customer value optimization can be achieved through improvements in the value chain, differentiated social values contribution can also be achieved by revamping the series of social values contribution activities. In marketing campaigns, social values contribution is not just compliance with regulators but looks to be proactive in making social improvements. For example, what Carlsberg did in the Drink Responsibly campaign. Even though Carlsberg promotes its products at the same time, it also warns that consumers must understand the limits of consuming alcoholic beverages, so they must maintain limits so as not to get drunk.

Shifting from Divisional-Centric to Stakeholder-Centric

Suppose we want to shift from divisional-centric to stakeholder-centric, which helps companies to comply with ESG standards. To achieve this, companies must address costs (see Figure 4.5). In stage 1, the company must be able to ensure that various costs must be as low as possible to reduce losses at a particular time. To support this, companies want to be able to make quick decisions regarding costs and eliminate the sharing of "nonessential" spending under challenging times.

At stage 2, the company can ensure that it achieves various low costs to maintain sufficient margins over time. Companies must run their business efficiently by looking for new ways to reduce costs.

At stage 3, companies must be able to optimize customer value without increasing costs. Therefore, innovation becomes increasingly crucial so that companies can offer various options with different value packages at the same costs.

At stage 4, the company must demonstrate its positive role regarding social values without increasing costs. Companies must convince customers to accept the value proposition related to social values. Implementation must also be maintained consistently. Despite these efforts, costs should remain the same in the long run.

	STAGE			Extension →
	S1 Divisional-Centric	**S2** Company-Centric	**S3** Customer-Centric	**S4** Stakeholder-Centric
Cost Orientation	Cost-cutting	Cost reduction	Customer value optimization	Social values contribution
Time Frame	Particular time	Over the time	Medium term	Long term
ESG Risk Exposure	Very high	High	Medium	Low
General Guidelines for Cost Management	• Ensure the company's cost is low to reduce loss significantly at a particular time. • Ensure the company's ability to make quick cost-related decision-making. • Ensure the company's going concern during a difficult time by eliminating "non essential spending."	• Ensure the company's cost is low to maintain good margin over the time. • Ensure that the company can manage an efficient business operation that, in effect, will reduce costs in the long term. • Ensure the company's ability to discover new ways of operating the business that, in effect, will reduce costs in the long term.	• Ensure the company's optimization to customer value without increasing cost. • Ensure the company can innovate in providing better offerings at the same cost. • Ensure the company can offer various choices with different value packages at the same cost.	• Ensure the company's contribution to social values without increasing cost. • Ensure the company can persuade customers to accept value propositions related to social contribution at the same cost. • Ensure the company can consistently practice social value contribution at the same cost in the long term.

FIGURE 4.5 Shifting from divisional-centric to stakeholder-centric (cost)

Key Takeaways

In this chapter, we discussed how the cost element is no longer solely focused on a cost-cutting approach, but must also take into account contributions that are in line with social values that refer to humanity. Following are the key takeaways from this chapter:

- Toyota is the global Kaizen benchmark and is continuously improving low-cost or target costing. Toyota opens its production facility for others to learn target costing on-site.

- Toyota's target costing has impressed others because of its bottom-up approach, encouraging low-level staff members to propose cost-cutting or cost-reduction initiatives.

- A significant event such as the COVID-19 pandemic can drive voluntary company-wide cost-cutting and cost reduction. In other situations, examples set and practiced by top management consistently can create a low-cost corporate culture.

- Low-cost-oriented leadership can produce a low-cost corporate culture and encourage bold cost-reduction initiatives such as outsourcing or digital transformation.

- A low-cost initiative combined with a desire to give better value to customers will enable customer value optimization.

- An environmental-related cost reduction that is practiced long term can become an excellent social contribution to the community or world.

CHAPTER 5

The New Perspective of Delivery

From On Estimate to On Conscience

We can divide products into two main categories: goods and services. As a result, product delivery can be divided into two main types of delivery, namely, goods delivery and service delivery. Both of these processes have changed a lot recently.

For example, global food delivery has grown more than threefold since 2017, partly due to the availability of various attractive and user-friendly applications that can meet changing consumer expectations. The lockdown enforced during the COVID-19 pandemic in spring 2020 also provided a powerful impetus for adopting technology-based delivery services, which in turn helped save many restaurant businesses from closure. This push continued into 2021.[1]

What we buy in a shop or receive directly at home is the last part of a long delivery process, especially for multiple goods imported from other countries, which require a very long and complex shipment process. This process cannot be separated from various problems that result in delayed delivery times, which can potentially cause multiple losses. Hence, various parties involved in the shipment process continue to make efforts so that delivery from one point to another can be fulfilled on time. It is important to educate customers about how complicated the delivery process is.

There are many causes for delayed deliveries, such as technical problems with transportation modes (cargo aircraft, cargo trains, and ships carrying containers), weather, and customs processes. Certain factors are now even more crucial in ensuring a delivery free from delays, namely, technology that makes it possible to integrate various processes and monitor multiple activities of the various parties involved in the delivery. Investing in cloud-based hardware and software can provide a more holistic approach that enables couriers, third-party logistics providers, other logistics, and transportation companies to stay connected and benefit from real-time data. Such a holistic approach helps reduce (even eliminate) delivery delays.[2]

In an era when online business is growing, we are increasingly accustomed to e-commerce delivery, namely, the transportation of goods ordered from an online shop to the customer's address, going through the stages of order processing to order fulfillment and even return processing. This journey, which involves many processes and parties, now plays an increasingly crucial role so that goods can reach customers earlier and cheaper while preserving the goods' quality and safety. E-commerce brings the delivery process to a much better efficiency level. The delivery process can influence customer perceptions and satisfaction with online stores. In one recent survey, 60% of respondents chose to buy from competing e-commerce sites with more convenient shipping options. The delivery process can be a differentiator so that an online store is more competitive in highly crowded industries.[3]

Online shopping also affects brick-and-mortar retail stores significantly; it requires them to adopt various in-store technologies and be compatible with multiple technologies in their supply chain, both upstream and downstream. According to a McKinsey study, with capable in-store technology, stores can improve their customer experience, better employee engagement, and make store management easier, increasing profitability by up to two times. According to McKinsey's calculations, today's technology that can transform profit and loss shows positive return on investment figures.[4]

To survive in today's business environment, retailers must improve their store economics by simplifying, eliminating, or automating routine activities. Omnichannel shopping is increasing, so retail stores must immediately realize that the conventional supply chain network is no longer sufficient because it is not designed to meet the demands of increasingly fast delivery and excellent service. Therefore, companies must implement a customer-centric supply chain strategy, namely, an omnichannel supply chain that meets customer needs across all channels.[5]

Today, more and more people expect to receive their purchases within a day, and the speed of receiving goods increasingly influences their shopping decisions.[6] Amazon has overhauled its delivery network and stated that it can now deliver more packages in one day or less in the United States and aims to double that number in the next two years.[7] Receiving delivery goods faster will increase brand satisfaction and improve the shopping experience. According to the 2016 Pulse of the Online Shopper survey results, 39% of people chose to buy from marketplaces that offer faster shipping options, and 46% abandoned shopping carts because shipping took too long or was not provided.[8]

In addition, late deliveries will have a significant impact because 17% of respondents will stop shopping at a retailer after receiving one delivery delay, and 55% will stop shopping at a retailer after receiving two to three delivery delays.[9] So, it is unsurprising that delays will reduce customer retention rates (which also increase customer acquisition costs) and, in turn, reduce customer lifetime value, not to mention the decline in the company's reputation due to negative word of mouth (which harms brand equity), which can make it challenging to acquire new customers.[10]

Delivering Goods: Past and Present

Before the digital system era took on its dominant role of today, recipients of goods didn't always know where their goods were and how far along the shipping process was. For example, DHL services had minimal tracking capabilities and visibility in the predigital era. Package handling (including sorting, physical tags, and paperwork) had to be done manually for identification and tracking purposes. In the 1970s and 1980s, DHL communicated with its customers to convey updated information via fax or telephone.[11] When was the last time you used a fax machine? Generation Z has probably never used a fax machine.

Such was the case with Maersk Line in the predigital service era. Maersk was a leading shipping company and still processed various documents for tracking and managing container shipments manually until the late 1980s. Customers had to contact the port directly (or even go directly to the port office) to track a shipment or get updates on the status of container movements. Orders for delivery of goods and documentation were handled via fax communication.[12]

Nowadays, when the role of technology is so vital in various delivery processes, the difference is stunning. At the end of 2022, Walmart opened its first next-generation fulfillment center, integrating people, robotics, and machine learning to speed up the fulfillment process. Walmart also implemented a drone delivery network that enables customers to receive tens of thousands of items weighing no more than 10 pounds in no more than 30 minutes.[13]

Technology plays a vital role in delivery services, as demonstrated by UPS's mesh methodology for near real-time tracking and cellular sensors for tracking deliveries beyond the UPS network.[14] UPS is also testing sustainable last-mile solutions using eQuad cycles, four-wheeled "bikes" powered by electricity. Another delivery company, Zipline, operates an on-demand drone delivery network that it claims is the largest in the world. Currently, there is one delivery to a location every two minutes. Zipline has made more than 400,000 autonomous deliveries of more than 4 million products, ranging from health-related and agriculture products to retail items.[15]

As you can see, there are many significant differences between goods delivery before the digital era and today. The following three factors characterize the difference between how goods used to be delivered compared to today:

- **Shift to online shopping and home delivery.** Ordering goods, usually done at physical ordering places or manually via telephone or fax, has now begun to be replaced electronically with the availability of various supports in the digital ecosystem. In the past, tracking was difficult (perhaps even impossible), so the delivery time for goods depended on estimates. Orders can now be made online via digital platforms, delivery times are faster and adjusted to customer wishes, and tracking exact locations is easy.[16]

- **Shorter delivery time.** In the past, the delivery of goods took longer. Sophisticated inventory management and distribution and logistics management has revolutionized how goods are delivered. It is not surprising that many people now offer speedy delivery of goods, even in one day or less. The goods delivery service is not only fast but also very reliable. Advances in technology have made it possible for various processes related to the delivery of goods to become more efficient, even for customers in remote locations.[17]

- **Higher reliability.** In the past, shipping goods was often characterized by many cases of damage and loss. Items were sent in large quantities at once, so individual attention to each package was not available. Now, goods are shipped in separate packages to reduce the risk of damage. Product loss has also significantly decreased thanks to sophisticated GPS tracking technology. The fleet management system has also been strengthened with sophisticated technology: data analytics and predictive maintenance, vehicle diagnostics and Internet of Things integration, fleet management software solutions, and so on. This technology helps companies track their shipments in real time and ensure they are timely.[18]

Delivering Services: Past and Present

Likewise, there have been many changes in the way services are delivered now compared to during the 20th century. In the health sector, for example, the in-person consultation method is the most common choice when someone wants to get medical help. Even though cell phones have been around for a while and widely used by the general public, most people still chose to meet directly with a doctor to ensure that the doctor can fully understand their complaints.[19]

However, with the onset of the COVID-19 pandemic, patients could not meet doctors directly because of government-mandated lockdowns, resulting in a method that later became known as *telemedicine* (or *telehealth*). Telemedicine makes it easy for people to access health services in a practical, faster, safer, and more reliable manner. For example, telemedicine services have increased significantly in Indonesia during the COVID-19 pandemic, in line with the acceleration of digitalization in the country. According to ALODOKTER records, the number-one digital health platform in Indonesia with more than 30 million active users every month and supported by more than 80,000 doctors, the number of telehealth users in 2021 increased by 30% compared to the previous year.[20]

Apart from accommodating various drug purchases and medical needs and scheduling in-person consultations, telemedicine services also make it possible to carry out virtual consultations with doctors with service quality equivalent to in-person consultations, offering consumers more choices of practices. The role of artificial intelligence (AI), for example, in ALODOKTER, is often used as a clinical decision-making tool to assist doctors in analyzing and diagnosing their patients.[21]

What about taxi services? Taxi services could have been more efficient several decades ago, especially when cellular telephones were not as mainstream as now, so on-call services could only be done in places where fixed-line telephone facilities were available. As mobile phones became widespread, it became easier to order a taxi, but it still needed to be more flexible.

Past business models for taxi companies were less flexible than today. Ride-hailing services like Uber, for example, position drivers as independent contractor partners. Using apps in ride-hailing services also provides more flexibility to users with dynamic rates depending on the high or low demand at certain hours.[22] Conventional taxis have now adopted various technologies, including apps, to remain competitive amidst increasingly fierce competition since the advent of ride-hailing.[23]

The banking industry is also changing with digital technology. Customers can now share their digital banking activities online anywhere and anytime via smartphone or website-based apps. Online banking and electronic payments are popular because they are convenient and safe and provide various services that can be accessed via smartphone. As a result, digital banking penetration in the European Union is, on average, 60%; in some Northern European countries, it is approaching 100%.[24]

Digital banking provides an online banking experience entirely different from before, where customers usually had to be present at the bank for various financial transactions. Conventional banks, even though they provide digital banking services, still need physical offices to operate and deliver several banking services. By contrast, digital banks have increased recently and do not need physical offices.[25]

Opening an account and applying for a loan at a digital bank is done entirely online with various services that can be accessed 24/7, operating similarly to conventional banks' online services. Digital banks are usually also part of the ATM network, but traditional banks usually provide their ATMs with easily recognizable names and logos. Various fees at digital banks are generally lower than at conventional banks, and customers are often not charged fees for withdrawals. Digital banks usually also offer higher deposit interest rates. However, the product choices are more limited than traditional banks. Customer service sometimes relies on service helplines or chatbots, which, in some cases, might not be as responsive as real people.[26]

Let's now look at the tourism industry. In the past, we relied on travel agents for various needs, from buying plane tickets to booking hotels, choosing destinations, and so on. But now, a person can meet all their needs by simply using a mobile travel app that provides all the services that a conventional travel agent does. We can access real-time price data for multiple modes of transportation and accommodations, different accommodation choices, and many other travel needs. We can also see many more objective assessments or ratings related to choices of hotels, airlines, and tourist destinations.[27]

You can see that there are several significant differences between service delivery in the predigital age versus now. The following are the three main factors that characterize service delivery today:

- **Significant online role.** Various online processes increasingly dominate our interactions with service providers. Many needs can ultimately be fulfilled online. Some services that used to require an in-person experience now can be fulfilled at your location (e.g., pet grooming, car repairs and upkeep). Physical locations are still needed for services such as medical procedures and testing, but in other fields, such as banking, having a physical location plays a minor role.

- **High flexibility.** The more integrated various service providers are with other service providers in a digital ecosystem, the more flexible they prove for customers. They can provide more varied options and even allow customers to customize their needs to a certain level. This flexibility also includes freedom in accessing services for a certain number of service products; for example, a digital wallet service connected to various parties in one digital ecosystem allows someone to carry out various financial transactions anytime, anywhere, with any party, for different payment purposes, with multiple customization options.

- **Hassle-free.** Customers can save more time and effort to get solutions from service providers. The process has become paperless, more environmentally friendly, queue-free, and can be done anywhere and anytime. In addition, the level of security is also high.

The Details of Today's Tech-Driven Delivery Processes

The development of today's delivery processes are very much influenced by technology. Companies are increasingly empowered with the help of technology such as AI, data analytics, big data, and so on.

Likewise, technology has become an essential part of customers' lives, changing how they carry out the decision-making process, making them very sophisticated and bringing them to a powerful bargaining position. Customer expectations are becoming higher; hence, it is increasingly difficult to satisfy and make them loyal.

Technology makes competition more open and challenging in line with the increasing interdependence of the global economy. Technology affects the increasingly complex process of delivering goods and services from one party to another, especially in cross-border delivery.

E-commerce (via various platforms) is becoming increasingly dominant in many countries, seriously threatening small businesses that still run traditionally or conventionally. The old-school business model seems incompatible in the rapidly growing sharing economy era. In general, here are some phenomena that we can observe:

- The speed of the delivery process is increasingly crucial as we see widespread demands for same-day delivery, even within hours or minutes, especially for various time-sensitive products.
- Flexibility is a critical capability, considering that every customer also demands high flexibility regarding the delivery of the products they purchase. Each customer can even customize delivery options according to individual wishes.
- It is difficult for companies to be flexible if they rely only on existing resources, capabilities, and competencies. Therefore, collaboration

with various parties (in a business ecosystem) is necessary. Companies must be able to harness the ecosystem advantage.

- Customers can review the products they buy and provide ratings on the delivery process, which becomes a reference for other customers in making decisions.
- Sustainability aspects are also becoming increasingly important in the delivery process. Customers are increasingly critical of viewing the delivery process concerning environmental impacts and social well-being.
- Updated, accurate, and timely data is necessary to win the competition. A data-driven delivery process can increase the company's operational efficiency and enable flawless customer experiences.
- Digital connectivity has enabled all processes from end-to-end—from searching for product information; selecting, ordering, determining time and delivery point (door-to-door or pick-up); and tracking processes to payment options (such as online payment)—to be done conveniently and hassle-free.

In a nutshell, everything is becoming increasingly customer-centric (even stakeholder-centric). Therefore, all selection and allocation of resources, development of capabilities, and formation of core competencies are directed at providing solutions to customer problems, even at the individual level. In addition, creativity and innovation play an increasingly important role in companies responding to changes in the business environment, especially in meeting diverse customer expectations.

How Companies Have Responded Proactively to Tech Changes

Technology has changed how goods and services are being delivered. A proactive response is necessary to survive in increasingly tight competition.

McDonald's, for example, started its McDelivery services to provide convenience to its customers who want their favorite fast food delivered to their doorstep. This McDelivery service is becoming increasingly popular in line with the rise of online food delivery services. The McDelivery service provides added value for customers because they can enjoy dishes from McDonald's without having to leave their homes.[28]

Uber also doesn't want to be left behind so they started providing UberEats, a food delivery service that is part of their ride-hailing service. This application was officially launched in early 2016, providing a platform for people to order food from many local restaurants and have it delivered directly to their doorstep.[29]

Pizza Hut is increasingly relying on its Pizza Hut Delivery (PHD) to respond to increasingly severe levels of traffic congestion and the increasing number of women who are now also working. This Pizza Hut subsidiary is also a way to create a barrier for possible entry by competitors. PHD is designed to capture segments their dine-in restaurants have yet to capture fully.[30]

The DHL eCommerce unit has launched DHL Parcel Metro, a fast and flexible new service for online retailers that meets growing consumer demand for same-day and next-day delivery. Parcel Metro uses special software that enables DHL eCommerce to create a "virtual delivery network" consisting of local and regional delivery vendors and crowdsourcing providers to ensure maximum flexibility and capacity in the last mile. Retailers can offer a fully branded delivery experience to their customers. The service creates a seamless experience for consumers: the retailer's branded customizable mobile interface enables them to track deliveries in real time, relay special instructions to their couriers, reschedule deliveries, and rate their delivery experience.[31]

Another example is Fulfillment by Amazon (FBA), which is a program to help Amazon sellers outsource the fulfillment process to Amazon. Sellers can register inventory on FBA to store their products in Amazon fulfillment centers. So, when customers order, Amazon can pack, ship, and provide customer service for FBA items.[32]

These changes force companies to achieve much higher levels of delivery efficiency, which means faster processes with no margin for error. It must also be more effective, which means using appropriate assets to meet market demand, being customer-centric, and even considering sustainability. The expected final result is a reduction in costs. However, this condition is no longer ideal because it has shifted and expanded from on-estimate to on-schedule, then to on-demand, and finally to on-conscience delivery.

Shifting from On-Estimate to On-Conscience Delivery

The transition from on-estimate delivery to on-conscience delivery aligns with the shift in orientation toward customers and the increasingly strong desire for sustainability that a company must promote. A company's delivery approach must also adapt to these conditions if it wants to continue to exist now and in the future.

On-Estimate Delivery

An example of *on-estimate delivery* is low-cost economy shipping, which is often the choice if the goods being sent are not too time-sensitive. For faster delivery, a customer usually has to pay more. Yes, generally, shipping costs are directly proportional to delivery speed. For the business-to-business segment, this low-cost option on a particular scale will significantly affect the price of the goods sold.[33]

Online shops usually rely heavily on delivery solutions with this low-cost option to achieve sufficient profitability margins, especially for bulk deliveries. In some conditions, the difference in delivery arrival time between this low-cost option and the more expensive type of delivery is not too significant for domestic deliveries.[34]

Low-cost deliveries like this often provide estimates of delivery arrival to users of the delivery service, for example, between 1 and 5 days or between 7 and 12 days. Sometimes, it provides an estimated arrival date for the delivery of goods, for instance, between November 10 and November 15. Many leading shipping companies often provide tracking links to their customers so they can follow the journey of the goods being sent.

Let's look at one of the cost-effective domestic delivery options offered by UPS, which sends packages by road using trucks, not airplanes. For cost-effective deliveries such as UPS® Ground, the estimated time for goods to reach their destination is between one and five days, depending on the delivery destination, which is longer than other delivery options such as UPS Next Day Air® or 2nd Day Air® delivery.[35]

On-Schedule Delivery

Sometimes, we choose a delivery option not based on how fast or slow the delivery arrives but on whether the delivery schedule suits our needs. Therefore, we can select several delivery time options or schedules based on the fixed time offered by the delivery service provider, which also best suits the recipient of the goods. In essence, the delivery service provider offers some scheduled delivery time options. Then, the sender and recipient agree to decide which schedule is most suitable for them and can meet the needs of all parties.[36] This is *on-schedule delivery*.

For example, FedEx provides a service that allows us to select a specific delivery date and time that FedEx has scheduled. After that, we can track the whereabouts of our package. Package visibility is also equipped with notifications via email or text. FedEx Delivery Manager can help us schedule package deliveries according to our needs so that we have more control over when, where, and how we receive packages that are being shipped.[37]

On-schedule delivery is still popular because, with a fixed schedule, we can align a value-creation process with various elements in the company's supply chain so that it is more efficient and, in turn, can provide guarantees to customers of the availability of the products they want according to when those products are needed. Certainty in the availability of these products will increase the credibility of the company that provides these products, increase consumer confidence, increase customer satisfaction, even form customer loyalty, and, in turn, strengthen the company's brand equity.

On-schedule delivery is still very relevant. After all, it positively influences the company's operational efficiency while maintaining long-term customer relationships because it creates high trust. Combining these two things is essential to forming a competitive advantage in tight competition.

On-Demand Delivery

On-demand delivery is the most suitable option for various time-sensitive products. In busy urban areas with very high and demanding customer expectations, businesses need delivery solutions that meet their needs quickly and sometimes almost instantly. Changes in the business environment with increasingly tight competition and technological advances in the availability of on-demand delivery applications have also triggered why on-demand delivery has become mainstream in various big cities in different parts of the world. In the next few years, retailers, restaurants, and various other producers plan to offer same-day delivery, with most targeting delivery times in the range of 30 minutes.[38]

Leading companies that sell various goods, such as Amazon, or those that provide services, like Uber, are examples of how sophisticated on-demand delivery operations work. Companies like that can truly satisfy the desires of their customers because they have very flexible on-demand delivery management capabilities. With solid technological support, they can seamlessly integrate collaborations with various parties, free from hiccups, in a digital business ecosystem. Customers can also communicate and track in real time.[39]

Amazon Prime, which has been around since 2015, helps its members to get whatever they want and need quickly and reliably. The same-day delivery service provided to its members has expanded to more than 90 major cities in the United States. Buyers will receive the goods they ordered, for example, beauty goods, household necessities, pets, and apparel, not only conveniently but quickly. Same-day delivery for orders over US$25 in most cities is free for Prime members. If you do not meet the minimum order price, members can still enjoy the same-day delivery service with a fee of US$2.99, whereas non-members are charged a fee of US$9.99.[40]

Of course, this is all triggered by the availability of technology that increasingly strengthens connectivity. Moreover, the proliferation of smartphones and internet penetration increasingly supports a very high level of community mobility. Access to on-demand services is increasingly wide open. It enables people to obtain a wide range of products (goods and services) according to their wishes and needs wherever and whenever through a very convenient process.

GPS technology also enables buyers to track in real time and accurately follow the progress of their order delivery. By using data analytics, companies can optimize various areas, including determining ideal delivery routes and predicting demand, which can significantly increase operational efficiency. If operational efficiency increases, profitability margins will also increase.

On-Conscience Delivery

The results of the three forms of deliveries described previously still range from input to output and outcome but have yet had only a negligible impact on society. In fact, for some of the situations we've discussed, we can observe the increasing importance of sustainability, which aligns with the increasingly strengthening level of conscience among customers. The growing importance of ESG aspects in business also encourages people to see how companies will ultimately realize all ESG-related concerns in the delivery context. Conscience is inevitably an essential aspect of the delivery process.

On-conscience delivery is becoming a necessity with the increasingly critical thoughts, attitudes, and behavior of customers and a society oriented toward environmental sustainability. An IBM Research Insights report found that 57% of consumers are willing to change their e-commerce purchasing habits to decrease their negative environmental impact. Therefore, to fulfill these new demands, companies must be able to adjust their supply chains and logistics systems. Although the process is slow, more and more CEOs are making sustainability a priority for their companies.[41]

Environmentally friendly logistics is a priority in the retail and logistics industry, considering that the freight and transportation industry significantly affects greenhouse gas emissions as the most significant contributor to greenhouse gas emissions in the United States, namely 28%. According to the World Economic Forum, this number is expected to grow by up to 30% with the estimated increase in online shopping and last-mile delivery. These facts will encourage individual and joint efforts by companies in the logistics sector to reduce their carbon footprint. We are entering the era of green logistics with increasingly efficient supply chains and logistics processes that can reduce energy consumption. Besides being more environmentally friendly, a green logistics approach can also increase the company's profit margin in the long term.[42]

The delivery route could provide an ESG approach. When the transportation industry prioritizes sustainability in its operations, it can reduce the time and mileage spent making the same number of deliveries. This reduction in time also results in greater drop density (more deliveries made by the same driver at the same time), resulting in a lower carbon footprint.

If we simplify it, there are several essential components in a delivery process (especially for tangible products/goods), namely, the product to be delivered, the mode of transportation to deliver the product, the route to be taken, and the customer who sends or receives the product. Of these four components, two components are directly related to delivery, namely, transportation and the route it takes. We must see to what extent sustainability aspects can be accommodated well in each of these components, especially those related to the delivery aspect.

Regarding products, ideally, the value proposition must show compliance with various requirements related to sustainability, for example, using environmentally friendly materials or green materials that can be recycled and reused. The production process refers to green manufacturing, including using electrical energy sourced from renewable energy. The packaging also uses recycled materials and does not overdo it so that it can cause unnecessary waste.

The sender or recipient of the goods should be educated enough regarding the importance of sustainability so that from the start they can choose environmentally friendly products, which, in turn, also ensures that they will not harm the environment.[43] They can determine how the product can be appropriately delivered, including choosing the most environmentally friendly and efficient transportation mode and other sustainability-based preferences.

Now, let's review two other aspects: the mode of transportation and the route.

- **A sustainable-oriented means of transportation.** On-conscience delivery uses environmentally friendly means of transportation such as electric vehicles (EV) or those using eco-fuel (high-quality, biofuel, hydrogen, etc.). Especially for last-mile delivery, you can use an EV or even a bicycle. The choice of means of transportation will determine the extent to which we can reduce air pollution and carbon emissions.

- **The use of technology for route optimization.** By optimizing delivery routes, companies will be able to save fuel consumption and reduce carbon emissions because they can find the shortest, fastest, and most traffic-free way. Collaboration with all parties in the supply chain, from upstream to downstream (down to the delivery mile) can help increase efficiency, reduce failed deliveries, and reduce carbon footprint.[44]

Educating the public to choose sustainable products and packaging and then select a delivery process oriented toward sustainability must also be done to enhance on-conscience delivery and end-to-end green logistics. In the future, more and more customers will be willing to pay more for various products and supporting services that firmly commit to sustainability. Multiple regulations, certifications, and compliance with environmental standards, which are increasingly enforced in many countries, will encourage various parties to implement a sustainability-oriented business approach.

In line with the growing eco-consciousness of customers, sustainable delivery processes are increasingly becoming necessary and can contribute significantly to various positive efforts for environmental preservation. However, it will also strengthen the company's reputation and, in turn, guarantee the company's viability in very tight competition.

One example is the GoGreen Plus solution implemented by DHL Express to reduce carbon emissions from its cargo aircraft fleet using sustainable aviation fuel (SAF). SAF—a substitute for conventional jet fuel—is a biofuel from renewable sources such as crops, vegetable oils, and waste products. Using SAF can reduce greenhouse emissions by up to 80% compared to fossil fuels.[45]

The method chosen by DHL Express is not simply "offsetting" the carbon emissions produced. DHL Express prefers the "insetting" approach, which is directly embedded in their business processes and can have a direct impact without going through other parties.[46]

Consequences of the 1PL to 6PL Shift

Logistics services are shifting from first-party logistics (1PL), namely, a company (or individual) that carries out the process of transporting and delivering goods with its self-owned vehicles without involving any other party, to fifth-party logistics (5PL), which provides fully integrated solutions with visibility real time throughout the supply chain through IT solutions. This shift is a response to increasingly stakeholder-oriented needs. This orientation toward stakeholders, especially those related to sustainability, requires a holistic solution in the supply chain, from upstream to downstream. Now, we have to get ready to welcome the presence of sixth-party logistics (6PL), a logistics concept that offers fully integrated supply chain solutions that are partially automated by using AI.[47]

The role of big data and predictive analysis will become increasingly important. It can provide many benefits, including increasing efficiency because it can shorten delivery time and reduce inventory level, transportation, and inventory costs. The level of customer satisfaction will also increase as service improves. Costs will also decrease, and achieving higher profit margins is possible.[48]

In line with the increasing importance of sustainability in business, including in the logistics sector, a green logistics approach focusing on reducing the carbon footprint is increasingly inevitable. This green logistics approach (which includes first-, middle-, and last-mile logistics) is a priority when we realize that transportation is the largest source of greenhouse gas emissions, as in the United States.[49]

Therefore, if we want an extension toward on-conscience delivery that is stakeholder-centric with low ESG exposure and can have a significant sustainability impact, we must strengthen collaboration with various parties in a logistics ecosystem supported by capable technology (see Figure 5.1).

	STAGE			
	S1	S2	S3	S4
	Divisional-Centric	Company-Centric	Customer-Centric	Stakeholder-Centric
Delivery Orientation	On Estimate	On Schedule	On Demand	On Conscience
ESG Risk Exposure	Very high	High	Medium	Low
General Characteristics of Logistics	• The important thing is that the shipment reaches its destination. • Stand-alone, there is not much collaboration with logistics service parties. • Advancement of logistics is still at 1PL or 2PL. • Low-tech (or even no tech), inefficient, not yet green-minded.	• It has started to incorporate efficiency. • Still relying on the power of the value chain but already partially connected and collaborating with logistics service parties. • Advancement of logistics is at 3PL. • Relying on low- to mid-tech to support efficiency, new green insights at an early stage.	• Have taken into account efficiency and effectiveness (or productivity). • It is fully integrated and collaborates with logistics service parties. • Advancement of logistics is at 4PL. • Relying on hi-tech to achieve high productivity and has implemented some of the green approach.	• Oriented toward productivity and sustainability. • It is fully integrated with logistics service parties with holistic supply chain coverage. • Advancement of logistics has reached 5PL (and is preparing for 6PL). • Relying on advanced technology (IoT, AI, big data) that is fully integrated into the logistics ecosystem.

Extension →

FIGURE 5.1 Consequences of the shifts toward logistics

Key Takeaways

This chapter explains how product delivery is applied more sophisticatedly in line with technology-based delivery methods. Tech-driven technology shifts the concept from on-estimate delivery to on-conscience delivery and provides a much better customer experience. Following are the key takeaways from this chapter:

- The delivery process has changed a lot in line with the growth of e-commerce. Technology helps to integrate various processes and monitor multiple activities of the various parties involved in the delivery process.

- More people expect to receive their purchases within a day; hence, the speed of receiving goods influences shopping decisions, increases brand satisfaction, and improves the shopping experience.

- Delivery today is much different than before the digital era, when technology plays an extraordinary role. The shift to online shopping, home delivery, shorter delivery times, and higher reliability have caused the old-school business model to become obsolete.

- Companies and customers are empowered with digital technology, enabling seamless online connectivity with high flexibility. It is a challenging data-driven competition aligned with the rise of e-commerce, where speed, flexibility, and collaboration have become a new norm.

- Companies must harness the ecosystem advantage to accommodate sustainability aspects.

- The delivery process should be efficient: lower cost and faster with no margin for error. It should also be effective: using appropriate assets to meet market demand, customer-centric, and sustainable.

- Changes in the business landscape have shifted from on-estimate to on-schedule, then to on-demand, and finally to on-conscience delivery.

- On-conscience delivery is becoming necessary and aligns with the growing importance of ESG aspects, forcing CEOs to prioritize sustainability. We are entering the era of green logistics with efficient supply chains and logistics processes and lower energy consumption.
- Logistics services are shifting from 1PL to 5PL. Soon, we will enter the era of 6PL, which offers fully integrated supply chain solutions that are partially automated using AI. Hence, big data and predictive analysis are becoming even more crucial.

CHAPTER 6

The New Perspective of Service

From Standardization to Transformation

When the Industry Forum of the Society of Motor Manufacturers and Traders (SMMT), which was founded by the British government in 1996, introduced the concept of business process management, there were three elements that industry players had to pay attention to: quality, cost, and delivery (QCD).[1] Paying attention to data will help companies figure out how to improve these three elements, including prioritizing improvements.

Companies that implement business process management are players in the manufacturing sector who want to ensure operational excellence in QCD, all of which are widely applied in manufacturing companies. With the service sector continuing to develop rapidly, differentiating manufacturing-based industry players, operational excellence is no longer just limited to QCD. It now also includes service. The process of improving operational excellence in the service sector includes not only comparing data against internal targets or benchmarking but also seeking direct input from customers through surveys.

This chapter will discuss many studies and examples from the services industry. However, this new perspective of service applies to companies from all sectors.

Customer-Driven Service Improvement

Why does the operational improvement process in service have to involve customers? Services arise because there is interaction between service providers and customers, and customers expect benefits to be satisfied by their service providers.

All kinds of improvement processes in service have the goal of creating high satisfaction with customers while following the rules of QCD. Cost management drives the need for service quality that is based on input from customers.

Characteristics of Services

Getting input from customers to improve a service is challenging to do. The characteristics of services are very different from goods. Services are intangible, heterogeneous, and inseparable from customers.[2]

- The characteristic of *intangibility* makes services challenging to measure, calculate, or store for future needs. Therefore, to help customers have a reference for measuring the quality of a service, tangible enticements must be offered to strengthen the benefits that service providers can offer. The customers can evaluate those elements of the service, especially before interacting with the service provider.

- *Heterogeneity* characteristics are related to services involving humans. However, humans have different physical and emotional needs, which will influence the consistency of providing benefits at a high level, especially if service providers involve various people with different physical and emotional health conditions and different levels of experience with the service.

- The characteristic of *inseparability* is related to the processes of producing and consuming services, which are tasks that cannot be separated and require the simultaneous joint presence of service providers and customers. This condition means that services can be provided only at certain times when interactions between the service providers and customers can be carried out.

Based on these characteristics, we need an easy evaluation method for customers. Customers can evaluate a service by comparing the expectations of the tangible benefits that can be provided with the reality that occurs when service providers interact with customers. In addition, customers must be able to assess the processes (from order to delivery) when service providers provide services to customers.

Service Improvement Based on Customer Evaluation

In 1984, Christian Grönroos from Finland introduced a service quality model that identifies two critical dimensions of service quality: functional quality and technical quality. The first dimension is functional quality, which refers to the outcome of the service provided. Meanwhile, the second dimension is technical quality, which refers to the process of delivering the service. Then, in 1985, A. Parasuraman, Valerie A. Zeithaml, and Leonard L. Berry from the United States introduced a model comparing perceived service with expected service, which initially included 10 dimensions and was later simplified into 5 dimensions, namely, reliability, assurance, tangible, empathy, and responsiveness.

Although these two models are popular with those who care about customer input, the Parasuraman, Zeithaml, and Berry model has been more widely tested and applied in various industrial sectors.[3] In addition to having fewer dimensions, it requires a shorter time to implement. Conducting surveys to measure the gap between expectations and perceptions is also easier. This gap is a result of customer expectation factors that arise from word-of-mouth communication, individual needs, previous experiences, and external communication to customers and compared with quality perception, which comes from service product content communication.

Many companies conduct routine service quality surveys with their customers to gather customer input. Various inputs can be obtained through regular surveys to improve services to meet customer expectations. These inputs are followed up in the form of multiple improvements, which are then monitored to determine whether the improvements made can meet customer expectations.

Efforts to make improvements by getting customer input are not only done individually but also by comparing players in the same industrial sector involving players who are considered to be at the same level of competition. It is done so that the input for improvement involving relevant customers can be followed up.

In its development, customer involvement through surveys is not limited to the service repair process but also includes quality and delivery. Product reviews by loyal users assess quality, while delivery provides opportunities for customers to track the order-to-delivery process. Customer input on quality and delivery is usually packaged in acceptance tests, providing indirect input on costs and influencing service evaluation.

It shows an exciting development in the process of improving operational excellence. Customers are one of the factors that must be considered in the process of improving operational excellence. One of the most important aspects for customers is service. Therefore, the service element, previously not included as one that could influence operational excellence, now complements the other three elements, namely QCD, which, if optimized, can increase operational excellence.

Standardization-Based Service Blueprint

Frederick W. Taylor's steps to introduce scientific management in the production process in 1909 encouraged efforts to make the division of labor more efficient. Even though Taylor's approach is no longer applied in production processes now, a division of labor is the basis for standardization so that a complex production process can be efficient.

Currently, standardization in manufacturing processes is increasingly important because many companies make hundreds of millions of products per year, such as smartphones manufactured by Samsung or billions of packs of noodles made by Indofood, one of the largest instant noodle producers in the world. In the past, companies carried out standardization only in manufacturing, but now they are also trying to standardize the service aspect.

Standardization in the Service Sector

The service sector has been developing so rapidly that it has a more significant contribution to the economy than the manufacturing sector. Many companies serve hundreds of millions of customers. For example, American Airlines, the largest aircraft in the world, serves more than 200 million passengers annually. Even bigger is China Mobile Communication, which has 974 million subscribers with mobile data traffic of tens of millions of terabytes per year.

If standardization in the manufacturing sector aims to produce efficiency in the production process, then the service sector is about trying to achieve efficiency and customer satisfaction. This is challenging for companies that have a large number of customers. American Airlines, for example, is not even in the top 10 companies on a Skytrax survey for the aviation industry, which ranks almost all airlines worldwide by service. In the United States, American Airlines is in 10th place.

Since 1999, Skytrax surveys have helped many airlines worldwide improve their services amidst the continued growth in the number of passengers, increasing passenger demands, and increasingly tight competition in the airline industry. However, improvement efforts are not easy to carry out because many airlines operate in dozens of countries. Still, when operating in just one country, airline customers are faced with a variety of different touch points.

Challenges in Standardizing Services

The more different touch points there are, the higher the possibility of inconsistencies arising, which will also result in an inconsistent customer experience. This happens a lot in various service providers from different industry categories. From the financial industry to health to retail, especially those operating in multiple countries, service providers have the same challenges. It's just that they don't have third-party input across the globe like Skytrax does for the aviation industry.

However, service industry players with thousands or even hundreds of millions of customers per year have the same target: serving as many customers as possible not just well but efficiently. Therefore, Taylor's idea of division of labor is the basis for service standardization. It is implemented by dividing the customer service process into different categories based on person, the implementer, and a written manual that becomes the implementer's reference in providing customer services.

Through standardization of service, service industry players try to manage customer expectations regarding the benefits that can be provided. Efforts to manage customer expectations are challenging because service providers are dealing with customers who differ in terms of social and economic class or willingness to pay. Difficulties will increase if service providers do not have the opportunity to divide customers with different socioeconomic status or willingness to pay based on service areas or access to different services, as is the case with Takashimaya, a famous department store from Japan that operates in several countries around the world.

Takashimaya is a retail industry player known for its ability to provide the finest Japanese-style service. When entering other countries, such as Singapore, potential customers will have high expectations of Takashimaya. Moreover, Singapore has one of the highest GDP per capita in the world, and some of its citizens travel a lot around the world to compare themselves to other countries.

Even though most products sold are generally at a premium level in their category and are served by trained staff members, it takes work to meet customer expectations. In a service quality survey while writing her dissertation in 1998 at Sterling University, Linda Wee Keng Neo discovered several service gaps that had to be corrected by Takashimaya in Singapore, which happened to have large outlets and did not have areas or access to customer service based on willingness to pay as airlines do based on category such as first class, business class, and economy class. To be able to follow up on the results of the service quality survey, service providers such as Takashimaya must prioritize service improvements based on importance and impact in the eyes of customers.

Based on improvement priority mapping, service providers standardize new services following customer expectations. For example, the priority for improvement is timeliness in providing services. In that case, the service provider must ensure that this can be done at all touch points by various people at different times with a certain level of service quality. The new service standardization must then be communicated so that customers know that the service provider is trying to meet their expectations.

Of course, service providers not only can create a new standardization of services partially or incrementally but also they can further standardize services as a whole and involve all parties involved, for example, including providers who come from outside the company. Incidentally, in line with the trend to focus on core competence and, at the same time, efficiency, there are service elements such as contact points or complaint handling, which are outsourced to contact points or complaint handling specialists, who can even come from different countries.

Blueprinting High Service Standard

Service providers need a service blueprint to direct all elements involved in the service process toward high service standardization.[4] The blueprint is a business process mapping emphasizing contact points with customers and helps service providers understand how service flows from the customer's point of view. Service blueprints can help service providers get an overview of the service quality of all contacts and fail points from the customer's perspective and analyze fail points, the number of customers that can be served in a given period, and the costs required to serve customers.

The service blueprint has five essential components arranged horizontally:

- Customer actions
- Frontstage actions
- Backstage actions
- Support processes
- Physical evidence

In addition to the five horizontal components, several other elements are needed in a service blueprint to facilitate customer service business processes. These other elements are timelines, a line of interactions with customers, a line of visibility to distinguish service flows that customers can and cannot see, and a line of internal interactions, which describes the interaction process among internal service providers.

The existence of a service blueprint will help service providers improve business processes toward high standardization of service to experience higher productivity and gain customer satisfaction, better time and cost efficiency, and reduce fail points. In addition, a service blueprint makes it easier to innovate services by modifying several business processes. Ultimately, the service blueprint will help service providers demonstrate their unique value proposition and competitive advantage compared to competitors.

Data-Driven Personalization

Service providers with a unique value proposition and competitive advantage based on standardization of service at a high level will easily acquire new customers. The service provider will also garner good recommendations from customers who are satisfied with the services provided, so the number of customers will continue to increase.

In the past, customer data was treated only as statistical figures, not intended for personalization or customization purposes. Even when customer relationship management and various tools emerged, no significant amount of data could be used because it required substantial costs and was quite difficult to gather while interacting with customers.

However, even when in general customers from a service provider are satisfied with the service at various contact points, they can still feel that something is missing. These customers will feel like just one nameless, faceless person in a pile of customer data.

Of course, when interactions occur in a service process, we expect a tangible form of good service where the service provider can show responsibility and responsiveness and provide assurance and empathy. For example, a patient served by a hospital with good facilities and supported by health workers who are responsible, responsive, and able to provide assurance will be happier if the doctor shows strong empathy by asking "ice-breaking" questions before probing further about the disease they are suffering from and what their living conditions are like.

Challenges of Delivering Empathetic Services

Empathy in the eyes of service users becomes increasingly important when service providers use automated machines or systems in many of their contact points. Even though technical operations can provide high service standardization in any situation, the machine or automation system cannot see the emotional side of the customer. All customers hope that the service provider understands the customer's needs or solves problems from the customer's point of view. This ability to empathize enables service providers to build warm relationships with customers.

The challenge of building empathy becomes more remarkable when the number of customers to be served is large. Customers come from different regions and can express different needs or problems. Large worldwide airline companies face such challenges. If 1% of the daily 100,000 passengers hope their problems can be resolved, regardless of location and service time, you can imagine the challenges an airline faces, especially if passengers need assistance with a quick resolution.

That is why several airlines, often in the top-five Skytrax survey results, take several anticipatory steps. Airlines that serve purely international flights, such as Singapore Airlines, hire flight attendants from various countries so that they can be more helpful if there are passengers who speak different languages.

In addition to language, Singapore Airlines also tries to ensure that all passengers from different classes are served personally to show they are special passengers. The flight attendants start with small things. An example is greeting passengers personally by saying their names even if the passenger is not asked first. The flight attendants get the passenger names from printouts of passenger data per seat in all classes available on the plane and then memorize them before meeting passengers, including in economy class, which serves hundreds of passengers.

Small personalization techniques like that certainly don't require large amounts of data. It's different if you want to carry out a personalization effort that must consider how to serve customers whose numbers reach tens, hundreds of thousands, or even millions. Relying on printouts of customer data certainly requires a very thick pile of data. So, such attention could be considered a hassle for customer service officers, but the level of personalized service means a lot to customers.

Personalized Services in the Information Era

Today's advances in information technology make it easier to access databases and obtain tens, hundreds of thousands, even millions of relevant data points. In addition, other information beyond customer demographic or geographic data, such as the length of interaction and the level of expenditure up to when the first complaint was made, is recorded. Such information can help service officers to be more customer-centric, from greeting them personally to meeting the need for quick problem resolution.

The personalized service process requires an extensive database and multichannel interaction capabilities. It includes face-to-face customer service or using technology such as telephone, email, social media, and real-time chat. Customers expect personal service from service providers at various customer contact points.

Some service providers have provided this personal service independently to tens, hundreds, or millions of customers. One of the pioneers in this kind of service is **Amazon.com**. In the second half of the 1990s, **Amazon.com** provided services for customers who wanted to browse the rankings of ordered books themselves. **Amazon.com** even collaborates with logistics companies to provide this information.

Services that can be done independently are also then carried out by other industry players. Remember when the banking sector started popularizing internet banking services in the second half of the 1990s? This service enabled bank customers to make transfers and payments independently. In turn, the number of bank transactions using internet banking services increased rapidly. The same happened with players in the commercial aviation industry. Airlines around the world have introduced self-check-in services with varying complexities. The aim is to provide customers a better and easier experience before the flight, such as cutting the waiting time to get a boarding pass mandatory to services such as printing the boarding passes complete with passenger seat numbers to ordering food for passengers according to dietary preferences, whether for health reasons or religious needs. What is more complex is checking the validity of passports for international flight passengers to prevent passengers from being rejected by immigration officers because the passport isn't valid.

Recently, several airlines offered an upgraded personalization experience as an appreciation for passengers who fly often with these airlines. These passengers can use onboard internet services or get a wide variety of reading and entertainment services. One of the airlines that does this is Singapore Airlines.

That is why even though it faces competition from various competitors, whether they are close competitors or even low-cost airlines, Singapore Airlines is still chosen by many passengers, even though its ticket prices, on average, are higher than others. Singapore Airlines is one of the airlines that managed to record large profits after the pandemic.[5] Once again, one of the factors that makes this airline the choice of many passengers, despite its high prices, is its ability to provide personal and ready service to tens of thousands of passengers per day. Singapore Airlines can give this kind of service efficiently, even though, at first glance, it offers benefits to many passengers because it is selected individually based on passenger spending.

Agile in Mass Customization

Despite carrying out massive personalization, Singapore Airlines' ability to achieve huge profits after the pandemic should encourage other airlines to follow their example by differentiating services, which is the opposite focus of the increasing number of low-cost airlines, which rely on low prices to attract potential passengers.

Singapore Airlines achieved high customer regard through a long time of offering operational excellence in the service sector. They started by maintaining a consistently high service standardization and continued to build a database through the branded frequent flyer, Kris Flier, over a long time to various generations of passengers, from the silent generation to Gen Z or even Gen Alpha. This has been accomplished by embracing multiple changes that have led to proven operational excellence, the emergence of various new solid competitors, and changes in airline customer lifestyles.

Some of Singapore Airlines' competitors, such as Emirates, Qatar Airways, Turkish Airlines, and Etihad, are trying to ride the wave of popular sport-based pop culture. These names even appear on the uniforms of European Premier League soccer clubs, stadium names, or soccer cup matches. Pop culture fans are significant in number, and of course, they are the target market. To get closer to the target market, Emirates, for example, has its flight attendants provide a very entertaining reception for thousands of spectators at several famous soccer stadiums in Europe, similar to what they do on the plane before take-off.

Implementing Mass Customization: The Airlines Case

There are many ways to carry out mass customization. As noted by James Gilmore and Joseph Pine in the *Harvard Business Review*, there are four types of customization: collaborative, adaptive, cosmetic, and transparent, and each is divided into matrices based on product and representation.[6]

Singapore Airlines, which chose a different target market from Emirates, Qatar Airways, Turkish Airlines, and Etihad, cannot carry out adaptive or collaborative mass customization. Because the number of passengers who are soccer fans is large, there will be too many choices for customers. Of course, it will be challenging to accommodate customization cost-efficiently because of the varying fan affiliations. However, applying cosmetic customization based on passenger class can eliminate the opportunity to encourage passengers to continue purchasing plane tickets in a higher class.

Transparent customization is carried out to provide a unique experience to passengers who want to purchase more plane tickets regardless of the chosen passenger class. The ability to use the internet at low cost or for free while the plane is in the air is one of the offers given to passengers based on spending tier.

Providing on-flight internet services at low cost or even free is undoubtedly considered a perk for people who always want to be connected to the internet, whether for work or entertainment. This is a large group. Airlines provide this in-flight internet service as an opportunity to add income by encouraging them to continue purchasing plane tickets with a certain minimum amount per month or year.

Many airlines can communicate customizations via email and convey spending tiers per month or even per year. Passengers who have a unique experience, in the form of being able to use the internet while the plane is in the air, will certainly try to get this service again.

Adopting Next Tech for Agile Mass Customization

Singapore Airlines provides an interesting example of how an airline processes and uses its database to trigger creativity and innovation, as mentioned in the Philip Kotler, Hermawan Kartajaya, and Iwan Setiawan

Marketing 5.0 book (Wiley, 2021). By understanding existing data, companies can creatively offer new services at low costs, which can be done massively quickly, and, more importantly, can provide additional profits or strengthen customer loyalty. It means that companies use technological advances to become agile, including mass customization.

Technology also supports agile mass customization in manufacturing. The emergence of 3D printing technology enables companies to realize collaborative mass customization. Even though you must adapt to customer input, mass production can be done quickly, including from various locations.

This technological advancement differentiated mass customization from the current era compared to when it was first introduced in 1997. The increasingly popular data processing technology makes it easier to make quick decisions to customize. This is supported by the ability to analyze various data points to predict the results of new service development, the ease of developing personalization and customization models according to behavior and habits, and the drive to combine the advantages of technology and human intuition. The customization can be carried out in an agile manner for both the service and manufacturing sectors.

Transformative Services

If personalization or customization promotes the creation of high-quality service standards that can be enjoyed by large numbers of customers at one time but with low costs and be profitable, then the transformative service leads to other services that can achieve sustainable development goals. Interestingly, even before the UN established the Sustainable Development Goals 2030 at the UN General Assembly in 2015, the terminology of transformative services in terms of sustainability was already being used.

The Urgency of Achieving SDGs Through Transformative Services

In 2010, Laurel Anderson and Amy L. Ostrom introduced the terminology of a *transformative service*.[7] At that time, they began to notice that the service sector, which was increasing contributions to the economies of developed countries, was worthy of being asked to contribute to solving various global challenges. Climate change, for example, started to emerge as a worldwide challenge after the 1997 Kyoto Protocol but was not widely acknowledged by many people until 2010.

That is why members of the European Union (EU) began to raise the European Union Emission Trading System (EU-ETS) issue in 2000 and introduced four implementation stages. Stage 1 (2005–2007) was the introduction of the EU-ETS. Stage 2 (2008–2012) started communicating policies, including bringing the airline sector to the EU-ETS. Stage 3 (2013–2020) has reformed and harmonized regulations. Stage 4 (2021–2030) is when the rules will be implemented.

Anderson and Ostrom are starting to see political and legal changes in the EU regarding developing sustainability or well-being-oriented services. Public transport, such as the airline sector, cannot avoid these provisions, especially as several studies show significant emissions from general aviation. As soon as the EU-ETS entered stage 3, several European airlines began introducing a carbon tax on plane tickets sold to passengers.

However, in 2015, Anderson stated that a transformative service relates to environmental, social, and economic transformations. This means transformative services are increasingly aligned with SDG 2030 related to the environment. Because the UN encourages economic actors to report achievements associated with the implementation of the SDGs, it is appropriate for transformative services to start measuring the operational excellence that can be achieved.

Case of Transformative Services: Jakarta's Public Transportation

Public transportation services in Jakarta through JakLingko and TransJakarta are examples of a transformative service. In 2021, JakLingko and TransJakarta won the Sustainable Transportation Award related to environmental transformation (and social and economic) from an institution under the United Nations, simultaneously achieving operational excellence.[8] As one of the largest cities in the Southern Hemisphere with a population of 10.56 million in 2020 and an area of 661.5 km^2, Jakarta began introducing Bus Rapid Transport on January

15, 2004, to encourage public transportation and reduce congestion. However, until early 2018, most public transportation in Jakarta did not meet safety and service standards and even caused high pollution because the vehicles were old and damaged.

The Asian Games 2018 held in Jakarta gave the country some momentum to transform the public transportation services in Jakarta by restricting private vehicles to certain hours and routes so that the traffic jams that had been characteristic of Jakarta did not interfere with the games. The private vehicle restrictions were followed by providing alternative transportation as an incentive for social transformation of the large population of Jakarta residents to become users of public services. There was an additional economic transformation that allowed public transportation owners outside TransJakarta, whose vehicles were almost all unfit for operation, to modernize the vehicles they own. The public transportation owners outside TransJakarta modernized their vehicles after learning that the Jakarta government would keep buying their services based on agreed key performance indicators (KPIs). By understanding their ability to meet the KPIs and the potential revenues they would get, they believed investing in new vehicles was worth doing.

Fleet owners outside TransJakarta were willing and able to modernize their fleet but only if they could get operational benefits from public transportation, such as serving customers based on daily target of kilometers. In the past, public transport providers used the minimum number of passengers that could be brought in their vehicles as their KPIs. They could meet the target during the limited peak hours. Unfortunately, during the peak hours, there used to be traffic jams. So, it was challenging for a public transport provider to meet a minimum number of passengers who could use their vehicles daily. Without this ability, a public transport provider couldn't provide money for maintenance and service, let alone invest in a new vehicle. By moving to a new KPI based on daily kilometers, the public transport provider will get money even though it serves only a few passengers. Drivers of vehicles outside TransJakarta had to meet KPIs for public services to earn a decent income. The new public transportation and enhanced vehicles prompted the Jakarta government to develop a three-way relationship scheme with the government, public vehicle fleet owners and their drivers, and passengers.

Public vehicle owners and drivers sell public transportation services per kilometer with certain KPIs to the Jakarta government, including subsidies to public transportation service users. The Jakarta government then sets public transportation tariffs for combined users of TransJakarta and various public service providers in Jakarta called JakLingko. This association encouraged public transportation service fleet owners outside TransJakarta to modernize their fleets and ultimately encouraged more and more Jakarta residents to become users of public transportation services.

At the end of 2017, the number of TransJakarta users was only 300,000 per day, but at the end of 2018, the number of passengers increased to 500,000 per day, after regulations limiting private vehicles at certain hours and routes and the start of rejuvenation of the public vehicle fleet. An increasing number of new vehicle fleets outside TransJakarta were modernized, which then led to the formation of JakLingko, at which point the number of passengers per day in 2019 reached 1 million people. The coverage area of this new service covered 82% of the Jakarta area at the beginning of 2020.

This increase in operational excellence is an exciting example of social and economic transformation, which has caused Jakarta, which was initially in the top 5 most congested cities in the world, to drop out of the top 30 on the Tom Tom Index, a data provider on road speeds, travel times, and traffic density across 387 cities worldwide. The reduction in traffic jams and the significant disappearance of public vehicles that are unfit, old, and emit thick black smoke have resulted in improvements in environmental conditions. It is what made Jakarta win the Sustainable Transportation Award in 2021.

Shifting from Divisional-Centric to Stakeholder-Centric

The shift from divisional-centric to stakeholder-centric will result in a change in the focus of providing services from random customers to specific individuals, then shifting again to particular groups of customers, and finally to society. Likewise, the service delivery level goes from standardization to personalization, then to customization, and eventually must be able to deliver a transformation (see Figure 6.1).

	STAGE				Extension →
	S1	**S2**	**S3**	**S4**	
	Divisional-Centric	Company-Centric	Customer-Centric	Stakeholder-Centric	
To Whom	Anybody	Particular individual	Particular group of customers	Society	
Service Delivery Level	Standardization	Personalization	Customization	Transformation	
ESG Risk Exposure	Very high	High	Medium	Low	
General Guidelines of Service	• Ensure customers, whether in small or big numbers, experience the same quality of service anytime and anywhere. • Ensure the service providers team, which comes from various backgrounds, can serve anybody with the same service operating procedure anytime and anywhere. • Ensure the service provider can meet the same service operating procedure when it improves service quality.	• Ensure particular customers experience a unique service quality based on specific criteria. • Ensure the service provider can uniquely perform service quality to particular individuals, small or big numbers. • Ensure the service provider can perform both easy and difficult unique service experiences to particular individuals.	• Ensure a group of customers experience a unique service quality based on specific criteria. • Ensure the service provider can uniquely perform service quality to a particular group of customers, small or big numbers. • Ensure the service provider can perform both easy and difficult unique service experiences to a particular group of customers.	• Ensure customers are ready to sacrifice to experience a service quality tailored to societal changes. • Ensure the service provider can consistently perform service quality tailored to societal changes to customers, small or big numbers. • Ensure the service provider's ability to make a greater contribution by enlarging coverage of service quality tailored to societal changes.	

FIGURE 6.1 Shifting from divisional-centric to stakeholder-centric (service)

At stage 1, the company is expected to provide equal service to all customers anytime and anywhere. Regardless of their different backgrounds, the team that provides these services must be able to serve anyone, anytime, and anywhere with the same service operating procedure. Therefore, it is essential for service providers to always be able to carry out the same service operating procedure to improve service quality.

At stage 2 (personalization), the company must ensure that it can deliver particular customers a unique service quality based on specific criteria, and service providers must be able to provide detailed attention to certain individuals (regardless of the number) to enjoy a unique service, irrespective of the level of difficulty in delivering that unique service experience.

At stage 3 (customization), the company must be able to pay attention to a group of customers in such a way that they can experience a unique service quality based on specific criteria. Service providers must be able to deliver exceptional service quality to that particular group of customers at various points within a range of difficulty levels.

At stage 4, the company is ready to make further "sacrifices," such as subsidies, to provide a quality service adapted to the demands of changing social environments. Therefore, companies must have the ability to make a significant contribution through service quality that is in line with societal changes.

Key Takeaways

In this chapter, we talked about how service is an element that can influence operational excellence besides quality, cost, and delivery. We can also see that there has been a shift from standard to transformational service, which has a number of consequences. Following are the key takeaways from this chapter:

- The impressive growth of service sectors since the 1980s has encouraged a significant scale of continuous improvement in service areas.
- The unique characteristics of service have encouraged the development of service quality measurements to be able to implement customer feedback.

- The American service quality model has been applied by companies globally to improve their service aspects. In addition to individual measurement, institutions such as Skytrax have practiced industry-wide service improvement in the airline industry.

- Widespread service quality measurements have educated customers about good service, which makes customers demand standardized good service.

- A more significant number of customers who experience good service will increase the emergence of loyal customers, who will demand good service personalized to them.

- Service providers that want to appreciate their loyal customers at low cost can implement mass customization.

- The advancement of the service sector has created the demand to contribute to solving social changes through transformative service.

- The shift in service perception—from commoditization to transformation—applies to businesses across all sectors.

CHAPTER 7

Creativity and Innovation in the New Operational Excellence

How the Korean Wave and Other Trends Are Affecting the World

The new view of operational excellence covered in previous chapters calls for particular and somewhat dichotomous capabilities. Organizations must be able to converge those dichotomies: between creativity and innovation (CI), between productivity and improvement (PI), between entrepreneurship and leadership (EL), and between professionalism and management (PM). This chapter will outline how creativity and innovation can change business operational processes to provide good customer results and positively affect society.

Samsung's Innovation Story

If you are a Samsung smartphone user, look at the phone's body and packaging. Your attention will probably focus on the beauty of the design and its improved performance compared to previous versions. But are you aware that Samsung strives to use more recycled materials for its internal components? The same goes for the packaging. Samsung has used recycled plastic and paper for the packaging box and cover protectors.[1]

Samsung also continues to innovate to reduce dependency on natural resources in the delivery stage. It has expanded the use of eco-packaging that can be used for a variety of the company's products, including vacuum cleaners, air purifiers, and more. To make installing an appliance as convenient and environmentally friendly as possible, the company is also eliminating the use of printed manuals in its packaging and offering users QR codes to access such information.[2]

The company keeps innovating to create more sustainable business operations. The attention that Samsung pays to using renewable energy is another example. In 2020, Samsung achieved its goal of 100% renewable energy use in the United States, China, and Europe.[3] It doesn't stop there; Samsung continues to set more ambitious targets. By 2050, Samsung Electronics targets net-zero direct and indirect carbon emissions. The Devise eXperience (DX) Division will be the pilot project, and it is expected to achieve this goal by 2030. Samsung Electronics anticipates reducing around 17 million tons of carbon dioxide equivalent (CO_2e) emissions by reaching net-zero direct and indirect carbon emissions.[4]

Samsung and innovation are like siblings. No wonder Samsung ranked 6 out of 50 in Boston Consulting Group's (BCG) 2022 list of "Most Innovative Companies" after Apple, Microsoft, Amazon, Alphabet, and Tesla.[5] Samsung is at the top of the list among global companies from Asia. Additionally, Samsung received 6,248 US patents in 2022, more than any other corporation.[6]

As discussed in the previous examples, the innovation carried out by Samsung improves product quality and delivery to customers and positively affects wider stakeholders. This practice is a real-world example of new operational excellence, which is the core discussion of this book. Quality, cost, delivery, and service are no longer just measured based on internal efficiency metrics and customer satisfaction index but must also contribute positively to people and the planet.

For a company to achieve that level of operational excellence, specific capabilities are needed, including creativity and innovation. As we explain in the book *Entrepreneurial Marketing: Beyond Professionalism to Creativity, Leadership, and Sustainability*, creativity and innovation are two interrelated capabilities. Creativity is the ability to develop valuable new ideas, while innovation turns them into concrete and ready-to-use solutions. Samsung is an example of a company that can adopt both in its business operations.

What is the secret to Samsung's creativity and innovation? To understand it comprehensively, we can't just look at it from the perspective of Samsung as a company. Some macro factors contribute to this company's flourishing of creativity and innovation. For this reason, we need to zoom in to the country of origin of this consumer and electronics industry giant: South Korea.

The Birth of South Korean Creative Capability

Based on some studies, South Korea is considered one of the most innovative countries in the world. According to the Global Innovation Index 2022 by the World Intellectual Property Organization, this nation is ranked 6 among the 48 economies in the high-income group. It is ranked first among the 17 economies in Southeast Asia, East Asia, and Oceania.[7] The Bloomberg Innovation Index 2021 also ranks South Korea as the most technologically advanced economy in the world, based on criteria such as patent activity, gross value added by manufacturing, research and development intensity, high-tech company density, and researcher concentration.[8]

The economy of South Korea was founded initially on agriculture. South Korea began pursuing an outward-looking strategy in the late 1960s, encouraging economic growth by exporting labor-intensive manufactured goods to gain a competitive edge. Initiatives from the government were vital in this process. Unskilled and semiskilled workers were quickly mobilized at this time into labor-intensive manufacturing sectors, including textile, footwear, and apparel. In the 1980s, the automobile sector was one of South Korea's key export and growth industries. South Korea accomplished a speedy economic boom thanks to its plentiful labor supply.

Economic considerations primarily drive the need for creativity and innovation in South Korea. Prior decades of South Korea's economic success were attributed mainly to the country's capacity to produce goods already on the market at cheaper costs than rivals, while maintaining acceptable levels of quality. Recently, South Korea has lost its competitive edge to China and several other nations, who are assuming the mantle of inexpensive labor. This condition means that South Korea must undergo another transition, much like Japan did in the 1980s, into an economy that depends on innovation. Rather than producing me-too products with more affordable prices, South Korea started moving to create innovative products with solid differentiation. Samsung is one of the main drivers of this transformation.

Samsung was originally a manufacturer of cheap electronic products with low quality. Its products could not even compete in the domestic market. However, Samsung carried out business transformation with the support of the South Korean government. Samsung's superiority was finally proven when it beat Japan's Sony as its main rival in the consumer electronics industry. Today, Samsung competes with Apple to be the top global smartphone producer.

Samsung's extraordinary business growth has contributed significantly to the South Korean economy. The revenue of Samsung Group accounted for about one-fifth of South Korea's GDP.[9] In this case, Samsung is not alone. Together with nine other *chaebols*—a large South Korean conglomerate run and controlled by an individual or family (some of the best-known examples include Lotte, Hyundai, and LG)—Samsung made up about 60% of the country's GDP.[10] This fact certainly raises concerns for the South Korean government. Too much dependence on a few chaebols risks the country's economy if their business experiences shocks.

Journalist Euny Hong states in her book *The Birth of Korean Cool* (Picador, 1994) that South Korea's economic dependence on chaebols began to be revealed during the Asian financial crisis in 1997. Rising labor costs also mean the country must rely on more than just manufacturing as a source of prosperity. For these reasons, Kim Dae-Jung, the president at that time, made a policy that began focusing on developing information technology and creative industries. During his presidency, Kim Dae-Jung implemented policies to promote Korean culture and entertainment, including establishing two relevant organizations: the Korean Culture and Information Service and the Korean Cultural Centers in other countries.[11] This critical moment marks the birth of *Hallyu,* or the Korean Wave.[12] What is this Korean Wave? It refers to the global popularity of South Korean pop culture, including television dramas, movies, music, and video games.[13]

The South Korean government's seriousness in strengthening the creative industry continued beyond one leadership period. In her 2013 inaugural address, President Park Geun-hye announced the Creative Economy Policy Enforcement Process,[14] which aims to promote the convergence of science, technology, and culture to create new industries and jobs. The endgame will be creative sectors as a new economic paradigm. Park's successor, President Moon Jae-in, identified Korean pop culture as a critical policy driver and aggressively promoted it to create a favorable perception of Korea on a global scale. The current South Korean president, Yoon Suk Yeol, continued this initiative, emphasizing collaboration with the United States to strengthen the two countries' creative industries. We can see a summary of South Korea's economic development journey in Figure 7.1.

The Hallyu Effect

The South Korean government believed in Hallyu as the soft power strategy to strengthen the country's brand globally. Harvard Professor Joseph Nye coined the term *soft power* in the late 1980s to describe the capacity to influence others' behavior through allure and persuasion. Culture, political principles, and foreign policies fall under noncoercive soft power.[15]

The Hallyu effect has been enormous, accounting for US$1.87 billion, or 0.2% of South Korea's 2004 GDP. More recently, in 2019, Hallyu made up 1.7% of the nation's GDP.[16] The popularity of South Korean pop culture also has the potential to encourage exports of other products produced in this country. By strengthening South Korea's positive brand image as a country at the global level, acceptance of South Korean company products in foreign markets will be easier. For example, the Korean Wave has increased Thais intention to purchase South Korean cosmetics.[17]

The Hallyu indirect effect also affects the country internally. The South Korean government's campaign toward the creative sector is also the foundation of economic and business transformation in this country. The government's investment in digital technology infrastructure

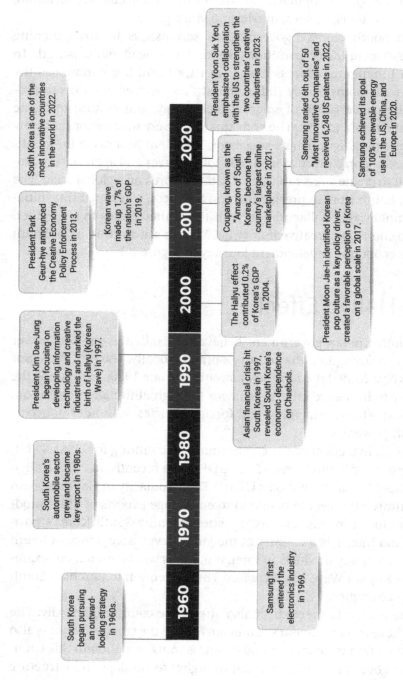

FIGURE 7.1 Some key moments in South Korea's economic development

South Korea began pursuing an outward-looking strategy in 1960s.

Samsung first entered the electronics industry in 1969.

South Korea's automobile sector grew and became key export in 1980s.

President Kim Dae-Jung began focusing on developing information technology and creative industries and marked the birth of Hallyu (Korean Wave) in 1997.

Asian financial crisis hit South Korea in 1997, revealed South Korea's economic dependence on Chaebols.

President Park Geun-hye announced the Creative Economy Policy Enforcement Process in 2013.

Korean wave made up 1.7% of the nation's GDP in 2019.

The Hallyu effect contributed 0.2% of Korea's GDP in 2004.

President Moon Jae-in identified Korean pop culture as a key policy driver, created a favorable perception of Korea on a global scale in 2017.

South Korea is one of the most innovative countries in the world in 2022.

President Yoon Suk Yeol, emphasized collaboration with the US to strengthen the two countries' creative industries in 2023.

Coupang, known as the "Amazon of South Korea," become the country's largest online marketplace in 2021.

Samsung ranked 6th out of 50 "Most Innovative Companies" and received 6,248 US patents in 2022.

Samsung achieved its goal of 100% renewable energy use in the US, China, and Europe in 2020.

1960   1970   1980   1990   2000   2010   2020

and creative human resources has contributed to this country's emergence of a creative class. These new generations will drive business and cultural transformation in various South Korean companies, from startups to giant chaebols.

Creativity and innovation policies at the country level are then implanted into corporate-level institutionalization. Samsung is one of the best examples of this kind of initiative. The Samsung C-Lab—also known as the Creative Lab—was established by Samsung to allow employees to develop their business ideas and provide them with the tools and resources needed to make those businesses successful. To assist people in obtaining the information and resources they need to be prepared for the future, including the landscape of data science and machine learning tools, Samsung has also built the Samsung Innovation Campus. You can see the results of these initiatives through several examples at the beginning of this chapter.

Apart from their creativity, people in South Korea are also famous for their extraordinary hard work, referring to the *pali-pali* (hurry! hurry!) spirit. Entrepreneurs (founders of many companies) and big established companies need to humanize their people by referring to the humane entrepreneurship concept, which strongly emphasizes human well-being. This concept was developed by South Korean professors focusing on how human development can enhance company performance (see Appendix C).

South Korean Company and the New Operational Excellence

This chapter describes Samsung as an innovative company and South Korea as a creative country. Both have developed operational excellence focusing on internal efficiency and effectiveness (stage 1 and stage 2). They are also concerned about satisfying citizens and customers (stage 3). But, beyond those stages, both are symbols of new operational excellence that prioritizes positive impacts on wider stakeholders (stage 4). Through creativity and innovation, Samsung and other Korean companies can find new ways to provide solutions for people and the planet by transforming their business operations. The following are additional examples of new operational excellence implementation from other Korean companies at the highest level (stage 4).

Impact-Based Quality

LG Corporation—also known as LG Group—is a South Korean multinational conglomerate that produces electronics, chemicals, and telecommunications products. The LG Group is South Korea's fourth-largest chaebol. LG has planned to develop products with lower environmental consequences throughout their lifetime. LG aims to make homes safer for its customers by removing dangerous materials, lowering appliance noise, and including anti-allergy and anti-bacterial features. To promote sustainability, LG is also restructuring processes to reduce carbon emissions and rethinking product life cycles to minimize waste.[18]

Social Values Contribution

Hyundai—a South Korean automaker—continuously works to create technology and solutions that will lower emissions and safeguard the environment. Hyundai has expanded its product and service lines for customers to enjoy environmentally friendly values like certified recycled products, sustainable solutions, hydrogen-powered cars, and a transition to greener vehicles.[19] Hyundai hopes to increase customers' willingness to pay through this innovation, not just reduce the cost of manufacturing the goods.

On-Conscience Delivery

Coupang—the "Amazon of South Korea"—is the largest online marketplace in the country by revenue. Since its founding in 2010, Coupang has grown to become the nation's top e-commerce platform.[20] By offering box-free shipping, Coupang has improved the sustainability of its packaging and delivery services. In addition, Coupang distributes millions of Fresh Bags to customers to deliver groceries and fresh delicacies, and customers can leave their used bags outside their homes for reuse.[21]

Transformational Service

A state-owned electric utility business, Korea Electric Power Corporation (KEPCO), has implemented several initiatives to encourage customers to use less energy. Customers can now get real-time information on their energy consumption through KEPCO's smart meter technology, enabling them to modify their use and reduce energy costs. Additionally, the business has introduced a "Green Premium" program that incentivizes users of energy-saving products.[22] These services aim to transform their customers into being more conscious of energy usage.

Lessons from Other Asian Countries

According to the Creative Productivity Index (CPI) report by the Asian Development Bank, Asia has a high potential for creativity and innovation. Innovation-led growth is crucial for developing Asia to maintain and, even more important, accelerate the development and growth of its economies.[23] This section identifies several examples of creativity and innovation in operational excellence from other Asian countries.

ACLEDA Bank (Cambodia)

ACLEDA Bank Plc., a public limited company in Cambodia, is the leading commercial bank initially founded as a national nongovernmental organization (NGO) for micro- and small enterprises' development and credit. Established in 1993, it is today one of Cambodia's largest domestic commercial banks in terms of total assets and number of customers. With 264 branches across Cambodia's provinces and cities, ACLEDA Bank has also strengthened its position as a regional bank by expanding to Laos (37 branches) and Myanmar (17 branches). No wonder it was the first bank in Cambodia to receive ratings from Standard & Poor's.[24]

With networks that reach remote rural areas, ACLEDA Bank tries to get microentrepreneurs, especially women, whom financial services have not supported as much in the past. A significant part of ACLEDA's loans are given to small business owners who sell staples, including rice, fish, fruit, and materials for crafts. Even though it carries a social vision, ACLEDA Bank still applies standard service procedures to maintain the quality of its micro-creditors. The loan size is given according to the financing objective, whether for investment or working capital. With quality creditors (input), ACLEDA Bank will be able to get lower nonperforming loans (quality output). For its creativity and innovation in developing products for this bottom-of-the-pyramid segment, the SME Finance Forum has honored and recognized ACLEDA Bank Plc. as the gold winner in the "Best Financier for Women Entrepreneurs" category and with an honorable mention in the "SME Financier of the Year—Asia" category.[25]

AirAsia (Malaysia)

AirAsia, the aviation arm of Capital A (formerly known as AirAsia Group), was founded in 2001 by Tony Fernandes and Kamarudin Meranun. After several business transformations, it has grown into one of the largest airlines in Asia, serving the underserved and democratizing air travel with its iconic tagline "Now Everyone Can Fly." As with other airlines, the COVID-19 pandemic forced AirAsia to halt operations in March 2020. Following the lifting of travel restrictions by the Malaysian government a year later, AirAsia resumed foreign flights. Despite the obstacles brought on by the COVID-19 pandemic, AirAsia has improved its financial performance in 2023, reporting profits and revenue increases.

The foundation of AirAsia's business strategy is its low-fare philosophy, which emphasizes simplified, easy, and effective operations. To accomplish this, the corporation has developed a few crucial tools, like operating a single aircraft model, speeding up turnaround times, and outsourcing noncore activities. The company's minimalist approach to human resource management and unique routes also contribute to its low-cost strategy. These cost-reduction initiatives effectively support AirAsia's strategy to target the non-full-service segment.

Even though AirAsia offers a low-cost carrier with minimum service, passengers can still get extra offerings at additional costs. This personalized service focuses on charging customers based on their desired value, enabling higher buying propensity and increasing customer satisfaction. The business also adapts its services to fit customers' needs by using data analytics to better understand their preferences and behavior. For example, AirAsia may provide personalized deals or recommendations based on a customer's travel history.[26]

The COVID-19 pandemic gave AirAsia the impetus to innovate new solutions that could benefit affected communities in addition to helping the company survive. The business has experienced a digital revolution, changing from an airline to a digital travel and leisure enterprise. As a result of this transition, companies like AirAsia Farm and AirAsia Food have emerged, increasing AirAsia's auxiliary earnings while giving thousands of small and medium-sized enterprises affected by COVID-19 digital support.[27]

Jollibee (Philippines)

The Jollibee Foods Corporation (JFC) owns the fast-food restaurant chain Jollibee, which is based in the Philippines. Tony Tan launched Jollibee in 1980, distinguished by a sizable anthropomorphic bee mascot sporting a red blazer, shirt, and chef's hat. Many of America's favorite comfort foods, such as fried chicken, French fries, pies, spaghetti, hamburgers, and more, are available on Jollibee's menu, but with a Filipino twist. According to the founder's belief, happy food leads to happy people. The company's mission embodies that belief: "spread the joy of eating across the world."

Jollibee has expanded internationally through acquisitions such as Greenwich Pizza, Chowking, Yonghe Dawang, Jinja Bar Bistro, and Mang Inasal, opening some stores in the United States. The company has also entered the Asian quick-service restaurant segment and entered a joint venture with Chow Fun Holdings LLC. Today, with 70 locations in North America and 1,300 more globally, Jollibee asserts to be the most significant and fastest-expanding Asian restaurant chain in the world.

Jollibee prioritizes innovation in customized menus and services to adjust to local tastes. Jollibee's strategy in Western countries is one example. This company also has invested a lot in the UK and Europe to expand its brand and become a significant player in the quick-service industry. The company has introduced new menu items, such as Asian Slaw, Tropical Burger, Mango Coconut Sundae, and Asian Chicken Tender Rice Bowl, catering to local tastes.[28] Jollibee aims to attract more local customers through a refreshed store design and lighthearted, fun branding emphasizing local community spirit. The company prioritizes customer satisfaction in every new market.

In addition to its creative customer-centric initiatives, Jollibee has increased environmental protection and preservation activities throughout its supply chain. These actions align with its Joy for Tomorrow global sustainability agenda, which attempts to treat the environment more responsibly and assist in creating a sustainable future for individuals and communities. The Jollibee Group's planet pillar is centered on enhancing packaging sustainability, cutting food loss and waste in the production process and in-store operations, and implementing energy-saving projects to lower energy consumption throughout its stores.[29]

Thai Union (Thailand)

Thailand has won praise for its creative marketing and advertising strategies. In Philip Kotler, Hermawan Kartajaya, and Hooi Den Huan's book *Marketing for Competitiveness: Asia to the World* (World Scientific, 2017), we once examined the phenomena of "sadvertising" as a kind of creativity among industry players in Thailand when packaging marketing campaigns with emotional storytelling. Thus, Thailand's entry into the top 10 of the Gunn 100 Report is not unexpected.[30] The world's most creative advertising and marketing initiatives are ranked in this annual report. In addition, the 2023 Campaign Brief Asia Creative Rankings placed Ogilvy Thailand first overall in Asia.[31] So, does the same creativity also apply to realizing more sustainable operational excellence?

Thai Union, a global seafood company based in Thailand, can answer this question. The company has a dedicated sustainability strategy called SeaChange®. It was introduced in 2016 and aims to lead a positive transformation in Thai Union's internal business operations and throughout the global seafood industry. In 2023, Thai Union launched SeaChange® 2030 with more aggressive new goals to better guide the global seafood value chain. The Dow Jones Sustainability Indices placed Thai Union at the top of the worldwide list of the food sector, a testament to the company's commitment to sustainable business practices.[32]

Thai Union has launched various initiatives through SeaChange® to protect the planet and people across the value chain, from sourcing to production and consumption. Here are a few examples:

- Buying all of the tuna used in branded products from fisheries that are either Marine Stewardship Council (MSC) certified or taking part in Fishery Improvement Projects (FIPs) to help them become certified by the MSC.

- Creating a new generation of environmentally friendly aquaculture feed that lessens the effects of fish farming.

- Making research and development investments to produce innovative, environmentally responsible products.

- Collaborating with NGOs, authorities, and other parties to advance ethical fishing methods and safeguard marine ecosystems.

- Aiding in creating sustainable fishing communities by giving those who fisher and their families access to resources, education, and training.

Another example of a creative initiative by Thai Union is implementing a traceability system that enables customers to track the origin of their seafood products and ensure that they are sustainably sourced. The seafood industry faces challenges in its complex and dynamic supply chains, mainly due to the transient nature of vessels at sea.

To combat this difficulty, traceability has become essential in the global fishing and seafood industry, providing transparency and addressing food safety and sustainability concerns. This technology increases customer confidence in food products and helps manage illegal, unregulated, and unreported (IUU) fishing, which leads to significant losses and harms the marine ecosystem. Traditional fisheries management has implemented traceability measures, but new technological solutions are emerging. Vessel monitoring systems are satellite-based systems that provide fishing authorities with vessel location, course, and speed, enabling them to detect, deter, and eliminate IUU fishing.[33]

Creativity, Innovation, and the New Operational Excellence

The examples mentioned in the previous section demonstrate the efforts made by Asian businesses to enhance their operations to meet customer expectations and sustainability concerns. Even though they operate in diverse industries, their stories have similarities. The stories demonstrate how creativity and innovation can improve product quality, services, and delivery.

In the book *Entrepreneurial Marketing: Beyond Professionalism to Creativity, Leadership and Sustainability*, we argue that creativity and innovation are a series of processes.[34] The main focus of creativity is observing external trends and internal issues to define problems. The next task is to generate feasible creative ideas through divergent thinking. Management then determines the best ideas based on available resources and compatibility with the organization's vision, mission, and values.

After that, innovation will evolve the selected feasible creative idea into a ready-to-commercialize tangible form. The procedure will consider external factors like client behavior dynamics and rival companies' identical offerings. Internal aspects such as available resources, capabilities, and competencies must also be considered. The results should demonstrate a value that is user-friendly and not easy to imitate by other industry players.

In the new paradigm of operational excellence, the implementation of creativity and innovation is directed at solving problems related to quality, cost, delivery, and service. Figure 7.2 illustrates the process. Organizations with creativity and innovation will be able to find solutions to operational issues and deliver more excellent value for more stakeholders.

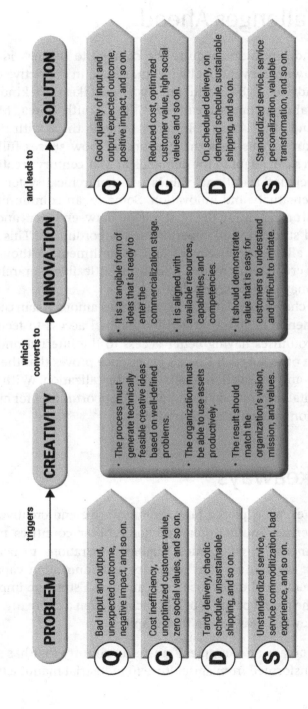

FIGURE 7.2 Creativity and innovation in the new operational excellence

PROBLEM *triggers* **CREATIVITY** *which converts to* **INNOVATION** *and leads to* **SOLUTION**

PROBLEM

- **Q** Bad input and output, unexpected outcome, negative impact, and so on.
- **C** Cost inefficiency, unoptimized customer value, zero social values, and so on.
- **D** Tardy delivery, chaotic schedule, unsustainable shipping, and so on.
- **S** Unstandardized service, service commoditization, bad experience, and so on.

CREATIVITY

- The process must generate technically feasible creative ideas based on well-defined problems.
- The organization must be able to use assets productively.
- The result should match the organization's vision, mission, and values.

INNOVATION

- It is a tangible form of ideas that is ready to enter the commercialization stage.
- It is aligned with available resources, capabilities, and competencies.
- It should demonstrate value that is easy for customers to understand and difficult to imitate.

SOLUTION

- **Q** Good quality of input and output, expected outcome, positive impact, and so on.
- **C** Reduced cost, optimized customer value, high social values, and so on.
- **D** On scheduled delivery, on demand schedule, sustainable shipping, and so on.
- **S** Standardized service, service personalization, valuable transformation, and so on.

The Challenges Ahead

Creativity and innovation require the courage to try new ideas that may conflict with conventional wisdom. People in restrictive cultures are usually advised to be careful and avoid mistakes; this kind of risk-averse mentality hampers creativity. China, South Korea, Malaysia, Singapore, and other Asian cultures are among those with rigid cultural boundaries. This begs the question of how successfully these Asian cultures can adapt to the demands of 21st-century creativity.[35]

Asian societies' traditional values and hierarchical systems might also hinder creativity and innovation. Some Asian communities still adhere to norms regarding the relationship between elders and youth, teachers and students, and superiors and subordinates. This kind of relationship allows for discipline and commitment. Although both qualities are crucial for creative initiatives, inflexible hierarchies and institutions may impede originality.

Another challenge relates to digital divides among Asian countries. The phenomenon is characterized by unequal access to technology, with some countries having better access to the internet and digital services than others. South Korea's experience proves that the growth of creativity and innovation aligns with digitalization. With limited access to digital information in some areas, opportunities for creativity and innovation to emerge are also uneven.

Key Takeaways

In this chapter, we explored how the innovative and creative energy that characterizes South Korea and some other countries may foster improvements in companies' business operations to benefit all stakeholders. We can see that creativity and innovation capabilities influence operational excellence and can have a strategic impact and strengthen the global position of a brand and even a company. Following are the key takeaways from this chapter:

- South Korea is an example of an Asian country that has successfully transformed from agriculture to industrial manufacturing to a creative economy. The Hallyu effect exemplifies this country's success in popularizing its creative pop culture worldwide.

- Samsung is an example of a Korean company that has succeeded in building new operational excellence based on sustainability through creativity and innovation.
- We can also take lessons about creativity and innovation from Cambodia's ACLEDA Bank, the Philippines' Jollibee, Malaysia's AirAsia, and the Thai Union.
- Asian cultural diversity, hierarchical system, and digital divide can challenge creativity and innovation in this region.

CHAPTER 8

Entrepreneurship and Leadership in the New Operational Excellence

How Indian Passion Is Helping Build Dominance

Leadership and entrepreneurship are crucial for a successful organization. Various studies have discussed the strategic role of these qualities for organizations. Influential leaders provide clarity of purpose, motivate employees, and guide them toward achieving their mission. Meanwhile, an entrepreneurial mindset will enable organizations to see opportunities amidst uncertainty and turn them into something valuable. This chapter will discuss the role of the leader and the entrepreneurial mindset in building organizational excellence from the operations side.

Made-in-India Leaders

What do the British prime minister and Alphabet's (Google) chief executive officer have in common? Both are popular and lead an institution with global influence. You will find other similarities in their names: Rishi Sunak and Sundar Pichai. Both have Indian names. Sunak was born to Indian parents who, in the 1960s, immigrated from East Africa to England. Pichai grew up in Chennai, India, at the same time. Another name that cannot be missed is Ajaypal Singh Banga. Banga is an Indian-born American who is now the president of the World Bank Group. Before this, he held the positions of executive chairman of Mastercard and vice chairman at General Atlantic.[1]

Overseas Indians also seem to be getting special recognition in the academic world. Since the early 2010s, several top US business schools have appointed deans of Indian descent. Here is a short list of what *The Times of India* noted as an "expanding league of Indian Americans heading educational institutions in the US": Nitin Nohria (the 10th dean of Harvard Business School), Sunil Kumar (the provost of Johns Hopkins University, previously serving as the dean of the University of Chicago's Booth School of Business), Soumitra Dutta (dean of the Cornell SC Johnson College of Business), and Dipak C. Jain (president of China Europe International Business School [CEIBS], previously serving as the dean of INSEAD and the Kellogg School of Management at Northwestern University).[2]

Many Indians are also widely known for their leadership roles in the business world. Some still hold or used to hold the highest positions in the organization. See Figure 8.1 for a list of global Indian business leaders.

This list is just a sample. Interestingly, almost all companies with Indian leaders, except Infosys, are not headquartered in India. This is proof of global recognition of the quality of Indian background talents as leaders. Even more interesting is that most of these companies run businesses in the technology sector. Statistics show that US technology companies increasingly favor Indian leaders. Despite representing fewer than 1% of the US population, the proportion of Silicon Valley tech firms headed by Indians has increased from 7% in the 1980s and 1990s to at least 13% to, according to some estimates, more than 25% in the 2010s.[3]

What factors might be behind this already noticeable trend? Of course, only looking at the country of origin as a leadership variable is oversimplification. However, this trend hints at the influence of India, as a country, on those bright leaders. According to the late C. K. Prahalad, "Growing up in India is an extraordinary preparation for management."[4]

No.	Name	Position	Company	Industry	Leadership Period
1	Satya Nadella	CEO	Microsoft	Computer software	2014–present
2	Parag Agrawal	CEO	Twitter	Social networking service	2021–2022
3	Leena Nair	CEO	Chanel	Fashion	2022–present
4	Shantanu Narayen	CEO	Adobe Inc.	Software	2007–2017
5	Laxman Narasimhan	CEO	Reckitt Benckiser	Consumer goods	2019–2022
6	Reshma Kewalramani	CEO	Vertex Pharmaceuticals	Biotechnology	2020–present
7	Arvind Krishna	CEO	IBM	Information technology	2020–2021
8	Neal Mohan	CEO	YouTube	Video sharing platform	2023–present
9	Ajaypal Singh Banga	Executive chairman	MasterCard	Financial services	2010–2021
10	Vasant Narasimhan	CEO	Novartis	Pharmaceutical	2017–present
11	Jayshree Ullal	CEO	Arista Networks	IT networks	2008–present
12	Sanjay Mehrotra	CEO	Micron Technology	Semiconductor	2017–2019
13	Ravi Kumar	CEO	Infosys	Consulting and IT services	2016–2022
14	Anjali Sud	CEO	Vimeo	Video sharing platform	2017–July 2023
15	Indra Nooyi	CEO	PepsiCo	Food and beverage	2006–2018
16	Ajei S. Gopal	CEO	Ansys, Inc.	Software and services	2017–present
17	Laxman Narasimhan	CEO	Starbucks	Retail coffee	2022–2023
18	Amrapali Gan	CEO	OnlyFans	Content-sharing platform	2021–present
19	Jay Chaudhry	CEO	Zscaler	Network security	2007–present
20	Rajeev Puri	CEO	Inmarsat	Satellite telecommunications	2021–present

FIGURE 8.1 Global business leaders of Indian descent adapted from [5]

India: The Birthplace of Global Leaders

One of the world's oldest civilizations, India has a broad range of cultures, beliefs, and languages. With more than 1.4 billion inhabitants, it is also the most populated nation today (surpassing China in 2022).[6] India, the largest country in South Asia, differs from many other countries in the rest of Asia because its seas and mountains give it a unique geographical identity. India is the seventh-largest country in the world and has borders with six other countries.

Since gaining its independence, India has made socioeconomic progress on all fronts. A historic agricultural revolution in 1947 helped the country go from being reliant on grain imports to being an agricultural powerhouse that is today a net exporter of food. Economic growth has coincided with the nation's incorporation into the world economy since the early 2010s. Strong domestic demand, solid investment activity fueled by the government's push for infrastructure construction, and brisk private consumption contributed to the country's economic growth.

Several reliable organizations make upbeat prognoses for India's future. From 2023 on, according to Morgan Stanley, India will be one of just three nations worldwide that can produce more than US$400 billion in annual economic production growth, which will increase to more than US$500 billion after 2028.[7] The World Bank mentions that India is one of the countries with the fastest economic growth globally, and it looks set to keep going in this direction. By 2047, when Indian independence will be 100 years old, the country hopes to have reached high middle-income status.[8] Based on this analysis, India is on the trajectory of becoming the third-largest economy in the world by 2027, surpassing Japan and Germany.[9] See Figure 8.2 for some key moments of India's economic and leadership development.

Despite its tremendous growth toward becoming a global economic giant, India still needs to overcome domestic problems. Although other nations cannot match India's talent pool in numbers, quality is still a challenge. Only 50% of young Indians, according to the India Skills Report 2023, are employable. Less than half of urban employees are employed full-time, and far too many people in India work in unproductive informal sectors. There is also extensive "home work" in health care, competency development, and education.[10]

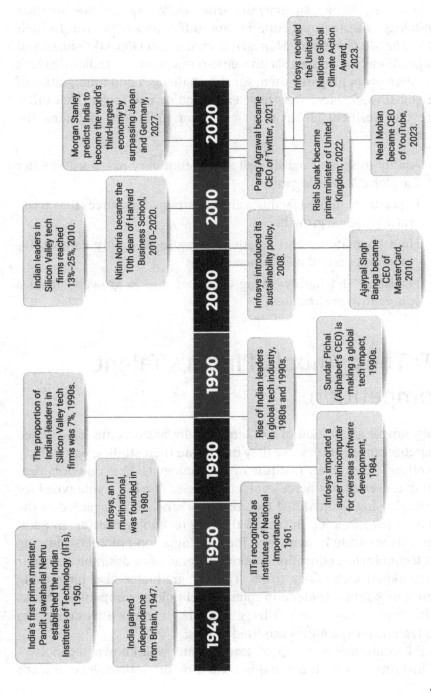

FIGURE 8.2 Some key moments of India's economic and leadership development

India's first prime minister, Pandit Jawaharlal Nehru established the Indian Institutes of Technology (IITs), 1950.

India gained independence from Britain, 1947.

Infosys, an IT multinational, was founded in 1980.

IITs recognized as Institutes of National Importance, 1961.

Infosys imported a super minicomputer for overseas software development, 1984.

The proportion of Indian leaders in Silicon Valley tech firms was 7%, 1990s.

Rise of Indian leaders in global tech industry, 1980s and 1990s.

Sundar Pichai (Alphabet's CEO) is making a global tech impact, 1990s.

Indian leaders in Silicon Valley tech firms reached 13%–25%, 2010.

Nitin Nohria became the 10th dean of Harvard Business School, 2010–2020.

Infosys introduced its sustainability policy, 2008.

Ajaypal Singh Banga became CEO of MasterCard, 2010.

Morgan Stanley predicts India to become the world's third-largest economy by surpassing Japan and Germany, 2027.

Parag Agrawal became CEO of Twitter, 2021.

Rishi Sunak became prime minister of United Kingdom, 2022.

Infosys received the United Nations Global Climate Action Award, 2023.

Neal Mohan became CEO of YouTube, 2023.

1940 1950 1980 1990 2000 2010 2020

However, India can generate trustworthy leaders due to their familiarity with the opportunities and difficulties they face. In their book, *The Made-in-India Manager*, Ramabadran Gopalakrishnan and Ranjan Banerjee argue that the environment of an Indian leader's formative years prepares them for the challenges and ambiguities of the global workplace. They have examined several factors that influence how resilient global managers from India are, including the following:[11]

- Ability to speak English well as a preliminary password to enter the global business game.
- Exposure to limited facilities and constrained resources that accelerates personal growth.
- High adaptability and creativity because of highly competitive environments and many uncertainties.
- Persistent and hard-working character due to growing up in a competitive environment.

IIT: The Symbol of India's Talent Competition

The younger generation of workers in India has become accustomed to intense competition since they first began their studies, particularly in college. The Indian Institute of Technology (IIT) is one organization that exemplifies fierce competitiveness. The IIT is renowned for developing highly qualified technical workers and is regarded as the quickest path to a job in India's thriving technology sector. In addition, this institute is renowned for offering a top-notch engineering and technological education, making its graduates desirable to major international technology firms. The IIT graduates also have a big chance of holding leadership roles in technology companies, thanks to the combination of soft skills generated by a competitive ecosystem and technical capabilities acquired at IITs.

IIT comprises a group of leading and well-known technological institutes across India and is owned by the Indian government's

Ministry of Education. Pandit Jawaharlal Nehru, the country's first prime minister, initially had the idea for the IIT because he thought science and technology had a significant role in modernizing India and addressing the demands of its expanding population. The first IIT was established at the Hijli Detention Campsite in Kharagpur, West Bengal, in May 1950.[12] The IIT was founded to produce professionals of the highest caliber who would lead India's socioeconomic transformation through technology.

Four more IITs were founded within 10 years after the first one, including IIT Bombay (1958), IIT Madras (1959), IIT Kanpur (1959), and IIT Delhi (1961). To avoid regional imbalance, the locations of these campuses were chosen to be dispersed throughout India. There are 23 IITs in India (see Figure 8.3 for the complete list of IIT campuses).[13]

	No.	Campus	State	Establishment
First Generation	1	IIT Kharagpur	West Bengal	1951
	2	IIT Bombay	Maharashtra	1958
	3	IIT Madras	Tamil Nadu	1959
	4	IIT Kanpur	Uttar Pradesh	1959
	5	IIT Delhi	Delhi	1961
	6	IIT Guwahati	Assam	1994
	7	IIT Roorkee	Uttarakhand	1847, converted to IIT in 2001
Second Generation	8	IIT Ropar	Punjab	2008
	9	IIT Bhubaneswar	Odisha	2008
	10	IIT Gandhinagar	Gujarat	2008
	11	IIT Hyderabad	Telangana	2008
	12	IIT Jodhpur	Rajasthan	2008
	13	IIT Patna	Bihar	2008
	14	IIT Indore	Madhya Pradesh	2009
	15	IIT Mandi	Himachal Pradesh	2009
Third Generation	16	IIT Varanasi	Uttar Pradesh	1919, converted to IIT in 2012
	17	IIT Palakkad	Kerala	2015
	18	IIT Tirupati	Andhra Pradesh	2015
	19	IIT Dhanbad	Jharkhand	1926, converted to IIT in 2016
	20	IIT Bhilai	Chhattisgarh	2016
	21	IIT Dharwad	Karnataka	2016
	22	IIT Jammu	Jammu and Kashmir	2016
	23	IIT Goa	Goa	2016

FIGURE 8.3 Campuses of the Indian Institute of Technology

The Institutes of Technology Act 1961, which establishes the IITs as Institutes of National Importance and outlines their responsibilities and governance structure as the nation's top technological institutions, governs the IITs.[14] The IITs have been crucial to India's technological advancement over the years, and their alums have made significant contributions to the government's public works, irrigation, power, railways, highways, and space research departments, as well as to the manufacturing and service industries in the private sector.

Getting into an IIT is extremely difficult, and the Joint Entrance Examination is regarded as one of the most challenging tests in the world.[15] For this exam, high school students from all around the nation prepare for several years, and the majority of them have used the services of coaches. Students taking the exam are under much strain because of its difficulty and low acceptance rate. Just 1.83% of candidates were accepted by the IITs in 2022, which is a lower acceptance rate than that of the Ivy League universities in the United States.[16] The terrible struggles and anguish they experience while preparing for the IITs are depicted in the Netflix series *Kota Factory*. The plot centers on Kota, a small "college prep" town in Rajasthan, India. It describes the lives of students who spend two years studying day and night for the IIT entrance exam while attending regular classes. The program gives credence to the lives of these students, who are under constant mental pressure while they study for the impending IIT entrance exam.

Intense competition, intellectually and mentally, makes IITs the ideal ecosystem to produce brilliant tech entrepreneurs and leaders. By alums of IIT Delhi alone, 1334 businesses have been founded, including 23 unicorns. From 2,781 investors, these businesses have raised more than US$36.51 billion in investment.[17] Alums from IITs also play a significant role in the global tech sector. IIT alums who have been successful in holding C-level positions in major global tech companies include CEO of Alphabet Sundar Pichai (IIT Kharagpur), CEO of Palo Alto Networks Nikesh Arora (IIT Varanasi), CEO of IBM Arvind Krishna (IIT Kanpur), former CEO of Twitter Parag Agrawal (IIT Bombay), and former CTO of Cisco and Motorola Padmasree Warrior (IIT Delhi).

A robust alum network is also one of the most significant benefits of wearing an IIT badge. Flipkart, India's biggest e-commerce company, is a prime example of the impact of IIT alums. Founded by Binny

Bansal and Sachin Bansal, who were one year apart at IIT Delhi, Flipkart hired many IIT alums, including Sujeet Kumar, who later became Flipkart's president of operations. Kumar's IITs network helped recruit more employees, saving time and connecting with the right people.[18]

Infosys Story

One of the IIT alum legacies that is still evident today is Infosys, an Indian multinational company that offers consultancy and information technology services. Nandan M. Nilekani, S. Gopalakrishnan, S. D. Shibulal, K. Dinesh, N. S. Raghavan, and Ashok Arora are the company's founders. Nandan Nilekani is an alumnus of IIT Bombay, where he studied electrical engineering. N. R. Narayana Murthy, another cofounder of Infosys, earned his master's degree from IIT Kanpur.

Infosys started its international expansion in the late 1980s, opening offices in the United States, UK, Canada, Germany, Sweden, and other countries. Today, it has a global presence with clients in more than 56 countries. Infosys serves 1,883 clients worldwide, with more than 336,000 talented employees.[19] The financial indicators for Infosys are currently performing well. It had a solid operating margin of 21.0% and 15.4% sales growth, the highest in the sector for the fiscal year 2023.[20] In TIME's list of the world's 100 best companies for 2023, this global tech giant is the only one from India.[21]

Infosys is also committed to achieving the United Nations' Sustainable Development Goals (SDGs) by reducing its carbon footprint and becoming carbon neutral. The company has achieved this sustainability target 30 years ahead of the Paris Agreement timeline and received the prestigious United Nations Global Climate Action Award.[22] For its environmental, social, and governance (ESG) practices, Infosys is also recognized as one of the 2023 World's Most Ethical Companies by Ethisphere.[23]

It is not unexpected that this organization exemplifies the new operational excellence practices. Its services are customized services tailored to clients' needs and transformational solutions that help clients become better sustainable companies. Infosys collaborates with clients to understand, create, and implement profitable and purposeful ESG initiatives. The framework used by Infosys to address the sustainability challenge is built on several fundamental components: ESG data and analytics, decarbonization, product life cycle management (PLM) circularity, sustainability design advisory, and water management solutions.[24]

Infosys introduced its sustainability policy in 2008, firmly rooted in triple-bottom-line principles: the social contract, resource efficiency, and environmental stewardship. The sustainability principles are integrated into all policies, processes, and decision-making frameworks. The sustainability practice unit formed by Infosys aims to help clients transition in facing climate change through business-based IT solutions based on carbon capture, usage, and storage (CCUS), energy storage, next-generation innovative and sustainable products and services, renewable energy, energy efficiency, trade, clean energy generation, brownfield modernization, and transformation, as well as electric mobility.

Entrepreneurship, Leadership, and the New Operational Excellence

Chapter 7 discussed that the innovation process will turn feasible creative ideas into solutions. This solution must be ready to use, not just an abstract concept. But creating solutions is only part of the business. We must continue creativity and innovation with entrepreneurship. No matter how impressive the resulting solution is, it still won't have a valuable impact if other people are not interested in adopting it. Like medicine, the benefits will not be felt if the patient does not want to take it. A solution must be "sold" so that as many stakeholders as possible want to use it. This principle also applies in the operational excellence context.

The entrepreneurial mentality has several characteristics that can accelerate new operational excellence practices: opportunity seekers, risk-takers, and network collaborators (see Figure 8.4). Opportunity seekers are curious and self-starters, embracing failure and learning from mistakes. Risk-takers create value for the organization by carefully calculating the various risks that may occur. At the same time, network collaborators build meaningful relationships

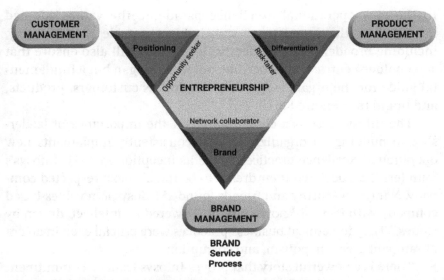

FIGURE 8.4   Entrepreneurship's role in brand management

with various stakeholders and work together to achieve common goals. These three characteristics will assist businesspeople in adding more value by managing customers, products, and brands more entrepreneurially. Regarding brand management, entrepreneurship can benefit all stakeholders by fortifying brand equity bolstered by services and processes.[25] Service and process (quality, cost, and delivery) are the main elements of new operational excellence we address in this book.

Several studies already examined the relationship between leadership and sustainable performance.[26] Once sustainable operational excellence practices are adopted, leadership will play a critical role in embedding them into organizational culture. They ensure that sustainability is incorporated at all levels of business operations for decision-making, procedures, and policies. Leaders inspire staff members to embrace sustainability as a central component of their job by fostering an atmosphere that encourages and rewards sustainable activities.

In *Entrepreneurial Marketing: Beyond Professionalism to Creativity, Leadership, and Sustainability*, we explained that leaders play an essential role in formulating values in the organization and internalizing them in business operations, strategically and tactically.[27]

In the new operational excellence paradigm, the values adopted must reflect the interests of stakeholders outside the company, including broader society. Effective leadership will also ensure that stakeholder-centric values become not just a slogan but a fundamental guide for the organization in managing its customers, products, and brand (see Figure 8.5).

The Infosys case is a clear example of the importance of leadership in building an organization that consistently implements new operational excellence practices. Since its inception in 1981, Infosys's founders have declared their dream to be India's most respected company. Narayana Murthy and friends founded Infosys as a values-based company with its well-known motto, "Powered by intellect, driven by values." They felt ethical business practices were crucial even in an era of rampant greed, nepotism, and corruption.

There is a powerful story that proves Infosys leaders' commitment to integrity. In 1984, Infosys imported a super minicomputer for overseas software development. However, local customs officials refused to clear the machine, requiring a bribe. Infosys leaders chose to pay a 135% customs duty and appeal for a refund.[28] They believed that Infosys' ethical image would increase employee commitment, business revenue, and respect from governments and societies in the long run. And they already have proved it today.

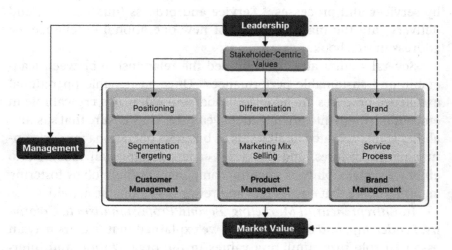

FIGURE 8.5 Leadership's role in internalizing stakeholder-centric values in the company

Lessons from Other Asian Countries

Previously, we have looked at what makes India a favorable environment for developing competent leaders. In this section, we explore examples of other companies outside India. We will learn from them how entrepreneurship and leadership are crucial for making sustainable companies.

Eiger (Indonesia)

Eiger is an Indonesian brand providing activity equipment and apparel that meets the lifestyle of outdoor adventure enthusiasts. The name Eiger is taken from the name of Mount Eiger, located in the Bernese Alps, Switzerland, which is 3,970 meters above sea level and is known as the third hardest mountain to climb in the world. Currently, Eiger provides three main product categories: mountaineering (for mountain climbing activities), riding (focuses on exploring motorbikes), and authentic 1989 (outdoor-adventurer-inspired lifestyle fashion). The company was founded in 1989 and has since become a well-known brand in Indonesia. Eiger has also expanded internationally by opening a store in Interlaken, Switzerland, in 2023.

The company is committed to sustainability and has released some unique product series to transform society with green lifestyle fashion. Several Eiger products already use recycled materials processed from plastic bottle waste. Certain ingredients in selected other Eiger's products allow the product to decompose back into nature within 12 weeks to reduce fashion waste. It has also released clothing products that use organic cotton. Organic materials aim to support more environmentally friendly cotton cultivation by using less water, crop rotation strategies, and not using toxic chemicals.

Eiger's concern for beyond-profit impact and environmental values contribution emerged from the personal experience and reflection of its founder, Ronny Lukito. When his business survived the Asian financial crisis in 1998, Ronny pledged to make Eiger an excellent organization to work for its employees and a responsible company contributing positively to the environment and society. Eiger's transformation began internally, with the preparation of a vision, mission, and culture oriented toward sustainability. Values internalization for employees is carried out through training and development and a green office environment. Continuous exposure to environmentally friendly physical evidence and activities produces employees who can become Eiger's green ambassadors.

Vinamilk (Vietnam)

Vinamilk is a Vietnamese dairy firm that manufactures and sells various dairy goods, such as yogurt, ice cream, condensed milk, powdered milk, fresh milk, soy milk, and other items made from milk. The business was founded in 1976 and is Vietnam's biggest dairy producer. Internationally, Vinamilk has grown and now includes operations in the United States, the Philippines, Poland, New Zealand, and Laos.[29]

Vinamilk pledges to uphold its obligations to all its stakeholders as a business that practices new operational excellence. Vinamilk has outlined its commitment regarding five topics mentioned in the company's sustainable development orientation: employee support, community development, local economic development, environment and energy, and human nutrition.[30]

As a producer, Vinamilk is dedicated to environmental sustainability and uses natural and energy resources effectively. To ensure ecological safety and ongoing improvement, they address emission concerns during construction design and put waste and emission treatment management methods in place. Vinamilk has also focused on integrating cutting-edge technology with sustainable agriculture. The company values animal welfare, and dairy cows are not given growth hormones. Strict international requirements are met by the factories that treat 100% of wastewater to satisfy applicable environmental standards before being released into the environment.

Consequently, Vinamilk gained respect on a global scale for its dedication to sustainable development. Vinamilk received recognition in two important categories for the Global CSR & ESG Awards 2022: the CSR & ESG Leadership Award (Gold) and the Best Country Award for Overall CSR Excellence (Platinum). Vinamilk's activities and dedication to sustainability are consistent with its thriving business performance. The company was acknowledged as the most promising dairy brand, and Vinamilk's brand value climbed to sixth in the world dairy sector rankings.[31]

For Vinamilk to operate sustainably, leadership is unquestionably essential. The leadership's responsibility is to specify company values, as shown in Figure 8.5. Similar to this, the sustainability values of Vinamilk are established by the CEO and board of directors, overseen by the sustainability development council, and applied throughout the organization. The leaders of Vinamilk included sustainable development as one of four criteria in their development objectives for 2022 to 2026. They also defined four materiality areas: the environment, society, the economy, and industry standards.[32] That is how Vinamilk's employees, guided and supervised by their collective leaders, are finally putting values into practice in sustainable day-to-day company operations.

The Hong Kong and Shanghai Hotels, Limited (Hong Kong SAR)

A conglomerate of upscale hotels and real estate companies, Hong Kong and Shanghai Hotels, Limited (HSH) was founded in 1866 and is traded on the Hong Kong Stock Exchange. This well-known business owns, develops, and operates The Peninsula Hotels (in addition to commercial and residential properties) across Europe, Asia, and the United States. In addition, the organization offers club management, tourist, and leisure services.[33] Thanks to its excellent business operations and dedication to sustainability, HSH is a significant participant in the hotel and real estate industries.

HSH has been actively involved in sustainability practices to provide sustainable luxury in all aspects of its operations and positively affect the surrounding communities and environment. One way it demonstrates its dedication to sustainability is by creating stunning and sustainable buildings that are thoughtfully planned and have the following qualities:[34]

- They integrate the industry's top sustainable building standards into large-scale rehabilitation and new construction projects.
- Most woodwork is sourced from suppliers certified responsibly.

- They have reduced airborne pollutants through optimizing indoor air exchange.
- Low volatile organic compounds (VOCs) are used in adhesives, paints, wall coverings, textiles, and carpets.

The chairman of HSH, Sir Michael Kadoorie, has significantly influenced the development of the business's sustainable practices. As part of his vision for the company, sustainability will be central to its business model and operations, with a particular emphasis on green financing to support initiatives that promote sustainable practices and scale up beneficial environmental impact. His leadership has encouraged ethical corporate citizenship and incorporated sustainability into the company's fundamental business activities.[35]

Future Leadership Challenges

Korn Ferry, an international organization consultancy, estimates that a worldwide shortage of talented human resources could reach more than 85 million people (about the same as Germany's population) by 2030. Finding candidates who can fill an available post and eventually advance into a leadership position is more concerning than finding suitable candidates in the short term.[36]

Indian companies have also had similar difficulties since the early 2010s. Globally speaking, this nation has produced many exceptionally gifted leaders, but the number still needs to come close to meeting the needs for talent at home. Since the new millennium, many Indian businesses have grown impressively. However, many later experienced the frightening consequence of a national leadership crisis.[37] Organizations must pay more attention to employee development because they are too busy expanding their businesses.

Based on these facts, firms must have their in-house leadership development program to secure long-term success. Businesses cannot develop the leaders they require by depending on outside mechanisms. A program for internal leadership development is essential. Organizations may create a strong pipeline of leaders better suited to handle the company's unique problems by investing in internal leadership development programs.

Developing internal leaders can aid companies in keeping their best employees. Employee retention is higher when they perceive opportunities for personal and professional development within the company. This commitment can assist companies in lowering employee turnover as well as the related expenses of recruiting and onboarding new staff members. Furthermore, internal candidates can transition into leadership roles more quickly because they are familiar with the organization's culture, principles, and procedures.

Businesses can learn from India's track record of developing accomplished global leaders when creating their leadership development initiatives. Companies need to recognize high-potential workers as future leaders from the beginning. Detailed preparation is required for the criteria to be a successful leader, which is a blend of technical aptitude and having moral qualities. Moreover, future company leaders must acquire cross-cultural communication skills to function effectively in an increasingly globalized society. In an organization with a wide range of stakeholders from different cultural backgrounds, future leaders will be more equipped to compete in the global marketplace.

Key Takeaways

In this chapter, we covered perspectives from India on leadership development and entrepreneurship that help businesses adopt sustainability practices. Following are the key takeaways for this chapter:

- India's unique social, cultural, and economic environment is a natural combination for the birth of potential entrepreneurs and global business leaders, especially in the IT industry.
- Strong leaders can emerge from an intellectually and emotionally competitive environment, as demonstrated by the India Institutes of Technology (IIT).
- Entrepreneurship and leadership play an essential role in creating organizational operational excellence that focuses on the interests of all stakeholders, not just company interests.

- Entrepreneurial traits, including opportunity-seeking, risk-taking, and network collaboration, will equip business leaders to create more value.
- Effective leadership will be the primary driver in creating and building stakeholder-centric values within the company.
- Organizations must develop an internal leadership development program to prepare candidates for a diverse global business environment.

CHAPTER 9

Productivity and Improvement in the New Operational Excellence

How the Japanese Spirit Goes Beyond Kaizen

Productivity is frequently measured by comparing input and output, and being productive means increasing production while requiring fewer resources and producing more. This method is evident in the production process when calculating the number of output units generated from a given input unit. We can still use it in other management areas even though it is more sophisticated. Meanwhile, if someone concentrates on getting better results today than yesterday, they are said to have an improvement paradigm. In this chapter, you will learn how to apply a productivity and improvement mindset to increase operational excellence that focuses on the interests of all stakeholders.

Toyota: The Story of Improvement and Innovation

What company best represents the word *improvement?* The answer is most likely Toyota. The Toyota Production System (TPS) based on continuous improvement has significantly contributed to the company's success. Toyota implements an average of nine improvement ideas per employee per year.[1] In his book, *The Toyota Way: 14 Management Principles from the World's Greatest Factory* (McGraw-Hill, 2004), Jeffrey K. Liker played a role in popularizing the Toyota Way, which refers to the principle of continuous improvement.

According to a well-known story, Toyota is so dedicated to continuous improvement that any employee on a Toyota assembly line can stop the line at any moment to address a production issue, fix a mistake, or recommend an alternative course of action to management that saves waste or boosts productivity. The worker receives rewards rather than punishment for pausing production if management is persuaded that the stoppage has increased productivity and quality.[2]

Toyota's history began when Sakichi Toyoda created the first automatic loom in the late 1800s. The British company Platt Brothers purchased the loom's manufacturing and sales rights in 1929. Sakichi then handed his son Kiichiro the money so that he might develop automotive technology further. As a result, the Model AA, the company's first passenger car, was introduced in 1936, and the Toyota Motor Company was officially established in 1937.[3] The business stopped making passenger automobiles during World War II and focused only on making trucks. The year 1947 saw the return of Toyota's passenger automobile manufacturing with the launch of the Model SA (known by its nickname "Toyopet").[4]

In the 1960s, Toyota capitalized on a rapidly expanding Japanese economy to sell automobiles to an expanding middle class. As a result, the Toyota Corolla was produced and became one of the best-selling automobiles in history. The business has made international strides, setting up sales offices and industrial facilities throughout several nations. The company's innovation, including the launch of the world's first mass-produced hybrid vehicle, the Prius (1997), and its luxury brand, Lexus (1989), contributed to its enormous expansion long into the next century.

With its Scion brand introduced in 2003 and the introduction of the Lexus RX 400h (2005), the first luxury hybrid car in the world, the business began to enter new markets, focusing on younger consumers.[5] Today, Toyota is the second-biggest automaker in the world and the highest-ranked Japanese firm on the 2023 Fortune Global 500 list, with US$274.5 billion in revenue.[6] See Table 9.1 for a list of Toyota's milestones.

TABLE 9.1   Toyota's Milestones adapted from [7]

Year	Events
1907	Toyoda Loom Company was established in Shimasaki-cho, Nagoya City. Sakichi Toyoda, who invented the automatic loom, was appointed managing director.
1936	Toyota Model AA, the first passenger car, was launched.
1337	Toyota Motor Company was officially established.
1955	Toyota Crown, the first passenger car made in Japan to be exported to the United States, was launched.
1961	Total Quality Control (TQC) was introduced.
1963	Production control method using Kanban was commenced.
1969	Annual sales volume in Japan tops 1 million vehicles.
1970	Awarded the First Japan Quality Medal.
1975	Toyota attained the number one position in sales of imported passenger cars in the United States for the first time.
1976	Cumulative production volume reaches 20 million vehicles. The number of dealers under Toyota Motor Sales, US, exceeds 1,000. Annual export volume reaches 1 million vehicles.
1978	Toyota attained the number one position in sales of imported passenger cars, trucks, and total sales volume in the United States (winning the triple crown).
1989	Toyota launched the luxury brand Lexus LS400 in North America.
1990	The development of the Toyota Flexible System, a press production system optimized for small lot production of a wide range of parts, was announced.

(Continued)

TABLE 9.1 (CONTINUED)

Year	Events
1994	A hybrid electric bus was developed.
1997	Prius, the first mass-produced hybrid car, was launched.
	Prius won the 1997–1998 Car of the Year Japan Award, the 2004 North American Car of the Year Award, and the 2005 European Car of the Year Award.
2001	The Toyota Way 2001 was adopted.
2008	Cumulative worldwide Prius sales top 1 million units.
2010	Collaboration with Tesla Motors on electric vehicle development was announced.
	The development of an advanced energy management system, Toyota Smart Center (TSC), was announced.
2015	Toyota Environmental Challenge 2050 was established.
2019	Toyota established a business model of technological innovations in the automotive industry in "CASE" (Connected, Autonomous/Automated, Shared, Electric).
2020	Toyota Philosophy and Toyota Way 2020 were established.
2023	Toyota became the second-biggest automaker in the world and the highest-ranked Japanese firm.

Toyota's Improvement Toward New Operational Excellence

Toyota prioritizes more than just efforts to boost bottom-line results. In recent years, the company has also made notable improvements toward sustainability. This is aligned with the Zen philosophy, which teaches the importance of connecting with ecology and remaining unaffected by materialism and mechanization. Integrating marketing and Zen philosophy, known as Marketing ZEN, can enhance the sustainability of businesses (see Appendix D).

Toyota has established high standards for lowering environmental effects and promoting a more sustainable future. By 2050, Toyota wants all its vehicle life cycles to be carbon neutral. Along the way, the business is developing technology for carbon collection and reuse of the collected carbon. Hence, it is cutting carbon emissions and increasing its efforts to electrify vehicles.[8] It's interesting to note that Toyota has made much of its progress toward sustainability through incremental advancements rather than radical changes. The ensuing instances demonstrate how improvements can have a noteworthy effect on the surroundings:

- **PVC reduction.** The team devised a clever and easy method to reduce the quantity of PVC—a plastic spray used to shield Sienna minivans' underbody from corrosion and keep emissions out of the car—used on the vehicle. It saved 24,000 pounds of PVC material by determining which areas didn't need the spray.[9] A tiny alteration has a significant material and environmental impact.

- **Water conservation.** Toyota Motor Manufacturing Indiana (TMMI) is reusing wastewater during the paint pretreatment process, saving an estimated 54 million gallons of fresh water annually as part of Toyota's water conservation efforts. These improvement methods are made possible by new microfiltration modules.[10]

- **Material usage.** Toyota has made cutting waste its top focus. Over 93% of garbage was recycled, repurposed, or composted in 2021. The amount dumped in landfills was only a minimal number. This demonstrates how waste management techniques in Toyota have significantly improved.[11]

Toyota has instilled a continuous improvement culture that has permeated the organization. Everyone in this company is encouraged to contribute to the ideation process and use the available resources to produce the most excellent answers. However, it is impossible to separate the emergence of this type of culture from the history of Japan, Toyota's country of origin, and how it rose after its massive loss in World War II.

Japan: The Story of Country Improvement

Japan was in ruins at the end of World War II, having lost a great deal of money and lives while significant cities were destroyed. A challenging struggle for stability and reconstruction characterized the early post-war years. After World War II, the American government was crucial to Japan's rehabilitation. Under General Douglas MacArthur's leadership as Supreme Commander for the Allied Powers, the United States spearheaded the Allies' occupation and reconstruction of the Japanese state. The U.S. administration maintained that social and political reform in Japan required a transformation of many aspects of Japanese society.

Under MacArthur's direction, Japan accomplished remarkable changes only in seven years, from 1945 to 1952.[12] In addition, the U.S. government invested US$2.2 billion in Japan's rehabilitation efforts during that period.[13] The fact that Japan is now a close friend of the United States and has maintained many of the significant reforms implemented during the occupation serves as a barometer for the occupation's success.

A group of American specialists, known as the Economic and Scientific Section (ESS), was sent to Japan to assist with the post–World War II reconstruction of the industrial sector. This group was responsible for enhancing Japanese industry competitiveness and was instrumental in creating and applying new management techniques. One of the inspirations for the continuous improvement paradigm, which became the cornerstone of industries in Japan, is the Training Within Industry (TWI) program. When millions of American men quit their industrial occupations to enlist in the military during the 1940s American war effort in Europe, TWI was created in the United States. Japan was then introduced to the technique by the ESS team. TWI caught on quickly, and Toyota was among the businesses that adopted it in 1951.[14]

TWI was a strategy that worked well for Japan at the time. These approaches suggested that businesses make minor adjustments rather than push for significant, drastic innovations to accomplish their objectives. The primary cause was the lack of time and funding during World War II for effective and creative modifications to military hardware manufacturing. The strategy's main focus was on making better use of the labor and technologies already in place.

Several new economic policies were also implemented to support Japan's industrial growth. The encouragement of anti-competitive activity and mergers has led to the consolidation of industries, resulting in increased productivity and efficiency. In addition, the US government offered favorable loans and tax deductions for expenses related to sales abroad, which lowered the cost of Japanese exports and increased their competitiveness in the world market. After that, Japan was able to bounce back incredibly quickly, witnessing what is known as the "Japanese Economic Miracle" as its economy expanded quickly.[15]

Japanese Economic Miracle

Japan's economy grew quickly and steadily between 1945 and 1990, the year that separated the end of the Cold War from the post–World War II era. Japan's economy prospered due to an aggressive export trade policy, a vast domestic market, and an unparalleled increase in industrial production.[16]

Numerous industries saw tremendous expansion during Japan's economic miracle, aiding the nation's quick and steady economic growth. During this time, there were a few major significant industries:

- **Automobile manufacturing.** Manufacturers of high-quality, fuel-efficient cars in high demand locally and abroad included Toyota, Honda, and Nissan. These companies rose to prominence in the automotive sector.
- **Electronics.** Japanese manufacturers of televisions, radios, computers, smartphones, and other consumer electronics, like Sony, Panasonic, and Toshiba, rose to prominence in the worldwide electronics market.
- **Steel and shipbuilding.** During the economic miracle, there was a notable surge in demand for both steel and ships. Japanese industries such as Nippon Steel and Mitsubishi Heavy Industries extended their manufacturing facilities to accommodate this demand.
- **Chemicals and petrochemicals.** Sumitomo Chemical, Mitsubishi Chemical, and Mitsui Chemicals are some companies that play an essential role in ensuring the availability of various chemical goods to the growing local and overseas markets.
- **Textiles and apparel.** Although this sector first contributed significantly to Japan's export-led prosperity, it later faced competition from lower-cost rivals, with companies like Fast Retailing (owner of the Uniqlo brand) rising to prominence.

Japan's post–World War II economic expansion was driven mainly by these industries, along with banking, services, and construction, which helped the country become a significant player in the world economy.

The Kaizen Philosophy

One of the main reasons for Japan's quick and steady post–World War II economic growth was Kaizen, which translates to "continuous improvement" in Japanese. Additionally, it entails carrying on with improvements in social, professional, domestic, and personal spheres. The term *Kaizen* gained international recognition thanks to the writings of Japanese organizational theorist and management consultant Masaaki Imai. Kaizen was first popularized in the West by Imai's best-selling 1986 book, *Kaizen: The Key to Japan's Competitive Success* (McGraw-Hill). The Japanese economy employed the Kaizen concept in manufacturing, management, and quality control, among other areas. This technique helped to boost competitiveness and productivity.

Japan encountered several difficulties following the war, such as scarce resources, a severely damaged infrastructure, and a shortage of scientific breakthroughs. To tackle these challenges, Japanese businesses and sectors implemented a continuous improvement culture that pushed each employee to affect the organization positively. They increased production and efficiency by using this strategy to find and remove waste, streamline operations, and improve product quality. Kaizen is commonly linked to the Toyota Production System, as it is a fundamental tenet of the system. The Kaizen principles gave Japanese manufacturers a competitive advantage in the global market by enabling them to create high-quality cars at a cheaper cost.

In contrast to Western nations prioritizing innovation for development, the Japanese argue that Kaizen is more beneficial in the long run. Because innovation's effects are sometimes said to wear off quickly, Kaizen amplifies the benefits and enhances its influence.[17]

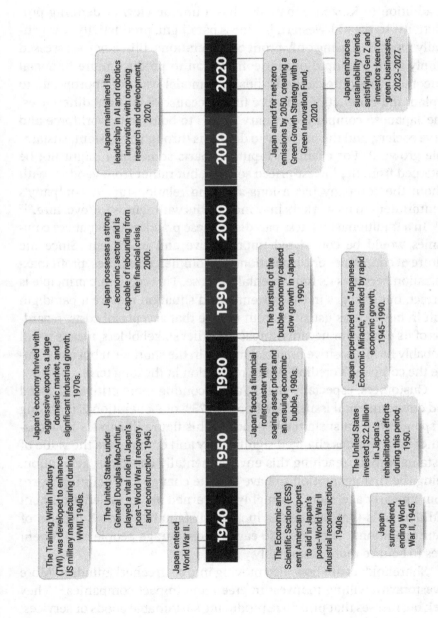

The Training Within Industry (TWI) was developed to enhance US military manufacturing during WWII, 1940s.

Japan's economy thrived with aggressive exports, a large domestic market, and significant industrial growth, 1970s.

Japan maintained its leadership in AI and robotics innovation with ongoing research and development, 2020.

The United States, under General Douglas MacArthur, played a vital role in Japan's post-World War II recovery and reconstruction, 1945.

Japan possesses a strong economic sector and is capable of rebounding from the financial crisis, 2000.

Japan aimed for net-zero emissions by 2050, creating a Green Growth Strategy with a Green Innovation Fund, 2020.

Japan embraces sustainability trends, satisfying Gen Z and investors keen on green businesses, 2023–2027.

Japan entered World War II.

Japan faced a financial rollercoaster with soaring asset prices and an ensuing economic bubble, 1980s.

The bursting of the bubble economy caused slow growth in Japan, 1990.

The Economic and Scientific Section (ESS) sent American experts to aid in Japan's post-World War II industrial reconstruction, 1940s.

Japan experienced the "Japanese Economic Miracle," marked by rapid economic growth, 1945–1990.

The United States invested $2.2 billion in Japan's rehabilitation efforts during this period, 1950.

Japan surrendered, ending World War II, 1945.

FIGURE 9.1 Japan's key moments

Stakeholder-Centric Productivity

In addition to Kaizen, Japan also has a unique view of defining productivity. In the old Western business paradigm, productivity was generally measured using only profit considerations. Efficiency is assessed simply from the input-output comparison to produce more financial outcomes. The pure capitalist business model was not appropriate to explain the conduct of Japanese firms because of cultural differences. The Japanese company's primary goal is to benefit its workforce and serve society, and the best way to do this is through consistent, sustainable growth.[18] For example, inputs or parts sometimes might not be obtained from the lowest-priced sources, but rather from vendors with whom the company has a long-standing relationship. A company's commitment to its workers may indicate its willingness to "overhire."[19]

In a traditional business paradigm, these practices by Japanese companies would be considered unproductive and inefficient. Since the nature of companies or corporations are commercial entities, profit maximization becomes its fundamental purpose. This economic principle is correct, but changes in the current world situation require a paradigm shift in business as usual. A profit motive that accepts all costs, regardless of its positive or negative impact on other stakeholders, means it will probably have a positive financial impact in the short term but can damage the company's credibility and reputation in the long term.

Customers, especially Gen Z, are becoming more critical of social and environmental issues. A whopping 73% of Generation Z is willing to spend extra on sustainable goods.[20] This figure illustrates how customer behavior has changed significantly and emphasizes the value of sustainability in reaching this environmentally conscious generation. Being the first generation to have climate change as a defining worry from an early age, Gen Z is highly concerned about the environment and demands that businesses include sustainability in all aspects of their operations. They are also eager to encourage people of different ages to behave more sustainably.[21]

Shareholders are now also moving into a "greener" mindset. More investors are willing to invest in green and impact companies.[22] They seek businesses that prioritize producing sustainable goods or services; using renewable energy sources like wind, solar, or geothermal energy; and supporting fair trade and other social responsibility programs.

Businesses that practice sustainability and go green are viewed as long-term investments with the potential to provide cutting-edge goods, services, and technology to spur future expansion. The financial market reacts appropriately to this development. Green stocks are beginning to beat less environmentally conscious corporations because they are expected to do better as laws and regulations continue to support sustainable business practices. The growing demand for eco-friendly investing is the driving force behind these companies.[23]

The current trends lead to the conclusion that productivity can pursue optimizing output and financial outcomes and maximize positive impacts on various stakeholders. This new operational excellence, which is stakeholder-centric, focuses on producing quality products with positive impact. Ignoring these trends will cause the company to lose credibility and reputation in the eyes of customers and shareholders. Japanese values prioritizing long-term and sustainable growth, not only short-term profit, align with these current business directions.

Sustainability and productivity are interrelated and can benefit each other. "Sustainable productivity" is one idea that combines the two in human resource management.[24] Keeping the organization's demands and the employee's needs in balance is the key to sustainable productivity. It entails intense employee welfare levels along with ongoing company growth.

Employee productivity has proven to increase over time via sustainable business practices. The traditional "reduce, reuse, recycle" maxim is a prime example. Based on this famous adage, reducing waste and emissions is one of the most effective strategies to prioritize sustainability. Maintaining productivity at work follows the same rules. Reducing inefficiencies such as needless meetings and bureaucracy, for instance, frees up employees to perform their fundamental duties, which boosts their productivity.

Improvement Toward Sustainability

Previous Toyota stories demonstrate that incremental improvement can lead to the achievement of lofty sustainability targets. Businesses might identify doable strategies to cut waste, optimize energy consumption, or find new, environmentally friendly materials by thoroughly examining their operations.

The Plan-Do-Check-Action (PDCA) cycle is a useful continuous improvement technique that we may apply to enhance our business operations and make them more sustainable. The PDCA cycle aims to improve the efficacy and quality of processes in several corporate domains: project management, human resource management, supply chain management, and product life cycle management. American management expert W. Edwards Deming popularized PDCA, drawing inspiration from statistician Walter Andrew Shewhart.[25]

Japanese business leaders invited Deming to Japan in 1950 so he could share his improvement techniques for enhancing teamwork and learning to executives and engineers. Top administrators and engineers learned how to improve quality control, productivity, and overall performance from Deming. In 1960, Emperor Hirohito's representative, Prime Minister Nobusuke Kishi, bestowed on him the Order of the Sacred Treasure, Second Class of Japan.[26] This acknowledgment was a noteworthy accolade that showed how Deming's contributions had affected Japanese industry and manufacturing. He is frequently acknowledged for significantly influencing Japan's prominence as a global economic force.

The PDCA cycle can be used in the following ways to foster continuous improvement toward new operational excellence:

- **Plan.** Determine where there is waste or inefficiency in a process and develop a strategy to fix it. This stage can involve creating a schedule for implementation, identifying green measures, and setting sustainability goals.

- **Do.** Put the plan into action and alter the business process in a way that will benefit all stakeholders. Examples of this phase are switching to renewable energy sources, adopting eco-friendly materials, and implementing circular processes.

- **Check.** Assess the outcomes of the recently adopted new operational excellence. The stakeholders can give feedback for further audits and inspections based on the results of some key performance indicators.

- **Act.** If necessary, modify the plan by taking the steps required in light of the evaluation. This might entail standardizing the new sustainability procedure, resolving problems or bottlenecks, and implementing lasting improvements.

Cases from Other Asian Countries

Apart from Japan's Toyota, other countries in Asia also have exciting examples regarding business operations improvements toward sustainability. These organizations can positively and significantly affect society and the environment through incremental transformation.

Grameenphone (Bangladesh)

The biggest mobile provider in Bangladesh, Grameenphone, provides contract and prepaid clients with voice, data, and several value-added services. Having been in business since the 1990s in Bangladesh, Grameenphone continues to place a high priority on providing access to connection services that have the potential to strengthen communities. With a revenue market share of over 46.3%, the company is ranked number 1 in Bangladesh's mobile operator industry.[27] It actively contributes to Bangladesh's solid digital ecosystem development and innovation facilitation.

The business has excellent environmental, social, health, and safety performance. The goal of Grameenphone's Climate Change Program, formally introduced in 2008, was to cut carbon dioxide emissions by 40% from business as usual by 2015, using 2008 as the baseline. As part of its climate change initiatives, the company has installed solar energy systems in its base transceiver stations (BTSs), replaced 7,272 BTSs with energy-efficient modern equipment, installed direct current ventilation systems in place of 6,500 air conditioners in BTS rooms, and inaugurated a new, environmentally friendly building.[28]

Gobi Cashmere (Mongolia)

Established in 1981, Gobi Cashmere has emerged as a prominent cashmere brand in Mongolia. Various cashmere products are available from Gobi Cashmere, such as bulky overcoats, blouses, scarves, and more. Its sustainable and ethically sourced cashmere fashions are well known.[29] This company, which employs primarily women, has increased its global reach to Asia, Europe, and the United States.

The business has an improvement policy that encompasses all facets of its operations and is dedicated to reducing the adverse effects of its operations on the environment. Gobi Cashmere prioritizes zero-waste production, encourages the responsible use of chemicals, and increases the efficiency of water and energy use by collaborating with specialists. The business is transparent about every aspect of its supply chain, including where cashmere fibers come from and how they are made.[30] Customers are better able to make decisions thanks to this transparency, which also helps to build confidence in the company's sustainability pledge.

Dentiste (Thailand)

Thai-based Dentiste is a premium dental care product brand. Toothpaste, mouthwash, and dental floss are among the oral hygiene products that Dentiste sells. The company is renowned for its improvement in offering high-quality ingredients (their toothpaste, for instance, comprises 14 natural extracts). Dentiste's products are currently available in 20 nations on six continents.[31] Known for many years in several countries as "The Lovers' Toothpaste," this brand firmly feels that maintaining a healthy mouth fosters stronger relationships and self-assurance, enabling its customers to live to their fullest.

Dentiste's improvement initiative aims to do more than boost internal efficiency and client happiness. Dentiste is also dedicated to ethical practices and sustainability to support a more positive environmental impact. The firm has a recycling program to reduce waste and employs environmentally friendly packaging.

Dilmah Tea (Sri Lanka)

Established in 1988 by Merrill J. Fernando, Dilmah Tea is a family-run tea firm based in Sri Lanka. However, the history of Dilmah Tea started in the 1950s, when Merrill J. Fernando noticed that the tea industry was becoming more and more controlled by a small number of influential firms, which was turning tea into a commodity. By establishing Dilmah Tea, Merrill J. Fernando rejected the process of commoditization of tea. He provided naturally delicious and flavorful tea because it was freshly packaged directly at the source.[32]

Dilmah Tea's mission is to "create a truly sustainable tea industry that is good for people, communities, and the planet." The company's production procedure is to preserve ethical and sustainable tea production. In keeping with their plan, Dilmah will keep looking for ways to improve the sustainability of its operations. To cut down on the firewood used in Dilmah's tea factory, for example, Dilmah sponsored the construction and commissioning of an inventive firewood drier. It was found that the stove's design reduced the firewood the factory needed by 20%.[33]

What's Next?

Applying what we've learned from Japan and a few other Asian countries, productivity and improvement are critical factors in achieving operational excellence that can positively affect all stakeholders. However, companies need more than just improvement when interacting with a dynamic external context. Organizations need innovation to come up with novel solutions. Although innovation and improvement are sometimes used synonymously, they are different. Whereas innovation produces something entirely new or radically different from what already exists, improvement is the process of making something better than before. The following justifies the necessity for innovation because improvement on its own is insufficient:[34]

- **Improvement has limits.** A process or product can be improved only to a certain extent. It eventually reaches a point when it is impractical or impossible to make any more improvements. Conversely, innovation has the potential to yield game-changing discoveries that fundamentally alter the way goods and services are produced, sold, and used.

- **Innovation creates new value.** Innovation brings new ideas to life through their successful application. New goods, services, and markets might result from it, opening new sources of income and spurring economic expansion.

- **Innovation is necessary for long-term success.** Businesses focusing only on improvement must catch up to their more innovative rivals. Extended success requires innovation because it keeps businesses ahead of the curve and enables them to adjust to shifting market conditions.

- **Innovation can disrupt the status quo.** Industry revolutions and status quo disruption are both possible with innovation. The development of new business models, goods, and services might alter our manner of living and working.

Key Takeaways

In this chapter, we explored the role of productivity and improvement in creating institutions that have a positive impact, using Japan as our primary source of inspiration. Following are the key takeaways from this chapter:

- Productivity and improvement are crucial competencies to implement new operational excellence focused on multiple stakeholders' interests.

- Japan's post–World War II economic recovery illustrates how well continuous improvement with constrained resources might work.

- Japanese values align with the implementation of values-based productivity and improvement, which is oriented toward company profits and aims to affect society positively.

- Toyota is one example of a Japanese company that has successfully transformed into a sustainable global company through continuous improvement (Kaizen).

- In an uncertain business environment, companies must complement improvement with innovation.

CHAPTER 10

Professionalism and Management in the New Operational Excellence

How Singapore's Attitude Is Becoming World-Class

The best way to discuss Singapore is to begin with its founding father, Lee Kuan Yew, Singapore's first prime minister. He was born in 1923, the first child of a Semarang-born Singaporean. He was once asked how people would remember him after he was gone, and he replied that he did not care what people thought about him. He would be dead by then, and it would not matter to him.[1] Lee's passion and ambition for building a nation was unstoppable. In the book by Fook Kwang Han, Sumiko Tan, and Warren Fernandez, *Lee Kuan Yew: The Man and His Ideas* (Singapore Press Holding, 1998), Lee stated, "We were not ideologues. . . . I'd read up the theories and maybe half believed them. But we were sufficiently practical and pragmatic enough not to be cluttered up and inhibited by theories. If a thing worked, let's work it, and that eventually evolved into the kind of economy we have today. . . . Our test was: Does it work? Does it bring benefits to the people?"

Singapore's transformation would not have happened without Lee Kuan Yew. With a slight chance of survival, Singapore was granted independence in 1965. Today, Singapore has risen from a legacy of colonialism, the damage of the World War II, and general poverty to a world-class metropolis with the number one airline, best airport, and busiest trade port. In the book *From Third World to First* (Harper Collins, 2000), Lee Kuan Yew explained the details of the extraordinary efforts to bring up an island city to survive and grow.

From Third World to First: The Professionalism and Management Journey

When Singapore became independent in 1965, it was a poor, small tropical island with few natural resources, little fresh water, rapid population growth, and recurring conflict among the ethnic and religious groups that comprised its population. Back then, there was no compulsory education, let alone enough skilled workers. Today, Singapore is one of the wealthiest countries in the world (see Figure 10.1).[2] The country has become the global hub of trade, finance, and transportation—Singapore's transformation from third world to first is identified as the 20th century's most successful development story.

This chapter will discuss the principles of operational excellence that Singapore has embraced to become a country with a world-class

Rank	Country	GDP per Capita (US$)
1	Ireland	145,196
2	Luxembourg	142,490
3	Singapore	133,895
4	Qatar	124,833
5	Macao SAR	89,565

FIGURE 10.1   Top five economies by GDP per capita ranking, 2023

status. Diving into Singapore's operational excellence will first take us to revisit the concept of "professionalism and management." In the book *Entrepreneurial Marketing: Beyond Professionalism to Creativity, Leadership, and Sustainability,* we introduced the omnihouse model, which can be used to implement strategies and achieve specific goals. As discussed previously, the core of the model is grouped into two clusters. The first cluster is the entrepreneurship group, comprising four elements: creativity, innovation, entrepreneurship, and leadership (CI-EL). The second cluster is the professionalism group, consisting of four components: productivity, improvement, professionalism, and management (PI-PM).

PM together is recognized as the driving force that helps organizations achieve operational excellence in their respective fields or industries. Management cannot function as intended if no one with professionalism is behind it. Professional individuals help ensure the management process runs accordingly.

Professionalism is often associated with a certain standard (written and unwritten). It can refer to several attributes related to knowledge and competencies, integrity, honesty, and mutual respect. Professionalism frequently results from a lengthy formation process that also produces accountability. Professional encompasses structure, well-laid plans, and avoiding procrastination, thus managing to follow promises. The practice of a professional mindset will collectively form a strong reputation and trust from stakeholders, as well as have an impact on better overall company performance.

On a larger scale, professionalism in an organization is critical because it clarifies what is generally accepted (and not) in a particular community. It builds the people's mindset and attitude, creating a sense of unity and agreement that applies to all aspects of an organization, like a set of rules everyone follows. These rules help avoid unproductive conflicts and disputes in various interactions among the community.

Now that we can see how professionalism affects an organization positively, it's no wonder a management practice won't be successful without a professional individual behind it. Management often begins with specific objectives and plans to achieve them. The process involves meticulous planning, effective organization, precise implementation, and careful control of processes. Having a professional mindset ensures the process of management practice is done optimally. Establishing connections and valuing the contributions of each mindset reduces the risk of conflict. It also increases cooperation, enables innovative ideas that benefit the company to be produced, and creates a synergy that moves the company forward.

Looking back at the previously mentioned omnihouse model, PM as part of a professional cluster is undeniably a capability an organization must have to perform operational excellence. Compared to PI (mindsets in the same cluster), which focuses on the preparation phase of a project, PM addresses more about how the organization executes the project. It requires a lot of implementation at the practical level. For example, the individual must have a professional mindset to be accountable and demonstrate integrity. Being professional also requires an ability to analyze through a helicopter view, having proficiency in managing projects, and being adaptable.

The transformation of Singapore from third world to first cannot be separated from the quality of human resources, who can make change achievable. According to the World Bank, Singapore has a Human Capital Index (HCI) value of 0.88, the highest in the world.[3] HCI is a measurement prepared by the World Bank that calculates the contributions of health and education to worker productivity. The final index score ranges from zero to one. It measures the productivity of a future worker of a child born today relative to the benchmark of full health and complete education. Singapore's high HCI score suggests that it is doing an excellent job in providing its citizens with health and education, which will contribute to a highly productive workforce in the future.

With this high score, it is no wonder Singapore can perform the management process successfully. *The Economist* stated that in 2023–2027, Singapore will remain the best country in the world to do business. The country will remain politically stable, with a technocratic approach to economic management and a long track record of effective implementation. In particular, the government will focus on helping local private sector companies upgrade technologically and supporting businesses to bolster Singapore's long-term growth. The role of government-linked companies in the economy is not expected to be challenged significantly in the next five years, while more restrictive foreign labor policy weighs on labor market scores.[4]

Singapore is among the top three in the world for having the best protection of intellectual property.[5] Singapore's strong protection of intellectual property reflects a professional approach to safeguarding the rights and innovations of individuals and businesses. This professionalism is evident in the country's legal framework, which ensures that intellectual property rights are respected and upheld. Effective management is critical to maintaining a robust intellectual property protection system.

Zooming into Singapore: The Evolution to Global Hub

From its former British colony to its emergence as a first-world economy, Singapore's journey has been marked by unique political, social, and economic dynamics. When Singapore began its nation-building journey, it was challenged by limited resources. The nation strategically implemented several initiatives to lay the foundation for its remarkable transformation. These strategies started with a fundamental setup in the form of vigorous enforcement of labor laws and regulations to attract foreign investment as the key to the open economy strategy that the country adopted.

Because of the openness of its economy, Singapore implemented supportive regulations and policies to ensure trade fairness. Singapore's geographical advantages and single-party political domination helped the government to successfully implement these strategies.

Soon after its independence, Singapore had nothing to offer but its strategic location at the crossroads of Asia with an audience of close to 4 billion within a seven-hour flight radius (see Figure 10.2).

Envisioning itself as a global hub, Singapore started enforcing labor laws and regulations to entice foreign investors, which would be the perfect economic growth driver as these investors would bring money and a workforce. Since then, labor law and regulations in Singapore have come a long way and have evolved in their ability to do collective bargaining, establishing a tripartite partnership model, accommodating foreign workers, and finally shifting toward better social justice.

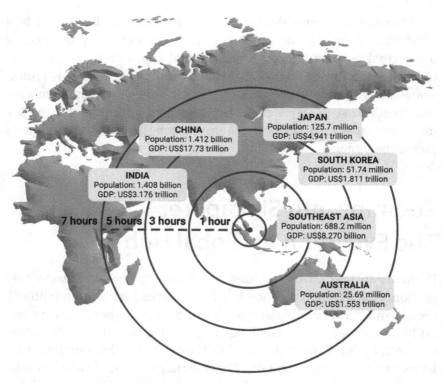

FIGURE 10.2 Singapore's strategic location as an access point to Asia

The journey started with a collective laissez-faire period from 1945 to the 1950s, when collective bargaining was the primary source of worker protection. Singapore offered businesses the freedom to create a friendlier environment for their friends with minimum government intervention. This gave companies more control over the specifics of their labor agreements, which could be tailored to their business needs.

From the 1960s to the 1980s, Singapore implemented a tripartite partnership model, through which a collaboration system with Singapore trade unions, the government, and employers balanced the negotiation between employer and employee. This was supported by The Tripartite Guidelines on Fair Employment Practices, a set of employment practices issued by the Tripartite Alliance for Fair & Progressive Employment Practices that employers were strongly encouraged to adopt concerning recruitment, grievance handling, performance management, retrenchment, and dismissal. This completely transformed the trade union scene in Singapore.

The arrival of skilled and unskilled foreign labor to support Singapore's rapidly growing economy posed a policy challenge, as it created tension between protecting domestic jobs and meeting the demands of employers and investors. The Fair Employment Guidelines include the Fair Consideration Framework, which requires employers to consider Singapore citizens reasonably in recruitment and avoid discriminatory recruitment practices (e.g., discrimination based on age, race, marital status, or nationality).

Although the Fair Employment Guidelines and Fair Consideration Framework are not legally binding on employers, the Singapore Ministry of Manpower has indicated that it will take administrative actions against employers who breach them. This guarantees that even though their country has absorbed the influx of many foreign companies and foreign workers, the native population still benefits and even improves their skills from the technology and culture brought from outside the country's boundaries.

Singapore's labor law and regulation have shifted toward social justice, entering the fourth phase during the legislative amendments from 2009 to 2018. An increasing amount of "protective" regulation and rights-oriented discourse has emerged since the early 2010s to counteract the inequality of bargaining power within the workforce. This phase highlights Singapore's evolving commitment to fairness and equity in labor practices, emphasizing professionalism and accountability in the workplace. The evolution of Singapore labor law and regulation over time has emphasized the cultural values of discipline, order, accountability, and professionalism that underpin each phase, which successfully served as the fundamental framework to support its next strategy, the open economy.

The government's strenuous efforts reflect Singapore's primary constraint as a small country: the lack of economic space, including few natural resources and a sizeable domestic market. Even today, despite its strategic location and relatively well-educated workforce, as a city-state economy, Singapore remains small relative to other major regional and global cities (see Figure 10.3).[6] To overcome the constraint of size and expand economic space to achieve GDP growth, Singapore's economy continually focuses on growing.

Singapore's first economic landscape phase occurred between 1965 and the late 1990s. It was characterized as a period of foreign

City	GDP (US$ billion)	Population (million)	Physical Size (square km)	Stock Market Capitalization (US$ billion)*	Number of International Airports	Number of Universities
Singapore	327	5.5	697	414	1	6
Hong Kong	350	7.2	1,108	1,108	1	8
London	731	8.6	1,572	3,019	6	47
New York City	1,210	8.4	790	18,668	3	35

FIGURE 10.3   Comparison of Singapore with other world cities

investment–driven growth. The second phase, which started in the early 2000s, could be described as one of foreign talent–driven growth. In the first phase, foreign direct investment was considered the critical economic growth and job creation driver. The government aimed to attract multinational companies by providing an efficient operations environment.

In the second phase, the government transformed the economy from an efficient multinational companies hub to a global city, where growth is derived mainly from innovation and creativity. A more creative workforce was considered necessary to support such a growth strategy, so the policy shifted from attracting foreign companies to attracting creative foreign talent. Much effort was devoted to making Singapore an attractive living and working environment for such creative workers.

Singapore's limitations drove these shifts in strategy as a small city-state with no significant natural resources or a large domestic market. To overcome these constraints and achieve sustained economic growth, the government adopted a policy of "economic openness." This policy encouraged free trade in goods and services and allowed the movement of capital and labor across borders. In line with that, the Singapore government does not tolerate anti-competitive practices.

The Competition Act prohibits agreements or concerted practices that lead to the prevention, restriction, or distortion of competition. Any conduct constituting the abuse of a dominant position in any market is also prohibited.

The decision to embrace foreign investment and talent was unconventional but proved successful. In the 1960s, Singapore actively courted foreign companies with incentives, and in the early 2000s, it relaxed immigration policies to attract creative foreign workers.

These decisions were based on the economy's practical needs and the ruling party's dominant political position. Singapore's approach and policies attracted multinational companies from the United States, Europe, and Japan, making it a favored location for production and distribution. The government's ability to adapt and provide an efficient business environment contributed to its success in attracting foreign direct investment.

A critical precondition for sustained economic growth is a certain level of social stability. The People's Action Party (PAP), which dominates the government, achieved this early in the days of independence by establishing a social contract between the government and the society. "Social contract" means society voluntarily relinquishes some civil rights to be traded against state powers and political control to pursue high economic growth. High GDP growth enabled the PAP to deliver various public services and goods and legitimize its rule.

The social contract worked because it ensured the population's basic needs were met, exceeding the citizenry's expectations. The economic strategy produced jobs that reached full employment in the early 1970s. A massive public housing construction program brought homes of high quality so that by the mid-1990s, more than 90% of Singaporeans owned their own homes. A considerable effort was made to expand educational opportunities at primary, secondary, vocational, and tertiary levels, giving citizens the opportunity for upward social mobility they had not imagined possible.

This success enabled PAP to retain the support of citizens despite the strict policies pursued. This also resulted in stability and predictability in national policies and long-term planning and continuity in governance, which contributed to attracting foreign direct investment and realizing the foreign direct investment-driven growth strategy in the first phase of its economic development.

Looking back at these strategies, starting with a solid fundamental setup in the form of labor laws and regulations enforcement that successfully supported the open economy strategy, showed how Singapore as a country performed a well-executed management process that wouldn't have happened unless professionals were behind it. This again highlights how Singapore's professionalism and management attitude have championed its world-class title.

Singapore Airlines: Service Excellence and Cost-Effectiveness

Singapore's attitude is also reflected in businesses running in the country. Singapore Airlines (SIA) is not an unfamiliar name, even outside the aviation industry. It has a stellar reputation in the fiercely competitive commercial aviation business by providing customers with high-quality service and dominating the business travel segments. SIA has been the most awarded airline in the world for many years. For example, it won the World's Best Airline Award 23 out of the 24 times, it has been nominated by the prestigious UK travel magazine *Condé Nast Traveler*, and it won Skytrax's Airline of the Year award three times over the past decade.[7] This sustained service excellence has no secret except its extraordinary principles of focusing on customers and effective people management.

One key element of SIA's competitive success is that it manages to navigate skillfully between poles that most companies think of as distinct: cost-effectively delivering service excellence at cost levels so low that they are comparable to those of budget airlines.[8] SIA's operational costs/expenses, specifically the cost per available seat kilometer (CASK), are below those of all other full-service airlines. From 2001 to 2009, SIA costs per available seat kilometer were just 4.6 cents. According to a 2007 International Air Transport Association study, the costs for full-service European airlines were 8 to 16 cents, for US airlines 7 to 8 cents, and for Asian airlines 5 to 7 cents per available seat kilometer. SIA had even lower costs than most low-cost carriers in Europe and the United States, which ranged from 4 to 8 cents and 5 to 6 cents, respectively.[9]

The question then would be, how is that possible? How come it seems so easy for SIA? The answer: it is not. A key challenge of implementing business-level strategies, such as effective differentiation at SIA and superior operational efficiency, is the alignment of functional strategies, such as HR, marketing, and operations, with the business-level strategy. It takes a lot of effort for the HR team from SIA to carry out practices that create capabilities that support the company's strategy, such as recruiting, training, retaining, delivering, controlling, and motivating people.

Human assets are significant for the service sector, and SIA can masterfully perfect its HR management practices and align its HR management to SIA's competitive strategy. Five interrelated and mutually supportive elements inherent in SIA's HR strategy, along with leadership and role modeling by top management, play a key role in SIA's ability to deliver its business strategy (see Figure 10.4).[10]

The five core elements of SIA's HR strategy align closely with the professionalism-management concept. The organization emphasizes professionalism by carefully selecting and recruiting individuals who meet specific criteria and possess the desired qualities. It ensures that only candidates who align with the company's values and standards are brought on board. Then, the company invests in training and retraining, which demonstrates the commitment to enhancing the workforce's expertise and ensures they stay updated and proficient in their roles. This helps build successful service delivery teams, and empowers frontline staff to control quality, which resonates with continuous improvement as a form of professionalism in management.

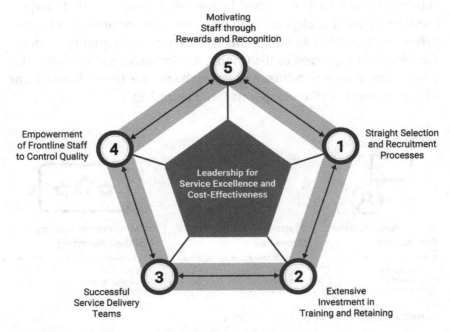

FIGURE 10.4   The five core elements of SIA's HR strategy

Ensuring the sustainable management process is crucial to maintaining a motivated and engaged workforce. The strategy is completed by recognizing and rewarding employees for their contributions and achievements. The outlined strategy aligns with the professionalism and management concept by prioritizing developing and cultivating a skilled, motivated, and empowered workforce committed to delivering high-quality service and upholding the organization's values and standards. It reflects a proactive approach to management that emphasizes professionalism at every stage of the employee life cycle. As a result, SIA is successful in cost-effectively delivering service excellence.

Changi Airport: Instill Professionalism and Management into People's DNA

In the neighborhood business, Singapore's attitude regarding professionalism and management also helps Changi Airport succeed in building its service DNA. They believe all partners in their airport community must understand the elements that make up the Changi Airport service DNA and align themselves to provide quality service.[11] The elements expressed in the Changi Airport service DNA will foster a more robust service culture and guide the service team's interactions with customers at all touch points (see Figure 10.5).

TO SERVE VERSUS TO ENGAGE
Personalized

Every customer is unique

- Be welcoming
- Be interested
- Be attentive

TO DELIVER VERSUS TO ANTICIPATE
Stress-free

To provide customers with peace of mind

- Be knowledgeable
- Be resourceful
- Be responsive

TO SATISFY VERSUS TO DELIGHT
Positively Surprising

To create good memories in every customer

- Be involved
- Be enthusiastic
- Be creative

FIGURE 10.5   Changi Airport service DNA

Gathered from a series of talent pools obtained through several engaging and training programs, Changi Airport Group (CAG) creates a conducive culture, a sense of belonging in the workplace through the CAG Home Project; internal communications via the CAG social networking application; a revamped company intranet; a collaborative and open atmosphere through crowdsourcing, personal development, and growth; an employee engagement survey; and skills training for the fast-changing environments. Moreover, the airport offers scholarship programs by attracting talented young people from local universities. This ensures that the airport draws and retains the best talent to support its mission. This strategy works; Changi Airport has been awarded World's Best Airport by Skytrax in 2000, 2006, and 2010, plus seven consecutive years from 2013 until 2020.[12]

Port of Singapore Authority: Global Maritime Powerhouse

Leading the world's aviation industry, Singapore's professionalism and management attitude also conquered the maritime industry. Based on the 2022 survey by the Global Trade and Regional Integration Unit of The World Bank Group in the 2023 Logistics Performance Index (LPI), Singapore has the highest score, 4.3 (third time as top scorer after 2007 and 2012).[13] The LPI is an interactive benchmarking tool developed by the World Bank Group. It helps countries identify the challenges and opportunities they face in their trade logistics performance and what they can do to improve their performance. It measures the ease of establishing reliable supply chain connections and the structural factors that make it possible. The LPI scores are decided based on six factors:

- Efficiency of the clearance process—speed, simplicity, and predictability of formalities.
- Quality of trade and transport-related infrastructure—ports, railroads, roads, information technology.
- Ease of arranging competitively priced shipments.

- Competence and quality of logistics services—transport operators, customs brokers.
- Ability to track and trace consignments.
- Timeliness of shipments reaching their destination within the scheduled or expected delivery time.

Singapore's position as a global maritime powerhouse results from concerted efforts involving critical players like the Maritime and Port Authority of Singapore (MPA) and the Port of Singapore (PSA). The MPA collaborates and coordinates efforts with port operators and shipping companies. This translates to elevated levels of efficiency and enables the port to achieve its potential as a one-stop shop for the global maritime community. With an eye on future competitiveness, Singapore invests heavily in technology and talent to enhance port operations.

The investment setting the tone for this is the Tuas Port, which is scheduled to launch in the 2040s. With a total capacity of 65 million twenty-foot equipment units (TEUs), it will be the largest container terminal in the world. Moreover, it will have technologies such as data analytics, automation, and uncrewed vehicles.[14] In tandem with these strategic efforts, PSA currently operates 67 quay berths across its container terminals in Tanjong Pagar, Keppel, Brani, and Pasir Panjang, which are operated as a single and undivided integrated facility. In 2018, PSA handled 36.31 million TEU of containers. This transshipment hub accounts for nearly one-seventh of the total container transshipment capacity worldwide and more than 4% of the global container handling capacity.[15]

The plan to maintain a world-class port is by capitalizing on its strategic location and maximizing the number of enablers, including infrastructure, information technology, workforce, and organizational culture. Information technology is then embedded in every facet of the port's operations. PSA's strategic drive toward IT-supported port operations started in the early 1980s.

PSA is attempting to provide value-added services to its traditional port operations, including storing goods and empty containers, labeling, repackaging, tagging, sampling and testing, quality control, and billing. The aim is to establish an integrated global logistics network that connects Singapore to major regions and countries.

Supporting the goal, MPA has operational-improvement programs such as the "Key Customer Managers" and "Chat Time." The Key Customer Managers program provides regular dialog sessions with customers, helping PSA staff members better understand and attend to customers' operational and contractual needs. Chat Time allows the organization to build rapport with customers and keep abreast of the latest developments in the shipping industry. To promote a quality culture in their workforce, PSA has widespread quality circles and encourages staff suggestions, saving PSA millions of dollars annually.[16]

Professionalism, Management, and New Operational Excellence

These views on how Singapore's attitudes affect its business all lead to— yes, indeed—world recognition, but also an optimization in cost. Two major industries that support Singapore's becoming a world-class global hub showcased similarities in several aspects. First, the companies ensure they have the best professionals on their team. Second, the companies plan the strategy carefully to achieve their goals and then implement it with strict supervision to ensure the strategy works. Third, they use this professionalism and management capabilities to elevate the service they give to their customers, eventually resulting in cost optimization.

Let's recall how Singapore Airlines has its five core elements as its HR strategy, Changi Airport grows Changi Service DNA, and the PSA uses the Chat Time program to engage with the customer. These companies operate their business excellently, and as a result, they successfully save money by reducing costs.

Zooming out from the business and looking into the country, the professionalism and management attitude also led to cost optimization for Singapore as a country, which refers to the efforts made by the Singapore government, or the public sector, to allocate and manage resources and expenditures efficiently at the national level.

The primary goal is to maximize the overall welfare and prosperity of the citizens while ensuring fiscal responsibility and sustainability. Singapore successfully provides welfare and prosperity to its citizens, marked by its 17th rank (top rank for Asia) on the Legatum Prosperity Index™, an annual ranking of 167 countries encompassing 99.4% of the world's population. It uses 300 country-level indicators, grouped into 67 policy-focused elements across 12 pillars to measure these countries' current state of prosperity and how it has changed since the early 2010s.[17] Figure 10.6 shows the prosperity index of Singapore and the United States, the world's largest economy with a land size 13,500 times bigger.

As promised in the social contract, Singapore's government commitment to its citizens should have become the benchmark for other countries. The high taxes and living costs are worth it since the citizens receive a high-quality life. In 2021, on the aspect of ensuring every

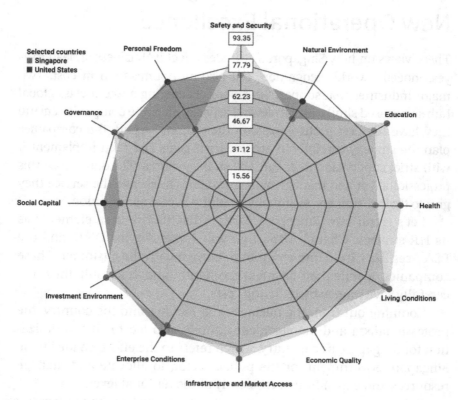

How to read this graph:
When comparing multiple countries on a spider chart, data points that appear further away from thhe center represent a better performance to the points that are closer to the center.

FIGURE 10.6 Singapore on the US Legatum Prosperity Index™

citizen has the same opportunity for education and quality jobs, over 97% of the Primary 1 cohort (students who enrolled in the first year of primary education about age 7) progressed to a post-secondary education program;[18] about 660,000 people benefited from the SkillsFuture initiatives in 2021—a national movement to provide Singaporeans with the opportunities to develop their fullest potential throughout life;[19] and 460,000 lower-wage workers benefited from Workfare Income Supplement payouts.[20]

Singapore's government also successfully allocates and manages resources and expenditures regarding quality and sustainable living at the national level. In 2021, 80% of residents lived in Housing and Development Board flats, with 90% owning the homes; 93% of households living within a 10-minute walk from a park; and 92% of Singaporeans were satisfied with the cleanliness of public space and public transport services.[21] The number shows that Singapore's government has successfully implemented policies and initiatives prioritizing its residents' quality of life, sustainability, and well-being. On top of that, Singapore's climate ambition was raised to achieve net-zero carbon emissions by 2050, supported by more than 450,000 trees planted under the OneMillionTrees movement.[22] This commitment promises more rewards that Singaporeans will obtain in their social contract with the government, such as a more sustainable and livable future. See Figure 10.7 for the five pillars of Singapore's Green Plan.

On a broader level, Singapore's professionalism and management are reflected in its strong and resilient economy. Strong economic fundamentals have helped Singapore overcome the pandemic's challenges, seize opportunities, and transform from third world to first world. In 2020, the economy shrank by 4.1%, the worst full-year recession since independence, before expanding by 7.6% in 2021.[23]

During the pandemic, the Unity Budget introduced the Job Support Scheme (JSS) in February 2020 to provide wage support to employers to retain their local employees during economic uncertainty due to the pandemic (see Figure 10.8). It was subsequently enhanced to support businesses and workers during the Circuit Breaker and other periods of restrictions.[24]

In summary, Singapore's commitment to professionalism and effective management extends from its thriving businesses to its governance at the national level. This mindset has not only earned

FIGURE 10.7 Five pillars of the Singapore Green Plan 2030

Singapore global recognition but also has resulted in cost optimization. The alignment of corporate strategies, a skilled workforce, and exceptional customer service in critical industries contribute to financial efficiency. On a national scale, Singapore's government successfully allocates resources, delivering a high quality of life as evidenced by its high Prosperity Index ranking, substantial educational and job opportunities, and well-planned urban living.

Moreover, Singapore's climate ambitions further demonstrate its dedication to a sustainable future. This professionalism-driven approach also underpins the country's strong and resilient economy, exemplified by its ability to navigate the challenges of the pandemic and emerge with robust growth, supported by wise fiscal policies and economic stimulus measures.

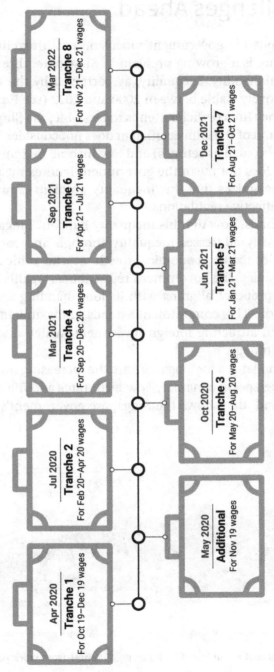

FIGURE 10.8 Timeline of JSS tranches with payout months and basis periods

Apr 2020 **Tranche 1**	Jul 2020 **Tranche 2**	Mar 2021 **Tranche 4**	Sep 2021 **Tranche 6**	Mar 2022 **Tranche 8**
For Oct 19–Dec 19 wages	For Feb 20–Apr 20 wages	For Sep 20–Dec 20 wages	For Apr 21–Jul 21 wages	For Nov 21–Dec 21 wages

May 2020 **Additional**	Oct 2020 **Tranche 3**	Jun 2021 **Tranche 5**	Dec 2021 **Tranche 7**
For Nov 19 wages	For May 20–Aug 20 wages	For Jan 21–Mar 21 wages	For Aug 21–Oct 21 wages

The Challenges Ahead

Ironically, despite the government's focus on ensuring citizen's prosperity, inequality is a growing problem in Singapore, threatening the country's social stability. Inequality, as portrayed by the Gini coefficient, was relatively stable between 2000 and 2022 (see Figure 10.9).[25] Even though the Gini coefficient tends to be stable, the Singapore government's version of the Gini coefficient does not consider households without workers (such as retirees) and low-income migrant workers.[26] However, this does not mean the government ignores inequality. The government recognizes that this inequality problem requires special attention and effective regulations.

The question is, how did this inequality happen? Singapore's government primarily addresses inequality through an economic lens, historically prioritizing economic growth as the critical solution. Instead of subsidies, the government redistributes wealth by enhancing assets like property, aligning with its long-standing focus on economic expansion. This commitment extends to maximizing capitalist profitability and attracting foreign investment, which underpins the government's strategy.

The next challenges for Singapore are the increasing threats from a demographic perspective, namely, low birth rates and life expectancy. On the one hand, this shows the Singapore government's success in

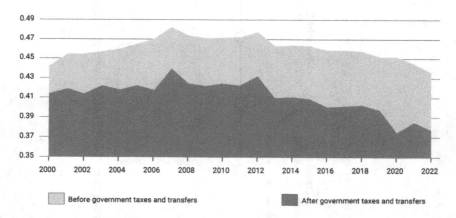

Before government taxes and transfers	After government taxes and transfers

FIGURE 10.9   Gini coefficient based on household income from work per household member

meeting its people's needs, but on the other hand, there are more Singaporeans who cannot work and need assistance than the workforce figures. Since the 1970s, Singapore has had a birth rate below the death rate. Realizing this, the government has prepared several scenarios to face the resulting challenges.

Singapore's government modeled the citizen population under various scenarios. Scenario A shows when the government assumes that the total fertility rate (TFR) is increased to 2.1—meaning that citizens begin to replace themselves yearly. Scenario B assumes that the TFR is still 1.2 (no increase) and there is no immigration. Scenarios C to E assumes that the TFR is 1.2 with different levels of intake of new citizens each year—15,000, 20,000, and 25,000, respectively. The model then showcased the result (see Figure 10.10).

Without immigration, and if Singapore's current low TFR and high life expectancy continue, the number of citizen deaths is projected to outpace births by about 2025. At that point, Singapore's citizen population will start declining (Scenario B). Raising Singapore's TFR (Scenario A) and immigration (Scenarios C–E) will delay and slow the rate at which Singapore's citizen population declines. An immigration inflow of 20,000 to 25,000 new citizens yearly will stabilize the population. Thus, public policy is needed to overcome this by opening the door to immigration or encouraging Singaporeans to have more offspring to close the existing gap.

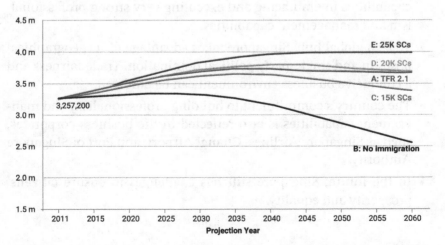

FIGURE 10.10 Citizen population size (in millions) according to population scenario

Another challenge for Singapore is stagnating GDP growth, which slowed in 2022 as expansion in all sectors moderated, and contributions from net exports and investment fell sharply. Inflation has accelerated as food and energy prices rose. Growth should improve in 2024. Inflation will be downward on the forecast horizon, contained by the lagged effect of monetary tightening. A comprehensive fiscal policy package should support a planned move toward a low-carbon transition while safeguarding competitiveness.[27]

Key Takeaways

In this chapter, we discuss how professionalism and managerial capabilities became the DNA of Singaporean society as reflected in the operational aspects of various institutions (government and corporations). This capability, among other actions, has made Singapore a global hub and a world-class country. Following are the key takeaways from this chapter:

- Singapore has been transforming from third world to first world. The first prime minister, Lee Kuan Yew, established policies to evolve the isolated small island into a thriving global hub.

- Singapore's world-class excellence is built from the country's capabilities in embracing and executing very strong professionalism and management capabilities.

- To be a global hub, Singapore takes advantage of its geographical position and single-party political domination. Trade fairness and a conducive business environment can be enforced.

- The country's commitment to building professionalism and management capabilities is also reflected in the business corporates, such as Singapore Airlines, Changi Airport, and Port of Singapore Authority.

- In the future, Singapore still has challenges to ensure citizens' prosperity and equality.

CHAPTER 11

The Yin-Yang Advantage

How China Made the Impossible Possible

How have different ideologies shaped the transformation of China? Mao Zedong, Deng Xiaoping, and Xi Jinping are considered to be transformative leaders who set China as a powerful global player. Although China "stood up" under Mao, it "grew rich" under Deng and is "rising strong" under Xi.

China's consistent transformation from one era to the next has an impact on strengthening its creative and innovative capabilities, increasing productivity, giving birth to many new entrepreneurs with solid leadership so they can make their companies highly competitive globally, and empowering their professional and managerial abilities. In short, China's transformation has had a significantly favorable influence on the development of its omni capabilities, which is a strong foundation for operational excellence.

Mao Zedong and His Great Cultural Revolution

Mao's vision of socialist revolution was philosophically different from Marxism-Leninism in some aspects. Unlike Marxism-Leninism communists, who based their revolution on workers overthrowing the bourgeoisie in industrial cities, Mao's revolution started with the peasants and surrounded towns from the countryside. Maoism believed that revolution against capitalists required violence and mass support. This theory resulted in the Great Leap Forward in 1958–1962 and the Cultural Revolution in 1966–1976. However, the revolution also caused the disaster of the "Great Chinese Famine" when China witnessed the deaths of millions of people.

The launch of the Great Leap Forward triggered radical agricultural policies, social pressure, and economic mismanagement. The unrealistic goal to outpace Great Britain as the "mother of the industrial revolution" led to this epic chaos. About 30 million people died from starvation between 1960 and 1962.[1]

After the catastrophic Great Leap Forward, more practical and moderate leaders, such as Liu Shaoqi and Zhou Enlai, took more active roles in governing the country. China's economic condition showed significant growth from 1962 to 1965. However, Mao felt the local party took advantage of their position. To minimize his worries, Mao favored open criticism and allowed people to openly state their concerns. People then exposed and punished the ruling class members who disagreed with Mao's ideologies.

Mao framed this as a genuine socialist campaign. For example, Mao's wife, Jiang Qing, argued that artistic and cultural works were beginning to criticize communism and should focus on promoting a revolutionary spirit. Afterward, a series of chaotic and radical terrors were promulgated. By 1974, Mao Zedong and Zhou Enlai were chronically ill and unable to govern effectively. The death of these two influential leaders in 1976 and the arrest of the remaining leaders of the Cultural Revolution marked the end of that revolution.

Deng Xiaoping's Pragmatic Leadership: The Door to Economic Revolution

Deng Xiaoping once said, "It doesn't matter whether the cat is black or white, as long as it catches mice." In 1978, he implemented an open-door policy to achieve economic growth. He introduced foreign capital and technology while maintaining the commitment to socialism. To become a modern state and superpower, China was obliged to develop a legal system that reflected contemporary needs and established efficient administrative organizations. The "Three Reforms" cover state-owned enterprises (SOEs), financial systems, and administrative organization reform.

The SOEs were in deficit condition in 1978 when the reform began. The significant pledge was made in 1998 by Premier Zhu Rongji, who said that his administration would eliminate the deficits of most prominent- and medium-sized SOEs within three years. This step marked the conversion of the enterprises into modern corporations by the year 2000. The result of the three-year SOE reform plan was beyond expectations. For instance, one-third of 8,000 large and medium-sized SOEs had shifted out of a deficit in the first year.

The Chinese financial system enforced the economic revolution. Until 1979, the only bank in China was the People's Bank of China. The only activities of the bank were savings, lending, and the provision of remittance services. Banks applied the financial plans of the central government and had no independence. The government separated four major state-owned banks in 1979. In 1984, private sector commercial banks could be found at the regional and national scale. Since then, the number of financial institutions has grown rapidly. In the early 1990s, there were more than 60,000 banks and nonbank financial institutions.

In 1980, Deng Xiaoping gave a speech entitled "Reforming Leadership System in the Party and the State," in which he listed problems with bureaucratic rule. He also emphasized the excessive centralization of authority and the need for proper systems relating to terms of office and retirement for senior officials. After two to three years of reform from 1998, several targets were achieved, such as the reduction of personnel numbers, the organizational restructuring of the State Council, and the integration of several ministries in the industrial and economic control sector.

"Xi Jinping Thought" to Made Chinese Society Stronger

In 2017, Xi Jinping introduced a political doctrine to help China become a solid and harmonious country by 2049. The "Xi Jinping Thought" calls for strict party discipline and strengthening the party's rule over all aspects of Chinese society.[2] The goal is to make China a global force, have a world-class military capability, and eliminate poverty. Xi also focuses on anti-corruption, environmental protection, and diplomacy assertiveness. He is making the Chinese way of growing economies an alternative model to the West. Xi also does not believe in the separation of party and state but instead sees the need for a division of power.

Xi Jinping did not face the same challenges that Mao Zedong did when the poor, abused, and humiliated masses of people were in the middle of a civil war. Now, Xi leads an economic superpower with an ideological weapon of nationalism. His plans for a "New Silk Road" or the "Belt and Road Initiative" made China the world's most powerful and influential country. The new Silk Road covers the same area as the old one—Asia, Africa, Europe, Latin America, and more. The Belt and Road Initiatives have evolved from a surplus dump to a financier of big infrastructure. This initiative remains a global political tool for Xi Jinping. Even though the realization of various projects is getting smaller in scale, this initiative remains influential and is likely to stay.

The Yin-Yang Philosophy: Opposites But Balancing Each Other

The fundamental model of entrepreneurial marketing involves various dichotomies, for instance, marketing and finance, technology and humanity, creativity and productivity, innovation and improvement, entrepreneurship and professionalism, and leadership and management. Companies or nations with omni capabilities can balance out those opposite couples. However, organizational rigidity is the biggest obstacle to obtaining the business result. Therefore, flexibility is the answer; mindsets to converge various dichotomies will help companies or nations optimize the benefits of each spectrum.

The Chinese culture has been around for thousands of years; the Chinese philosophical concept of yin and yang explains the harmony of opposite forces. Yin and yang are always opposite and have equal qualities, which create and control each other (see Figure 11.1). In this book, the yin and yang concept is relevant to the business dichotomies. Companies or nations that can bring the optimum energy of these

FIGURE 11.1   The yin and yang symbol

forces will gain the most advantages. In this chapter, we will zoom in on how China harmonizes each dichotomy and transforms it into the benefit of operational excellence.

The Omni Capabilities: Preparation and Execution

Most companies and countries have only two or three of eight omni capabilities. For instance, South Korea provides the world with creativity and innovation, India builds its dominance with entrepreneurship and leadership, Japan uses the principle of Kaizen to increase productivity and improvement, and Singapore has become world-class with the attitude of professionalism and management.

Companies or nations could achieve all eight omni capabilities if they were to manage the preparation (supporting the process) and execution of strategies with all entrepreneurship and leadership capabilities (to create value by referring to values) and professionalism and

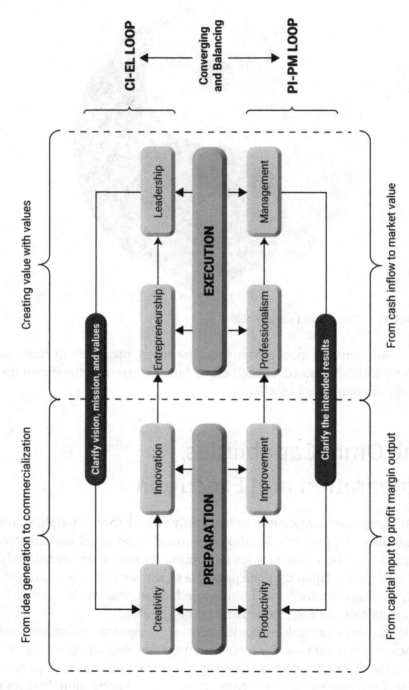

FIGURE 11.2 Framework of preparation and execution to achieve all omni capabilities

management capabilities (to ensure cash inflow and strengthen market value in these ways:

From idea generation to commercialization
- Create feasible creative ideas to solve problems and keep referring to the initial strategic intent.
- Create market-winning solutions by using business landscape knowledge.

From capital input to profit margin of output
- Create relevant and sufficient capital to support creative processes.
- Create multiple operation initiatives to improve profit margin.

Creating value with values
- Implement an entrepreneurial approach to gain optimal value.
- Apply strong leadership to maintain values.

From cash inflow to market value
- Ensure everyone involved in value-creation processes carries out professionalism in generating cash inflow.
- Coordinate the management team to achieve higher market value.

Companies or nations aiming for excellence must organize and balance the omni capabilities of preparing and executing for maximum results (see Figure 11.2).

The Omni Capabilities of China After the Reforms

This section explains how China can build its eight omni capabilities of creativity, innovation, entrepreneurship, leadership, productivity, improvement, professionalism, and management. Along with its achievement of becoming the "world's factory," China is indeed a country that has been the global economic powerhouse for at least the last four decades.

Creativity and Innovation

Before 1978, nearly four out of five Chinese worked in agriculture; by 1994, only one of two did.[3] The reforms expanded property rights in the countryside. They formed small, nonagricultural businesses in rural areas, which de-collectivized and implemented higher prices for agricultural products directed to more productive farms and more efficient use of labor. The rapid growth of village enterprises had moved people from traditional agriculture to higher-value-added manufacturing. Pre-1978, the annual growth of China was 6% per year; post-1978 China experienced real growth of more than 9% a year. Per-capita income has almost quadrupled since the early 1908s.

Creativity is the key driver of economic development. Since the early 2010s, China has been climbing the rank in terms of creativity and innovation (see Figure 11.3).[4] The index measures innovation based on several criteria, such as human capital, research, and creative outputs.

China ranks first among the 36 upper-middle-income group economies. China's economic performance has reflected creativity and innovation. Regarding GDP, China's version is above expectations, where innovation and development show a positive relationship (see Figure 11.4).

Among the eight pillars of innovation (knowledge and technology outputs, creative outputs, business sophistication, market sophistication, human capital, research, infrastructure, and institutions), China performs best in knowledge and technology outputs and creative outputs. This superior performance even outpaces the top 10 countries' performance.

Year	GII	Innovation	
		Inputs	Outputs
2020	14	26	6
2021	12	25	7
2022	11	21	8

FIGURE 11.3 Global Innovation Index ranking for China

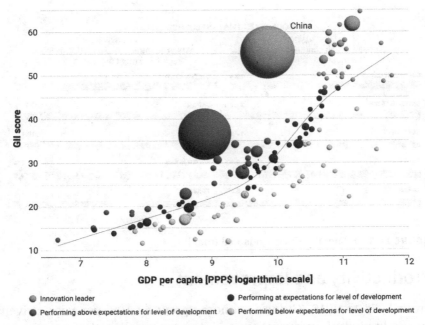

FIGURE 11.4   The relationship between innovation and development [5] / with permission of WIPO

Entrepreneurship and Leadership

China is a superpower in Asia and will soon be the next powerhouse worldwide. Based on the Asia Power Index report published by Lowy Institute, China is the highest-ranked country in terms of economic relationships and diplomatic influence.[6] This index shows China reflects strong trade and investment ties with other countries. The number one rank in diplomatic influence explains China's extensive diplomatic engagement with other countries and more tempered views toward the United States.

Looking at the 10-year (2012–2021) cumulative flows of foreign capital investments, the European Union and the United States are countries that invest the most in China. The economic relationships have brought China into a top-rank position in the global economy. Regarding media influence, China is also exposed to global trends (see Figure 11.5).

COUNTRIES THAT INFLUENCE CHINA

Globally, which countries invest the most into China?

EUROPEAN UNION	25.9%
UNITED STATES	23.2%
GERMANY	12.9%
TAIWAN	9.9%
JAPAN	8.8%

Which countries' media platforms in the region are most popular in China?

UNITED STATES	57.2%
JAPAN	19.6%
RUSSIA	10.1 %
SOUTH KOREA	9.3 %
TAIWAN	2.0%

FIGURE 11.5   Bilateral influence adapted from [7]

Productivity and Improvement

From 1978 to 2010, China's economy grew by 10% per year, driven by productivity improvements and resource reallocation across sectors.[8] China has successfully transformed a focus on rural agriculture into urban industrial societies (see Figure 11.6). The robust economic development benefited the life expectancy, rising by 10 years. Moreover, more than 700 million people have gotten out of poverty.

Professionalism and Management

As an initiative to modernize China's industrial capability, Prime Minister Li Keqiang launched Made in China 2025 (MIC 2025) in 2015.[9] The 10-year program aims to secure China's position as a global powerhouse in high-tech industries. The MIC 2025 initiative plans to replace China's dependency on foreign technology so that Chinese individuals can be competitive domestically and globally. This is reflected in one of the four advantages that MIC 2025 focused on its talent. These 10 key sectors will benefit from the MIC initiative:

- New information technology
- Numerical control tools
- Aerospace equipment

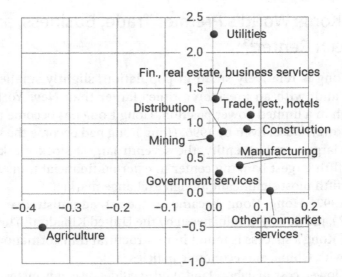

FIGURE 11.6   Labor moving out from agriculture [10], 2020 / The World Bank Group / CC BY 3.0

Note: Log ratio of sectoral to aggregate labor productivity in 1978, *y*-axis; change in employment share 1978–2010, *x*-axis.

- High-tech ships
- Railway equipment
- Energy saving
- New materials
- Medical devices
- Agricultural machinery
- Power equipment

Zoom into the Greater China

Greater China refers to the area of mainland China, Hong Kong, Macau, and Taiwan.[11] In the 1930s, George Cressey, an American geographer, author, and academic, referred to Greater China as the entire Chinese Empire, the territories as of the Qing Dynasty or Great Qing. The term began reappearing in Chinese-language sources in the late 1970s, mentioning the growing commercial ties between mainland Hong Kong and extending these to Taiwan.[12]

Hong Kong: World's Premier Trade, Business, and Financial Center[13]

Hong Kong is relatively small in population, slightly smaller than Switzerland, with an area three times larger than New York City. Although in a limited power position, Hong Kong has become an economic powerhouse. Even by 1996, Hong Kong had become the world's seventh largest trading entity, the seventh largest stock market, the world's fifth largest banking center in external financial transactions, and the fifth most significant foreign exchange market.

In 1997, Hong Kong became a special administrative region (HKSAR), previously administered by the United Kingdom. The secret of Hong Kong's success is found in its structural transformation, integration with China, and economic policies.[14]

The lower cost of labor, land, and facilities was advantageous for industries. The rapid increase in China's export activity leveled the development of supporting service industries. Hong Kong became the most productive region among OECD countries in the 1980s (see Figure 11.7). Through its structural change (see Figure 11.8), Hong Kong has become a prominent financial center, with financial and business services contributing almost one-third of its GDP.

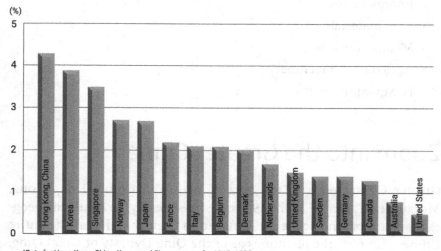

¹Data for Hong Kong, China; Korea; and Singapore are for 1965–1990.

FIGURE 11.7 Total factor productivity growth (1970–1989) [15] / with permission of AASIM M. HUSAIN

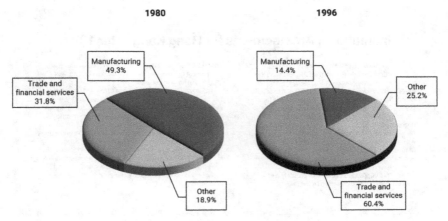

FIGURE 11.8 Changing composition of private sector employment. [16] / with permission of AASIM M. HUSAIN

Undeniably, the economies of Hong Kong and China are closely linked. Hong Kong also has the role of a financial intermediary for China. About one-quarter of Hong Kong dollar banknotes are circulating in southern China. The Hong Kong Stock Exchange has a capitalization of about four times that of the combined Shanghai and Shenzhen stock markets.

The framework of HKSAR provided an environment that encouraged market forces and helped maintain business confidence in 1997 (see Figure 11.9). Continuing a rules-based approach has contributed to Hong Kong's past success and maintained confidence and stability as it moves into the future. The system encompasses a noninterventionist competition policy, linked exchange rate, prudential supervision, providing financial infrastructure, and a strong fiscal policy. Although the economic growth is unlikely to reach the levels of the 1980s, Hong Kong retains a good position as a service-based economy by focusing its trading and financial links to both China and the rest of the world.

Macau: A Different World

In 2015, Macau, a city of 646,800 people, hosted nearly 30.7 million visitors, of which almost 67% came from mainland China. Since opening its locally controlled casino industry to foreign competition in 2001, Macau has transformed into the world's largest gaming center.[17]

Institutional Arrangements for Hong Kong After 1997

The constitutional framework for the Hong Kong Special Administrative Region (HKSAR) following the transition of sovereignty on July 1, 1997, is set out in the Sino-British Joint Declaration (1984) and the Basic Law of the HKSAR of the People's Republic of China (1990). The framework stipulates that the HKSAR's capitalist system and way of life shall remain unchanged for 50 years after July 1. During this period, the HKSAR is to remain autonomous in all but two areas: foreign affairs and defense. Key provisions of the constitutional framework with respect to the economic and legal system are:

• The rights of private ownership of property and investment shall be protected by the law.

• The HKSAR will enjoy freedom from taxation by the central government of China and will have an independent tax system and its own tax laws.
• The monetary relationship between China and Hong Kong has been defined under the concept of "one country, two systems" as one country with two currencies, two monetary systems, and two monetary authorities that are mutually independent.
• The Hong Kong dollar will remain the legal tender and a freely convertible currency fully backed by foreign exchange.
• The HKSAR shall also maintain autonomy in its external economic relations, including the status of a free port and a tariff-free zone, separate customs territory, and participation—in an appropriate capacity—in international organizations.

FIGURE 11.9   HKSAR framework [18] / with permission of AASIM M. HUSAIN

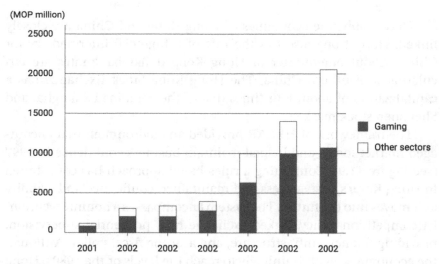

FIGURE 11.10   Foreign direct investment inflows: Gaming versus other sectors (1997–2007) [19] / with permission of ELSEVIER

The increase in Macau's gaming-related infrastructure and promotion activities expanded its market rapidly (see Figure 11.10).

Casino gaming has become more popular, especially in resource-poor regions, economically struggling regions, or small economies. Casino gaming generates positive benefits for local communities, such as economic growth, overall employment, per-capita income, and poverty alleviation.[20]

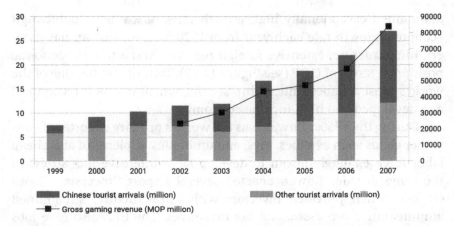

FIGURE 11.11 Gross gaming revenue, total tourist arrivals, and Chinese tourist arrivals (1999–2007) [21] / with permission of ELSEVIER

According to investigations in North America carried out by William R. Eadington, the booming gaming industry has a positive impact on rapid economic growth, increasing investment and employment, and enhancement of government revenue.[22]

Although Portuguese Macau legalized casinos in 1962, it was not until sovereignty over Macau was transferred back to China that Macau experienced booming growth in its gaming industry. The liberalized gaming market and deregulated China made Macau the world's largest gaming destination. Macau's gross gaming revenue grew nine times from 1999 to 2016. Because the Chinese central government allows Macau a legal monopoly on casino gaming within China, the development of the gaming industry is affected by Mainland China's attitude.

Customers of Macau's casinos are primarily from Mainland China (see Figure 11.11). However, because the state tightly manages the number of Mainlanders who visit Macau each year, a sudden change in visa policies in Mainland China will cause a loss in Macau's gaming revenues.[23]

Taiwan: The Metal Asian Tiger

Taiwan, Singapore, Hong Kong, and South Korea are called "Asian Tigers." These four countries underwent rapid industrialization and maintained exceptionally high growth rates of average double-digit economic growth rate each year from 1970 to 1990. Taiwan has modern infrastructure, extensive foreign reserves, and a top 25 economic position in terms of GDP (see Figure 11.12). Taiwan also has one of the world's most advanced microchip sectors, which makes it recognized as a developed and high-income economy.

During the 1960s, Taiwan was the world's primary exporter of consumer goods such as shoes, toys, and umbrellas. A plentiful and cheap labor force enabled Taiwan to develop labor-intensive industries. In the same decade, Taiwan enacted several Export Processing Zones (EPZs), which provided investors with infrastructure, streamlined administrative processes, and tax incentives. The EPZ also gave jobs to the previously rural population and attracted foreign investment and technological know-how, such as the light industry, which was the growth engine for Taiwan's economy in the 1960s.

In the 1970s, Taiwan expanded heavy industries, particularly petrochemicals and steel. The exports from the light industry and the emerging heavy industries carried Taiwan's economy forward. Taking advantage of the labor-intensive and export-oriented model, the government refocused its industrial policy on science

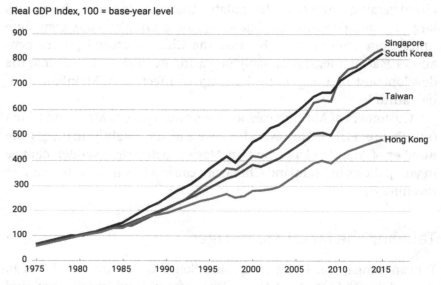

FIGURE 11.12 Indexed real GDP growth of Asian tigers [24] / Milken Institute / CC BY 3.0

and technology development. The government launched two critical programs in 1973 and 1980: the nonprofit Industrial Technology Research Institute to conduct applied research and the Hsinchu Science Park to encourage the development of high-tech industries. These programs attracted overseas talent to Taiwan and giant tech firms, such as United Microelectronics Corp. and TSMC, the world's leading semiconductor foundries.

In the late 1970s, China established an open-door policy to attract foreign investors. The opening of China also attracted Taiwanese manufacturers, who set up production there to reduce rising costs. As Taiwan became a more open economy and its production costs grew, many manufacturers relocated production facilities to lower-cost Southeast Asian countries and China. Some researchers argue that this offshoring has "hollowed out" Taiwan's industrial base, whereas others believe this strategy helped restore the strength of Taiwanese manufacturers.[25] In the 1980s, the government undertook more institutional reforms in trade liberalization and financial deregulation to integrate Taiwan into the world economy. Taiwan engages the private sector not only as an original equipment manufacturer but also as an original design manufacturer and original brand manufacturer.

The situation keeps testing Taiwan's entrepreneurial spirit. The high-tech sector has been the cornerstone of Taiwan's economy since the 1990s. Although the government has advanced various policies and initiatives to sustain its economic and industrial development since then, they have been less effective than the program backing high-tech. The lackluster policies signal Taiwan's need to recraft its strategies. President Tsai Ing-wen announced that the government would bring up five pillar industries to enforce the economy: green technology, national defense, the Internet of Things (IoT), biomedicine, and advanced machinery. To address stiffer competition and the intertwining of high-tech products and services in the consumer market, Taiwan initiated the Taiwan Miracle: Taiwan's rapid economic development to be a developed, high-income country during the latter half of the 21st century.[26]

CI-EL, PI-PM, and Operational Excellence

While China shows the capabilities of entrepreneurial marketing, the real goal is the impact on the market. Different policies established by the country force business players to respond prudently and act flexibly. Here are some cases of companies that are powerful and change the ecosystem of industry in China and its surrounding regions (Hong Kong, Macau, and Taiwan) and the world: Tencent, BYD, Xiaomi, and Haidilao.

Excellence in Quality: Tencent's Quality Exploitation and Exploration

Tencent, a Chinese internet giant, plays a significant role in consumers' daily lives. Tencent's world is rising to gain massive influence in the future. To exist in China everyone must have some interaction with Tencent, whether social media, games, e-commerce, or payment. Tencent boomed with social media in the desktop era. It became immersed in people's lives with WeChat in the mobile age. Originally a chatting app, it has become a platform for services, including news, social media, ride-hailing, hotel booking, e-commerce, dining, utility payments, and mutual fund sales.[27]

Instead of competing with everyone, Tencent's strategy is to open its ecosystem and invest in startups. The vast network of users also made the company an influential global investor. Tencent took on a stake in Spotify, Tesla, and Snapchat and invested in the biggest gaming companies in the world, such as Fortnite.

The era of "common prosperity," a slogan ushered by President Xi Jinping, aims to narrow the wealth gap in the country. To survive as a businessperson in China, one must navigate the balance between ideological campaigns and freedom of growth. Tencent is one of the powerful Chinese companies that remains obedient to the government, yet still advances in growth.

The humble Ma Huateng (also known as Pony Ma), the captain of the Tencent ship, wisely navigates the direction and course of the company. Ma is the cofounder and the CEO of Tencent, a renowned, influential person acknowledged by *Time Magazine*, *Forbes*, and

Fortune as the world's most influential and powerful businessperson and leader. Ma was also a deputy to the Shenzhen Municipal People's Congress and a delegate to the 12th National People's Congress.[28]

Being one of *"Fortune* World's Greatest Leaders," Pony Ma is known for his low-profile personality compared to fellow Chinese Jack Ma's outgoing personality. Pony Ma is an aggressive acquisitor and is compared to Warren Buffet for their similar investment approaches.[29] For years, Ma's strategy to acquire overseas content met little resistance and has been seen as a good thing for China because it helps boost China's soft power. Tencent aspired to become an infrastructure-like company equivalent to water and electricity.

Excellence in Cost: BYD's Decomposition and Decentralization Strategy

BYD has become the world's largest electric vehicle manufacturer and is a significant manufacturer of automobiles, forklifts, battery-powered bicycles, solar panels, and rechargeable batteries.[30] BYD ranked first in sales of EVs, plug-in hybrid vehicles, and fuel cell vehicles across 14 major markets in the first half of 2023. Based on MarkLines reports, Tesla followed in second place and the Volkswagen group a distant third.[31] Since 2022, BYD announced its intention to focus on only electric vehicles after surpassing Tesla for the world's most electric vehicle sales, including plug-in hybrids.

The innovative and eccentric founder, chairman, and CEO, Wang Chuanfu is behind the success of BYD. Wang won the "Most Creative Leader in the Asia-Pacific Region" title in 2004 and was named the "Most Predictive CEO" by *Car Newspaper* in 2007. Charlie Munger, the vice chairman of Berkshire Hathaway Corporation, considered him to be a combination of Thomas Edison and Jack Welch—something like Edison in solving technical problems and something like Welch in getting what he needed to do.[32] Different from other managerial leaders, Wang is a chemist and a technician. He spent several years as a government-sponsored researcher before entering the private sector and founding BYD in 1995.

With his entrepreneurial leadership, Wang incorporates his belief in corporate culture into a more horizontal organizational structure. The company generally has a product organizational structure with a

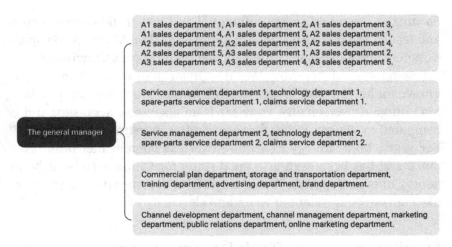

FIGURE 11.13 The organizational structure of BYD [33] / with permission of Baidu

flat hierarchy. Each segment is responsible for the product's production, marketing, and development. There are 28 segments in total, each of which has only one leader, Wang himself (see Figure 11.13). Wang gives all his managers access to the critical resources to produce effectively. The flat hierarchy enables a decentralization of responsibilities.[34]

Another unique approach to innovation implemented in BYD is "decomposition," which is the process of innovatively imitating, duplicating, and improving mature foreign end products. BYD gained innovative imitation by implementing the decomposition approach and gradually secured two core technologies: batteries and innovative molds. This practice needs legal support and a patent-management team to avoid patent disputes. The manufacturing method shows the decomposition. For example, with CN¥2 million, BYD could not afford an automatic assembly line, which cost at least US$5 million in 1995. So, BYD decomposed the manufacturing process into hundreds of steps. This decomposition makes low cost possible and enables a flexible assembly line and more effective quality control.

Excellence in Delivery: Xiaomi's Winning Omnichannel Tactic

In 2010, Xiaomi was not a smartphone brand. The company only offered a free Android-based operating system. Jumping to 2017,

Xiaomi became one of the world's largest smartphone makers, reaching US$15 billion in revenue. Three years later, accelerating its growth rate, Xiaomi transformed into the world's largest consumer IoT, with its revenue surpassing US$37 billion and more than 210 million devices (excluding smartphones and laptops) sold in more than 90 countries.

The secret of Xiaomi's growth lies in "strategic coalescence,"[35] which refers to a process in which a firm connects with demand- and supply-side stakeholders. Xiaomi did a strategic coalescence with its consumers and partners. Instead of competing head-on with incumbents, such as Huawei, Lenovo, Apple, and Samsung, Xiaomi courted tech-savvy smartphone users by offering free software and building an online community to understand the desired and undesired features.

Xiaomi expanded categories outside the company's expertise with partners by implementing a unique approach to identifying and developing partnerships. For example, Xiaomi purposely selected firms that were small or startups, so partnering with Xiaomi offered significant value to them as an incubation. Being a network collaborator to seek opportunities shows the capability of an entrepreneurial marketer.

Xiaomi aimed for four synergies by leveraging a coalescing strategy in expanding to the IoT market. First, Xiaomi created in-home IoT synergy by leveraging its smartphones as an "omni remote control." Second, to further strengthen the connection between Xiaomi and its customers, Xiaomi looked for design aesthetics synergy, which meant if a consumer purchased other Xiaomi products, those items would be aesthetically harmonious with Xiaomi's products at home. Third, Xiaomi took advantage of product portfolio synergy, which is a multi-channel synergy to maximize the returns on its brick-and-mortar stores.

Xiaomi also leveraged online sales data. Xiaomi's coalescence created another foundation for becoming a global IoT giant. Those approaches enabled Xiaomi to manage partners and product portfolios while maintaining consistency in design, aesthetics, quality, and technology/price ratio. Indeed, Xiaomi has a winning value proposition.

Excellence in Service: Hot Pot Chain Haidilao's Beyond Happiness Culture

Waiting is always a frustrating activity when you go to restaurants, but it does not happen in Haidilao. Customers are offered free manicures, massages, or car washes while waiting. These added-value services are out of customers' expectations. Therefore, people will talk about the perks and spread the news. Most restaurants compete for better quality, better ingredients, and better service, but fewer compete on unique and surprising differentiation. Haidilao also always takes local strategy in the business with modern cultural interiors. As of 2022, Haidilao is China's most extensive hot pot chain, with 1,300 restaurants.

The founder, Zhang Long, established Haidilao in 1994 in the Sichuan province. After five years, Haidilao started expanding to other regions and the global market. Technology also plays a vital role in delivering excellent customer experience. Haidilao launched a smart restaurant in 2018 and collaborated with Panasonic. The intelligent restaurant applied robotics, image recognition, and full kitchen automation technology. Balancing the technology excitement, emotional human interaction becomes more impactful in Haidilao. For example, the servers will perform hand-pulled noodles to enhance cheerfulness.[36]

Haidilao believes that happiness is always from within. The company gives autonomy and frontline incentives to the employees if they need to "wow" customers. The efforts of customer satisfaction and loyalty reflect promotion and career growth.[37] Regarding reputation challenges, Haidilao always provides transparency and directly addresses customer problems. Integrating technology and humans is the critical success factor for Haidilao to be a successful chain restaurant in the future.

The Challenges Ahead

As an economic powerhouse, China faces the future challenges of sustainability issues and an aging population. The policy of the Belt and Road Initiative (also known as One Belt One Road) has brought the country to a wealthy and highly educated society. However, this prospective condition leads to an imbalanced population.

Greener China

The Belt and Road Initiative policy financially supported coal-fired power plants outside China until being discontinued in 2021. Domestically, coal is the primary cause of carbon emissions because it supports nearly two-thirds of China's energy consumption (see Figure 11.14). The country accounts for about half of coal consumed globally. The staggering pace of urbanization also contributes to increased energy demands to power new manufacturing and industrial centers. President Xi Jinping has acknowledged climate change as one of the top concerns and has developed a variety of pledges to address it.

What is China doing to be greener?[38]

- Achieving carbon neutrality by 2060.
- Reaching peak carbon dioxide emission before 2030.
- Having renewable energy sources be 25% of total energy consumption by 2030.
- Reducing carbon intensity to more than 65% by 2030.
- Increasing the capacity of solar and wind power generators to 1.2 billion kilowatts by 2030.
- Increasing forest coverage to about 6 billion cubic meters by 2030.

In 2019, renewable energy accounted for nearly 15% of China's energy mix, compared to 7% in 2010. In addition to installing more hydropower, solar panels, and wind power generators, China also boosts its nuclear power capacity. Beijing and other large cities also incentivize electric

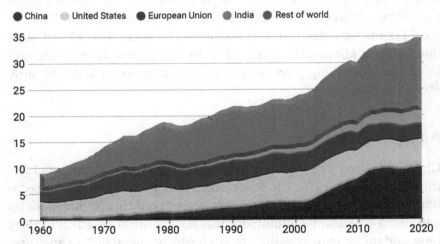

FIGURE 11.14 Global carbon emission in gigatons [39] / with permission of Global Carbon Project

vehicles, including battery electric, plug-in hybrid, and hydrogen fuel-cell vehicles. China is also open to cooperating with the rest of the world on climate change, including the United States. Despite the political and economic tension, China and the United States have worked together to reduce emissions.

In balancing the effect of the Belt and Road Initiative, China needs an estimated additional US$6.4 trillion to US$19.4 trillion to finance the transition to a greener economy. China has also started collecting an environmental tax to help fund ecological policies and attract more innocent investment. In early 2018, the Chinese government approved three sustainable development zones: Shenzhen for high-tech pollution management, Guilin for desertification innovation, and Taiyuan for air and water pollution innovation.[40] In promoting and making concrete efforts, China's technology giants play a vital role in sustainable development. Ultimately, end consumers will enjoy the products and services the corporations and brands offer.

Over the next decade, the number of upper-middle-income and above households in China will grow by almost 70%. But, beyond the scale and rising incomes, the market is more diversified and changed in terms of preferences and behaviors. Looking at the future seven segments shaping China's consuming landscape, the rising sustainable segment is the "eco-shopper" (see Figure 11.15).[41]

The eco-shopper is a segment willing to pay for more sustainable products and services, although sustainable options are more expensive—exceeding 30% more in some categories. In 2017, Chinese local brands for green products accounted for more than 85% of sales due to their affordable prices. Chinese companies always innovate to ensure the selling price is affordable; for instance, EVs cost only about US$5,000.

Aging Population

China is dealing with an aging population mainly due to the rapid fertility decline after 1970. The government policy and the social and economic imbalance triggered this result. Today's relaxing fertility policies and rising educational attainment will not significantly affect fertility rates and might reduce fertility by 0.3 births per woman.[42] In any case, China's population will age rapidly, with the old-age dependency ratio

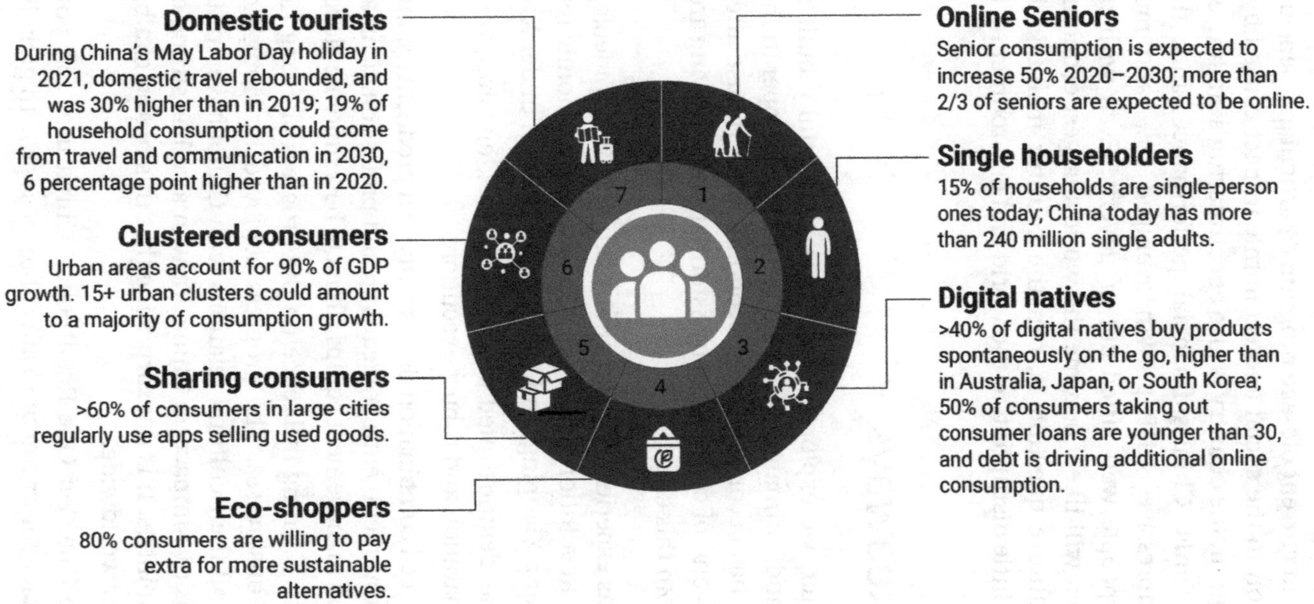

Online Seniors

Senior consumption is expected to increase 50% 2020–2030; more than 2/3 of seniors are expected to be online.

Single householders

15% of households are single-person ones today; China today has more than 240 million single adults.

Digital natives

>40% of digital natives buy products spontaneously on the go, higher than in Australia, Japan, or South Korea; 50% of consumers taking out consumer loans are younger than 30, and debt is driving additional online consumption.

Domestic tourists

During China's May Labor Day holiday in 2021, domestic travel rebounded, and was 30% higher than in 2019; 19% of household consumption could come from travel and communication in 2030, 6 percentage point higher than in 2020.

Clustered consumers

Urban areas account for 90% of GDP growth. 15+ urban clusters could amount to a majority of consumption growth.

Sharing consumers

>60% of consumers in large cities regularly use apps selling used goods.

Eco-shoppers

80% consumers are willing to pay extra for more sustainable alternatives.

FIGURE 11.15 Seven segments that drive growth in China

more than tripling. If this continues, China will experience severe fiscal problems in current old-age programs, particularly pensions.

In addition to the social and economic impact caused by China's aging population, the country is also encountering a stalling economy. By any standards, China's financial performance since the 1990s has been impressive. GDP growth averaged 10%, and more than 500 million people were lifted out of poverty. Even with moderate growth, China will likely become the world's largest economy before 2030.[43] The future question is, can the country maintain its rapid growth with little disruption to the world and environmental issues?

Key Takeaways

In this chapter, we explored how China successfully built its omni capabilities and ultimately was able to implement operational excellence. China has become a global economic powerhouse after undergoing various eras of continuous transformation. Following are the key takeaways from this chapter:

- China has experienced revolutions led by different ideologies: the Cultural Revolution under Mao Zedong, the economic revolution under Deng Xiaoping, and the social revolution under Xi Jinping.
- China has demonstrated omni capabilities, encompassing excellent preparation and robust execution.
- The balanced combination of creativity and productivity, innovation and improvement, entrepreneurship and professionalism, and leadership and management equips China to be a supreme global player.
- China has a strong influence on the progress of Hong Kong and Macau's businesses. The progress achieved by Hong Kong and Macau and their cultural relations with China have, in turn, also had a positive impact on China. Taiwan also has strong competitive capabilities. It is not surprising that this region can become a top player worldwide.
- With the One Belt One Road policy, China uses soft power and commercial enforcement to affect business growth globally.
- Challenges ahead oblige China to be greener and more sustainable-oriented country regarding operational excellence.

Epilogue: Countries, Capabilities, and Operational Excellence

The Impact of Nation Transformation on Corporate Competitiveness

What is the essence of everything explained in this book? The operations aspect, as the center of gravity in the omnihouse model, can reach its excellent level through the optimization of quality, cost, delivery, and service (QCDS). These QCDS elements are influenced by various entrepreneurship capabilities (creativity, innovations, entrepreneurship, and entrepreneurship, or CI-EL) and professionalism capabilities (productivity, improvement, professionalism, and management, or PI-PM), either in part or overall.

In line with the basic ideas of the new genre of entrepreneurial marketing, we must be able to converge aspects of these two clusters of capabilities. Suppose we only have a part of it and can only focus on some aspects of this capability. In that case, we can still leverage those aspects, which will contribute significantly to improving operational excellence, reflected in a business organization's higher efficiency or productivity. The results are not only limited to financial figures. They should also be visible in the increasingly flexible operational character of the organization, in which the company can embed sustainability aspects in its business model and reach the stakeholder-centric QCDS level.

It takes a long learning curve—time-consuming and even painful—for most Asian countries finally to have the opportunity to compete with the West. Japan was the pioneer, which was then followed by several other countries in the Asian region. Along the way, competing with the West has become increasingly difficult because, from time to time, the definition of quality has also shifted to the next level and ultimately will always be linked to impact. The shift of bargaining power to customers makes it even more challenging because customers feel that they are the ones who have the right to determine the definition of quality. What's more troublesome for business organizations is that the definition of quality between one customer and another (let alone between different countries) is relative. Consequently, defining quality becomes increasingly dynamic, just like a moving target.

More than cost-cutting is needed in line with the shift in orientation toward stakeholder-centricity. Costs are increasingly oriented toward the extent of alignment to social values in the long term with lower ESG risks. Therefore, companies are required to be able to implement environmental-related cost reductions. Yes, ESG reports publicly disclosed by a company are not enough to make us confident that the company complies with ESG aspects. ESG must be truly embedded in the company's business processes or model and audited thoroughly using audit standard methods accepted worldwide. Our accountant friends must be familiar with two necessary standards: IFRS S1 General Requirements for Disclosure of Sustainability-related Financial Information and IFRS S2 Climate-Related Disclosures, which must be effectively applied as of 1 January 2024.[1]

Technological advances that can integrate supply chains from upstream to downstream and the presence of various digital business ecosystems support the flourishing of online shopping. Delivery times become shorter, more reliable, very flexible, and hassle-free. The sustainability aspect is also part of the delivery process considerations. The perspective on delivery, in turn, has also shifted to become increasingly customer-centric and, even further, stakeholder-centric. The delivery orientation moved from on estimate to on schedule, then went to on demand, and finally to on conscience by including the importance of positive impacts on society as part of the ESG aspects.

Likewise, the level of service has shifted from standardized to personalized, then increased further to customized and finally transformative, namely by providing quality service but simultaneously complying with stringent environmental and social requirements and regulations.

As already explained, elements of CI-EL and PI-PM will be able to influence QCDS. South Korea has strong capabilities in creativity and innovation, which are visible in various companies originating from that ginseng country. South Korea's operational excellence is achieved by focusing on two capabilities: creativity and innovation. South Korea's creative capabilities result from serious hard work by the South Korean government and its people. Policies related to creativity and innovation are then firmly embedded at the corporate level. This bold intention is also supported by South Korea's unique *pali-pali* spirit, which has ultimately made the country one of the most innovative countries in the world.

India is a country that is very worthy of showing extraordinary entrepreneurship and leadership capabilities. These two characters are often seen prominently (and even dominantly) in various contexts. So, we cannot ignore it; we must admit that many global business leaders are dominated by made-in-India leaders. Don't believe it? Just check out their growing presence in US technology companies. Life in India, which is very competitive, has formed a solid natural entrepreneurial mentality. India builds operational excellence by relying on strong entrepreneurial and leadership capabilities.

A country that is very suitable to be an icon for productivity and improvement capabilities is Japan, famous for its implementation of the Kaizen philosophy. This culture of continuous improvement has made Japan the birthplace of many highly productive and competitive companies at the global level with impressive operational excellence. We are often amazed by how "overkill" the Japanese people's passion for details and perfection is.

Professionalism and excellent managerial skills are prominent characteristics of various leading companies in Singapore. These two capabilities are the primary basis for Singaporean companies' world-class qualifications; even as a country, Singapore has long held world-class status. This capability has been formed since Singapore's independence in the mid-1960s. Professionalism and solid managerial abilities are inseparable parts of Singapore's human resources quality, vital to transforming the country from third to first world. These two capabilities are the primary basis for operational excellence in most Singaporean companies.

Figure E.1 shows countries that can be the icons of several critical capabilities of CI-EL and PI-PM they have mastered, which become the basis for strengthening operational excellence in each country as reflected through the competitiveness of various companies from those countries.

How has China become one of the countries with the most powerful economy in the world? China has almost perfect omni capabilities—CI-EL and PI-PM—and has converged those dichotomies well, just like the *yin-yang* (see Figure E.2).

These capabilities, among others, enable China to do and achieve many things that are impossible for many other countries in the world to make happen. Many products made in China now have world-class quality but can still be produced with a very high level of efficiency, thereby reducing costs, and can be delivered and made available anywhere in the world (familiar with "One Belt One Road"?); these products also are supported by reliable service capabilities. This is a reflection of extraordinary operational excellence. To get to this point, China has had to undergo a long journey through

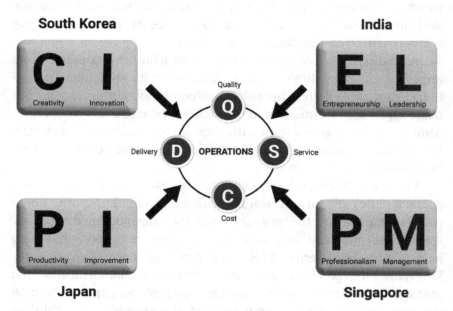

FIGURE E.1 Core capabilities of South Korea, India, Japan, and Singapore

China

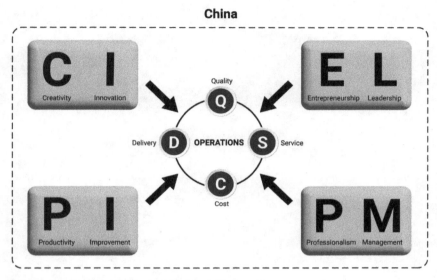

FIGURE E.2   Perfect omni capabilities of China

many transformation eras, from Mao Zedong to Deng Xiaoping to Xi Jinping. What's impressive is that China can go through its learning curve in various fields in a much shorter time than many other countries.

So, what's the catch after briefly reviewing those countries? Regardless of the differences in the government system, domestic political conditions, various issues, and constraints in each country, there is one thing in common: it takes considerable efforts, which require seriousness, commitment, and consistency (both from the government and society) to develop conducive conditions that support the formation of capabilities that have a significant and positive impact on increasing the competitiveness of companies operating in a country, which, in turn, leads to the overall country's competitiveness on a global scale.

Every country must be able to leverage all the golden momentum it has. Keeping it from slipping away at any cost is an indispensable and essential action because it is unlikely that the same invaluable momentum will happen again soon. Once a country loses momentum, its future will be more vulnerable, and if there is no accurate and immediate attempt to fix it, it might lose its chance to remain relevant on the world stage.

Appendix A: The Omnihouse Model

A Holistic Perspective of Entrepreneurial Marketing[1]

The omnihouse model is a framework used to explain a new genre of entrepreneurial marketing, namely, a holistic entrepreneurial marketing approach, different from the "classic" entrepreneurial marketing concept that has existed for a long time. The new genre of entrepreneurial marketing was developed after observing what has occurred in recent years, including the development of digital technology, which has greatly influenced the business landscape, how companies deal with unimaginable conditions during the COVID-19 pandemic to survive, as well as some marketing blind spots phenomenon that has occurred at least in the last decade. All of this is discussed in the book *Entrepreneurial Marketing: Beyond Professionalism to Creativity, Leadership, and Sustainability*, which underlines that business and marketing will never be the same again.

A "too professional" marketing approach that is very procedural, slow-moving, and reactive is no longer sufficient to deal with the various dynamics of the business environment. We also found that many companies could survive and demonstrate their resilience during the uncertainty of the COVID-19 pandemic due to their ability to apply a more entrepreneurial approach. An entrepreneurial approach is the ticket so that an organization can strengthen its dynamic capabilities and become an organization that is interconnected, flexible, and results-driven. This omnihouse model is the basis for explaining a more expanded version of entrepreneurial marketing, which essentially advises businesspeople to converge various dichotomous elements in an organization, including banishing silos and inertia in the organization.

This model tries to converge an entrepreneurial mindset and a professional mindset as well as various functions in business

235

organizations, which are usually in conflict and, at the same time, ensures that business organizations can have a positive and significant impact on society and the environment. This impact is part of the results that management must achieve, not just output and outcomes. It is hoped that applying the new genre of entrepreneurial marketing concept will lead business organizations through the expected challenges of 2025, continuing toward 2030 and beyond.

Applying this holistic perspective of entrepreneurial marketing is intended to shape various business organizations' resilience in the rapidly changing business environment because it has a strong foundation for organizations facing challenges in the present and especially in the future. The omnihouse model shows how we should integrate an entire organization. Omnihouse refers to an organization that combines multiple elements. Each component plays an individual role and collaborates with the other parts of the business. The omnihouse model is a framework that can be used to implement strategies and achieve specific goals.

The core of this model is housed in two clusters. The first is the entrepreneurial cluster, comprising four elements: creativity, innovation, entrepreneurship, and leadership (CI-EL). The second cluster is professionalism, which comprises four components: productivity, improvement, professionalism, and management (PI-PM). Other functions surround these clusters and interact with them. They are affected by "dynamics," which constitute five drivers: technology, political/ legal (including regulations), economy, social/cultural, and market. These drivers, in turn, affect the 4Cs, which refer to changes, competitors, customers, and companies.

These dynamics components are the foundation for developing marketing strategies and tactics, as outlined in the competitiveness triangle at the top right of the model. Within the triangle, PBD stands for positioning, differentiation, and brand. This is the anchor for the main elements of marketing: segmentation, targeting, marketing mix, selling, service, and processes.

The dynamics element is also the basis for developing ideas, which leads to creativity. These ideas can be converted into innovation in the form of tangible solutions for customers. These creative ideas must use various company's capital productively. The solutions provided to customers must result in improvements, as reflected in the company's better profit margins. Thus, the convergence of creativity/innovation and productivity/improvement elements affects the balance sheet (B/S) and income statement (I/S).

Elements of creativity and improvement can generate competitiveness only if we involve people with solid mindsets of entrepreneurship and leadership to manage them. Value creation is the responsibility of entrepreneurs, and leaders maintain values. However, we must also support entrepreneurship and leadership with solid professionalism and management. This condition, in turn, can propel the company forward. What we see in the balance sheet and income statement results from the past. What we are doing now, primarily through the strong convergence of entrepreneurship/professionalism and leadership/management elements, will determine a company's cash flow (C/F) and market value (M/V).

Thus, we gain a picture of how the organization will perform. As laid out in the omnihouse model, it is essential to integrate marketing with finance and also integrate technology and humanity. Humanity refers to primary stakeholders: people, customers, and society. Collectively, these functions support the actions that lead to financial and nonfinancial results.

Note that in the heart of the model, we have operations. This function takes marketing objectives and places them into action and, at the same time, ensures financial goals can be achieved. Operations that also bridge the use of technology will ultimately affect humanity. The operations capabilities interact with the other capabilities to keep a company moving forward and competitive within its industry. The operations capabilities also enable the organization to adapt quickly to any changes in the business environment.

Appendix B: Inner Development Goals

A Pathway to Sustainable Development and Personal Growth

In September 2000, leaders from 189 nations converged at the United Nations headquarters, embarking on a transformative journey by signing the historic Millennium Declaration. This declaration committed to achieving eight measurable goals, ranging from poverty reduction to gender equality and child mortality, all aimed to be realized by 2015.[1] These Millennium Development Goals (MDGs) envisioned countries as the primary drivers of global progress. Figure B.1 lists the eight goals.

The MDG progress has resulted in substantial results, with the world successfully achieving the first goal of halving extreme poverty by 2015. However, these achievements have not been uneven, and as the MDGs approached their expiration in 2015, the United Nations

Goal 1	Eradicate extreme poverty and hunger.
Goal 2	Achieve universal primary education.
Goal 3	Promote gender equality and empower women.
Goal 4	Reduce child mortality.
Goal 5	Improve maternal health.
Goal 6	Combat HIV/AIDS, malaria, and other diseases.
Goal 7	Develop a global partnership for development.
Goal 8	Eradicate extreme poverty and hunger.

FIGURE B.1 The Millennium Development Goals (MDGs)

General Assembly Open Working Group (OWG) unveiled a document outlining 17 comprehensive goals. The focus shifted toward fostering a sustainable world where environmental integrity, social inclusivity, and economic development stand on equal footing. These goals laid the foundation for the Sustainable Development Goals (SDGs), extending the global development agenda from 2015 to 2030.

The United Nations Development Group expanded the sphere of stakeholders, incorporating universities, nongovernmental organizations (NGOs), and the private sector from across the globe, all actively promoting the SDGs. Figure B.2 lists the 17 goals.

The SDGs presented a holistic blueprint for a sustainable world by 2030, encompassing 17 goals that address people's diverse needs,

Goal 1	End poverty in all its forms everywhere.
Goal 2	End hunger, achieve food security and improved nutrition, and promote sustainable agriculture.
Goal 3	Ensure healthy lives and promote well-being for all at all ages.
Goal 4	Ensure inclusive and equitable quality education and promote life-long learning opportunities for all.
Goal 5	Achieve gender equality and empower all women and girls.
Goal 6	Ensure availability and sustainable management of water and sanitation for all.
Goal 7	Ensure access to affordable, reliable, sustainable, and modern energy for all.
Goal 8	Promote sustained, inclusive, and sustainable economic growth, full and productive employment, and decent work for all.
Goal 9	Build resilient infrastructure, promote inclusive and sustainable industrialization, and foster innovation.
Goal 10	Reduce inequality within and among countries.
Goal 11	Make cities and human settlements inclusive, safe, resilient, and sustainable.
Goal 12	Ensure sustainable consumption and production patterns.
Goal 13	Take urgent action to combat climate change and its impacts.
Goal 14	Conserve and sustainably use the oceans, seas, and marine resources for sustainable development.
Goal 15	Protect, restore and promote sustainable use of terrestrial ecosystems, sustainably manage forests, combat desertification, halt and reverse land degradation, and halt biodiversity loss.
Goal 16	Promote peaceful and inclusive societies for sustainable development, provide access to justice for all, and build effective, accountable, and inclusive institutions at all levels.
Goal 17	Strengthen the means of implementation and revitalize the global partnership for sustainable development.

FIGURE B.2   Sustainable Development Goals (SDGs) as proposed by the OWG values, and convictions. Although a collective vision exists, with support from numerous countries, universities, NGOs, and the private sector, progress toward this vision has, regrettably, fallen short. Humanity grapples with a lack of inner capacity to navigate our increasingly intricate environment and challenges.[2]

Fortuitously, contemporary research demonstrates that we can nurture the inner abilities to overcome these obstacles. By developing our inner abilities, we no longer need to wait for external parties; we can take proactive steps toward sustainability on an individual level. This was the starting point for the "Inner Development Goals" (IDGs) initiative, spearheaded by a nonprofit organization also named "Inner Development Goals," which is dedicated to inner development.[3] The organization involves research, curation, and dissemination of science-based skills and qualities that enable us to lead purposeful, sustainable, and productive lives.

The IDGs furnish a crucial framework of transformative skills for sustainable development that align with the UN's SDGs. This initiative operates on cocreation principles, constantly evolving through input from a growing network of experts, scientists, practitioners, and organizations worldwide. In 2021, the details were meticulously crafted by an international team of researchers following an extensive outreach consultation involving more than 1,000 individuals (the first survey was on 1 March 2021, and the second was on 19 April 2021). The IDG framework comprises five dimensions that organize 23 skills and qualities essential for human inner growth and development.

In the realm of IDGs, it is acknowledged that different theoretical frameworks can often overlap and interrelate. Given the complexity of this knowledge domain, the IDG framework remains open-ended, avoiding an exclusive allegiance to any particular theoretical model. This openness aims to make the IDG framework an inclusive and adaptable pedagogical tool accessible to those with diverse theoretical preferences.

The IDG framework encompasses five fundamental aspects pivotal for inner development and personal growth: being, thinking, relating, collaborating, and acting (see Figure B.3).[4] Each of the five fundamental aspects consists of several elements. We can further study and understand each fundamental aspect and its components by reviewing the IDG full report.

Being: Relationship to Self	Thinking: Cognitive Skills	Relating: Caring for Others and the World	Collaborating: Social Skills	Acting: Enabling Change
Inner compass	Critical thinking	Appreciation	Communication skills	Courage
Integrity and authenticity	Complexity awareness	Connectedness	Cocreation skills	Creativity
Openness and learning mindset	Perspective skills	Humility	Inclusive mindset and intercultural competence	Optimism
Self-awareness	Sense-making	Empathy and compassion	Trust	Perseverance
Presence	Long-term orientation and visioning		Mobilization skills	

FIGURE B.3 Five fundamental aspects of the IDG framework

Appendix C: Humane Entrepreneurship

The New Cornerstone of Modern Business

Entrepreneurship often significantly emphasizes profit and growth. However, in this relentless pursuit, some companies inadvertently neglect the human side of the equation. Issues such as meager employee compensation, unethical waste disposal practices, and the strict maximization of working hours often overshadow the human element. Enter the concept of *humane entrepreneurship*, a holistic approach that marries the human cycle with the enterprise cycle to create a harmonious ecosystem.

The brains behind humane entrepreneurship are a formidable team of scholars: Zong-Tae Bae, a professor at the College of Business, KAIST; Myung-Soo Kang, a professor at the Department of International Trade at Hansung University; Ki-Chan Kim, a professor of the School of Business Administration at The Catholic University of Korea; and Ji-Hoon Park, the corresponding author and a postdoctoral researcher at the College of Business, KAIST.[1]

The scholars suggested the concept of humane entrepreneurship, where human-centered logic enhances the traditional view of entrepreneurship. They offer the five disciplines in management studies as theoretical foundations of humane entrepreneurship: strategic entrepreneurship, stakeholder theory, transformational leadership, motivation theory, and humanistic management. As a result, the research has involved 19 countries and tested its reliability and validity, showing that humane entrepreneurship comprises two dimensions: human and enterprise cycles (see Figure C.1).

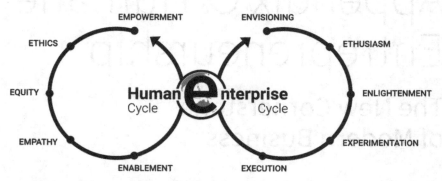

FIGURE C.1 Humane entrepreneurship model: human and enterprise cycles

The Human Cycle: Nurturing Happiness in the Workplace

The human cycle is where the journey begins, focusing on the well-being and happiness of workers within the enterprise.[2] Here, leaders play a pivotal role in shaping the approach and environment conducive to nurturing human capital. It comprises several vital elements:

- **Empowerment.** Entrepreneurs and leaders must empower themselves and their followers. This inner empowerment is born of a passionate vision and unwavering self-efficacy. Outer empowerment involves embracing change, learning from mistakes, and fostering an innovative learning spirit.
- **Ethics.** Responsibility is a cornerstone of ethical action for entrepreneurs. They serve as patrons of ethical practices, embracing accountability and social and environmental responsibility.
- **Equality.** Equality in the enterprise translates to respect among all stakeholders, fostering fairness, openness, and collaboration. This spirit extends beyond leaders and followers to encompass interactions with external partners and vendors.
- **Empathy.** Leaders must cultivate empathy by stepping into the shoes of employees and customers. Effective communication and relationship building in this regard boost employee motivation, loyalty, and engagement.

- **Enablement.** Employees should not be viewed merely as cost centers; they are potential profit drivers. Therefore, investment in their development through training, coaching, and mentoring is essential for leveraging revenue.

The Enterprise Cycle: Realizing the Vision

On the leader's side of the equation lies the enterprise cycle, a set of behaviors and strategies that, when effectively implemented, pave the path to achieving the enterprise's vision and mission.[3] It comprises vital elements:

- **Envisioning.** Entrepreneurs, as leaders, gaze into the future, anticipating changes, seizing opportunities, and providing visionary direction. Proactive pursuit of innovation is their hallmark.
- **Enthusiasm.** The spirit of enthusiasm drives entrepreneurs to challenge the status quo, explore new opportunities, take calculated risks, and collaborate with potential partners who share their zeal.
- **Enlightenment.** Value creation comes to the forefront through continuous improvement, leading to the development of new technologies and products.
- **Experimentation.** Entrepreneurs should encourage experimentation to enhance product quality, refine business processes, and boost productivity. A culture of experimentation fosters a safe space for learning from results that may not meet initial expectations.
- **Execution.** Successful entrepreneurs meticulously design management processes that optimize costs, quality, technology, and operations, aligning them with the overarching company goals.

Integration for Sustainability: Fostering Profit, People, and Planet

The human and enterprise cycles unite to form a sustainable paradigm beyond making money. Companies can accomplish financial success and environmental protection by developing ethical behavior, promoting equality, encouraging empathy, and facilitating personal and professional growth.

By combining these two concepts, companies can grow in a way that is morally, socially, and environmentally sound. It is also more sustainable because this model is adaptable to new businesses, SMEs, and enterprises and prioritizes humanity as much as profit.

In humane entrepreneurship, profit and people coexist harmoniously, paving the way for a brighter future where businesses flourish while safeguarding the well-being of their most valuable asset—their human capital—and preserving the planet for generations.

Appendix D: Marketing ZEN

A Holistic Approach to Ethical and Sustainable Business

Companies are frequently motivated by the quest for more sales and income in the fast-paced world of modern business, with a persistent focus on hypergrowth using various ethical and unethical strategies. However, many companies worldwide are increasingly rethinking their strategy or approach, particularly in light of worries about the moral ramifications of some marketing techniques.[1]

The Evolving Landscape of Consumer Data and Ethics

To enhance the customer experience, some companies have endeavored to collect and enclose consumers' behavioral histories, effectively converting them into data. Concurrently, there is a heightened scrutiny of third-party cookies, which track user web histories, and a reevaluation of targeted advertising practices. Criticisms have also arisen concerning "dark patterns," which manipulate customer behavior through user interface and design features.

Consequently, some marketing strategies have emerged that inadvertently overstimulate consumers, generate anxiety, and promote the purchase of products or services that may not be genuinely needed. With the rise of artificial intelligence and algorithms, individuals must understand their minds better to retain control and prevent technology from dictating their preferences and behaviors.[2]

In 2017, Mikio Shishido, a Zen and mindfulness coach, embarked on a remarkable journey by establishing a company with a specific focus on nurturing mindfulness within the realms of business, education, and government. To his surprise, he discovered a genuine interest from various businesses or companies in imbibing the profound values of Zen 2.0 and mindfulness principles.

Additionally, Shinji Tanaka was uncomfortable when requests for "maximizing profits" and "expanding the organization" became prevalent during seminars and consulting sessions. Such an approach to corporate activities, deeply rooted in mass production and consumption, left them questioning the fundamental underpinnings of modern business.

Amid the growing calls for restraining unbridled capitalism, Shishido and Tanaka were acutely aware of the pressing need to introduce new values and revolutionize the business and marketing landscape. Thus, they commenced a collaborative effort to redefine marketing, laying the foundation for the concept of Marketing ZEN. Four years have elapsed since their initial meeting, and their relentless dedication has finally given birth to *Marketing ZEN*.

Introducing a New Framework: Marketing ZEN

To address these ethical and sustainability concerns, a new framework for marketing emerges: Marketing ZEN. In Marketing ZEN, businesses listen to their inner voice and rediscover their mission. They prioritize sustainable environments and partnerships over the relentless pursuit of profit expansion.

The term *zen* conjures different meanings, from the profound meditation of traditional Buddhist discipline to the simplicity of design. For instance, presentation Zen advocates for simplicity in design, using limited images, colors, and text to reduce audience stress during presentations. Shigematsu Soiku of Shōgenji Temple provides a different perspective on Zen by emphasizing identity, ecology, and lifestyle. In marketing context, ZEN seeks true identity, connection with ecology, and a life unswayed by materialism and mechanization.[3]

The Characteristics of Marketing ZEN

The following are the characteristics of Marketing ZEN:

- **Ethics over money.** Marketing ZEN strongly emphasizes ethical marketing practices and strives for a sustainable business size rather than solely focusing on financial gain.
- **Connecting with nature and humanity.** It recognizes the human desire to feel more connected to nature and one another. Many explore spirituality and consciousness to unlock their potential beyond numbers and logic.
- **Client-centric and environmentally aware.** Businesses are urged to restructure their marketing strategies, prioritizing their relationships with clients and considering the environmental impact of their actions.
- **A thoughtful approach to marketing.** Marketing ZEN advocates for a more deliberate, thoughtful marketing approach that centers on understanding an organization's core purpose rather than pursuing rapid capital gain through mass advertising.
- **Incorporating Zen principles.** It incorporates principles of Zen and mindfulness, aiming to reintroduce humanity into the business realm and create a better society.
- **The role of intuition in marketing.** Marketing ZEN acknowledges the significance of intuition in generating fresh ideas and conducting marketing. It emphasizes that marketing is not solely about numbers and logic but also about having that special feeling that enables individuals to perceive things differently.

The Steps of Implementing Marketing ZEN

Following are the steps of implementing Marketing ZEN:

1. **Reflect on oneself.** Clarify the brand's position within the market.
2. **Apply lean business management.** Streamline complex business models prone to expansion.

3. **Pursue the appropriate business plan size.** Seek a sustainable business size rather than perpetual growth.

4. **Specify marketing measures.** Eliminate wasteful marketing processes and focus on specific strategies.

5. **Establish customer relations.** Foster ethical relationships built on shared purposes.

In a nutshell, Marketing ZEN represents a transformative approach to business and marketing, emphasizing ethics, sustainability, and a deep connection with humanity. It is a paradigm that enables businesses to thrive while contributing to a better society and preserving the environment for future generations.

Notes

Preface

1. The integrated concept of quality, cost, and delivery in management is an idea developed by Masaaki Imai.
2. https://www.visualcapitalist.com/visualizing-the-105-trillion-world-economy-in-one-chart/
3. https://twitter.com/ValaAfshar/status/1749155704617795673/photo/1
4. https://www.reuters.com/business/autos-transportation/toyota-shares-slide-unit-daihatsus-safety-scandal-widens-2023-12-21/, https://www.japantimes.co.jp/business/2024/01/30/companies/toyota-akio-toyoda-global-sales/, https://www.cnbc.com/2024/02/14/toyota-enforces-reshuffling-at-scandal-hit-daihatsu-unit.html, https://english.kyodonews.net/news/2024/01/ae5a9a8eaf58-urgent-toyota-group-firm-rigged-data-on-diesel-engine-power-output.html, and https://fortune.com/asia/2024/01/30/toyota-worlds-top-car-seller-safety-scandals-daihatsu-hino
5. According to QS World University Rankings. https://www.topuniversities.com/universities/national-university-singapore-nus

Chapter 1: Operations as the Center of Gravity

1. https://www.investopedia.com/financial-edge/0311/5-of-the-most-adaptive-companies.aspx
2. https://hbr.org/2014/10/how-to-gradually-become-a-different-company/ and www.encyclopedia.com
3. https://www.forbes.com/sites/rhettpower/2020/04/26/how-5-businesses-are-adapting-to-life-in-a-pandemic/?sh=67b4ad814f5a/ and https://www.caresignal.health/covid-companion
4. https://www.icis.com/subscriber/icb/2017/10/06/10149719/basf-ceo-kurt-bock-seeks-gradual-transformation-for-competitiveness/#_=_/
5. https://www.insightandforesight.com.au/blog-foresights/why-businesses-avoid-talking-about-radical-transformation/

6. https://www.globenewswire.com/en/news-release/2017/05/09/ 1208818/0/en/Ten-Companies-Lead-in-Responding-to-Radical-Market-Change-and-Reinventing-Themselves-for-a-Different-Future-According-to-New-Analysis-of-Public-Company-Data.html
7. https://www.processexcellencenetwork.com/business-process-management-bpm/articles/7-companies-that-forever-changed-the-face-of-proce/
8. https://leanscape.io/brilliant-leadership-is-useless-without-operational-excellence/ and https://www.sweetprocess.com/ operational-excellence/
9. Michael A. Hitt, Barbara W. Keats, and Samuel M. DeMarie, "Navigating in the New Competitive Landscape: Building Strategic Flexibility and Competitive Advantage in the 21st Century," *Academy of Management Perspectives* 12, no. 4 (November 1998). https://doi.org/10.5465/ ame.1998.1333922
10. https://www.ibm.com/cloud/blog/delivering-value-through-operational-excellence
11. Philip Kotler, Hermawan Kartajaya, Hooi Den Huan, and Jacky Mussry, *Entrepreneurial Marketing: Beyond Professionalism to Creativity, Leadership, and Sustainability* (Wiley, 2023), Chapter 17.
12. Ibid.
13. Ibid.
14. https://www.sweetprocess.com/operational-excellence/
15. https://www.arcweb.com/industry-best-practices/operational-excellence-opx-achieved-companies-operationally-resilient/
16. Masaaki Imai, *Gemba Kaizen: A Commonsense Approach to a Continuous Improvement Strategy* (McGraw-Hill, 2012).
17. https://www.gartner.com/smarterwithgartner/how-to-make-ecosystems-part-of-the-business-strategy/
18. Enriko Ceko, "On Relations Between Creativity and Quality Management and Quality Management Culture" (Wisdom University, Tirana, Albania, 2021).
19. https://asq.org/quality-press/display-item?item=E0930
20. https://innovationmanagement.se/2005/08/29/quality-and-creativity-enemies-or-allies/
21. Katherine Gustafson. https://www.legalzoom.com/articles/creative-cost-cutting-ideas-for-small-businesses
22. David Rutley. https://collectivenext.com/blog/getting-creative-about-cutting-costs/

23. **https://www.badgermapping.com/blog/creativity-customer-service/#:~:text=Creativity%20is%20what%20is%20always,of%2Dthe%2Dbox%20strategies/**

24. M. G. Antunes, J. T. Quirós, and M.d.R. F. Justino, "The Relationship Between Innovation and Total Quality Management and the Innovation Effects on Organizational Performance," *International Journal of Quality & Reliability Management* 34, no. 9 (2017): 1474–1492. **https://doi.org/10.1108/IJQRM-02-2016-0025/**

25. **https://simplicable.com/productivity/cost-innovation/**

26. **https://www.retail-insight-network.com/comment/delivery-innovations-technology-trends/**

27. **https://www.wallstreetmojo.com/service-innovation/#:~:text=Service%20innovation%20refers%20to%20any,to%20enhance%20ease%20and%20speed/**

28. **https://ecampusontario.pressbooks.pub/leadinginnovation/chapter/chapter-3-service-innovation/**

29. **https://dcid.sanford.duke.edu/importance-of-entrepreneurship/#:~:text=By%20bringing%20innovation%20to%20every,products%2C%20services%2C%20and%20technology/**

30. **https://www.thersa.org/blog/2018/03/how-can-entrepreneurs-improve-quality-of-life-around-the-world#:~:text=Successful%20entrepreneurs%20with%20vision%20improve,easily%20said%20rather%20than%20practised/**

31. Stella Toyosi Durowoju. **https://platform.almanhal.com/Files/Articles/91715/**

32. Saumyaranjan Sahoo and Sudhir Yadav, "Entrepreneurial Orientation of SMES, Total Quality Management and Firm Performance," *Journal of Manufacturing Technology Management* 28, no. 1. **https://www.researchgate.net/publication/319578024_Entrepreneurial_orientation_of_SMES_total_quality_management_and_firm_performance**

33. Azriyah Amir, Sofiah Auzair, and Rozita Amiruddin, "Cost Management, Entrepreneurship and Competitiveness of Strategic Priorities for Small and Medium Enterprises," *Procedia: Social and Behavioral Sciences* 219 (2016): 84–90. **https://doi.org/10.1016/j.sbspro.2016.04.046**

34. **https://www.toppr.com/guides/business-economics/theory-of-production-and-cost/factors-of-production-entrepreneur/**

35. Paul D. Hirtz, Susan L. Murray, and Catherine A. Riordan, "The Effects of Leadership on Quality," *Engineering Management Journal* 19, no. 1 (2007): 22–27. **https://doi.org/10.1080/10429247.2007.11431718**

36. Hongyun Tian, Shuja Iqbal, Shamim Akhtar, Sikandar Ali Qalati, Farooq Anwar, and Muhammad Aamir Shafique Khan, "The Impact of Transformational Leadership on Employee Retention: Mediation and Moderation Through Organizational Citizenship Behavior and Communication," *Frontiers in Psychology* 11 (March 2020). **https://doi.org/10.3389/fpsyg.2020.00314**

37. **https://www.bizjournals.com/dallas/news/2022/05/16/the-impact-of-leaders-on-employee-retention.html#:~:text=If%20 employees%20feel%20like%20their,leaders%20retain%20 employees%20more%20effectively**

38. **https://www.workhuman.com/blog/the-ridiculously-high-cost-of-employee-turnover/**

39. **https://www.mcorpcx.com/articles/5-things-need-know-want-deliver-brand-promise/**

40. **https://www.indeed.com/career-advice/career-development/how-to-be-better-leader-in-customer-service#:~:text=Strong%20 leadership%20in%20customer%20service,informs%20all%20 decisions%20and%20processes/**

41. **https://jurnaljam.ub.ac.id/index.php/jam/article/view/1527/**

42. Munwar Hussain Pahi, Abdul-Halim Abdul-Majid, Samar Fahd, Abdul Rehman Gilal, Bandeh Ali Talpur, Ahmad Waqas, and Toni Anwar, "Leadership Style and Employees' Commitment to Service Quality: An Analysis of the Mediation Pathway via Knowledge Sharing," *Frontiers in Psychology* 13 (September 2022). **https://doi.org/10.3389/fpsyg.2022.926779**

43. Farhang Momeni and Jun Ni, "Quality Can Improve as Productivity Increases: Machining as Proof," *Procedia Manufacturing* 53 (2021): 299–309. **https://www.sciencedirect.com/science/article/pii/S235197892100038X/**

44. **https://www.cliffsnotes.com/study-guides/principles-of-management/productivity-and-total-quality-management/productivity-and-quality/**

45. **chrome-extension://efaidnbmnnnibpcajpcglclefindmkaj/https:// deden08m.files.wordpress.com/2013/02/chapter-14-improving-service-quality-and-productivity1.pdf**

46. **https://www.sweetprocess.com/quality-improvement/**

47. **https://www.linkedin.com/pulse/importance-user-experience-ux-digital-marketing-scott/**

48. **https://www.liferay.com/en/web/l/3-ways-to-enhance-your-digital-customer-service-strategy?utm_term=improve%20customer%20 experience&utm_campaign=7014u000001t5buAAA%20-%20 ASEAN%20%7C%20SEM%20-%20Self%20Service%20Portal&utm_ source=adwords&utm_medium=ppc&gad=1&gclid=CjwKCAjwg-**

GjBhBnEiwAMUvNWytVwuotCwwsYZYNDlE9xcFClGmUfsxHF
QOc-hIZZZGe8zzd3sDZIBoCqucQAvD_BwE
49. https://converged.propelsoftware.com/blogs/why-quality-
management-really-matters#:~:text=Quality%20management%20
provides%20a%20framework,best%20possible%20products%20
and%20services.&text=Quality%20management%20functions%20
as%20both,cutting%20costs%2C%20and%20eliminating%20errors
50. https://bakkah.com/knowledge-center/importance-of-quality-
management-for-organizations
51. https://enterslice.com/learning/cost-management-for-business/
52. https://myabcm.com/understand-what-cost-management-is-
how-important-it-is-and-how-to-do-it/#:~:text=It%20makes%20
it%20possible%20to,well%20as%20better%20investment%20
opportunities
53. https://fareye.com/what-is-delivery-management#:~:
text=Delivery%20management%20helps%20in%20making,in%
20streamlining%20supply%20chain%20operations
54. https://www.vp-delivery.com/the-importance-of-delivery-
management/
55. https://yasm.com/wiki/en/index.php/Service_Management#:~:
text=Service%20management%20is%20a%20management,has%20
been%20maturing%20for%20decades

Chapter 2: Competing with the West

1. https://voi.id/en/memori/45591
2. https://www.astronomy.com/space-exploration/we-choose-to-go-
to-the-moon-remembering-jfks-rice-university-speech/
3. https://www.jrailpass.com/blog/shinkansen-bullet-train-history
4. https://en.wikipedia.org/wiki/Non-Aligned_Movement
5. https://unctad.org/system/files/official-document/
osgdp20043_en.pdf
6. https://www.adb.org/sites/default/files/publication/436406/ewp-
550-asias-industrial-transformation-part2.pdf
7. https://www.persee.fr/doc/rei_0154-3229_1995_num_71_1_1558
8. https://www.gsid.nagoya-u.ac.jp/sotsubo/Krugman.pdf
9. https://core.ac.uk/download/pdf/80521628.pdf
10. http://etheses.dur.ac.uk/7144/1/7144_4326.PDF

11. https://en.wikipedia.org/wiki/Park_Chung_Hee. Note: The Fourth Republic of Korea was the government of South Korea from November 1972 to March 1981, but it was only partially completed under the rule of Park Chung Hee because he was assassinated in October 1979.
12. https://www.asianstudies.org/publications/eaa/archives/taiwans-small-and-medium-enterprises-smes/
13. https://www.hkmemory.hk/MHK/collections/postwar_industries/industrialization_in_postwar_hong_kong/index.html
14. chrome-extension://efaidnbmnnnibpcajpcglclefindmkaj/https://www3.weforum.org/docs/WEF_IBC_Measuring_Stakeholder_Capitalism_Report_2020.pdf
15. https://www.sdg.services/principles.html
16. https://www.icaew.com/technical/financial-services/esg-assurance/what-is-esg-and-why-does-it-matter
17. https://www.armanino.com/articles/esg-scores/
18. https://www.reprisk.com/news-research/resources/methodology

Chapter 3: The New Perspective of Quality

1. https://www.dell.com/en-us/lp/customizable-pcs
2. https://www.theatlantic.com/health/archive/2016/05/food-customization-america/482073/
3. https://www.thestreet.com/restaurants/customer-customization-coffee-starbucks-billion-dollar-win
4. https://www.restaurantbusinessonline.com/financing/starbucks-beverage-modifiers-become-1b-business#:~:text=Those%20%E2%80%9Cmodifiers%E2%80%9D%20generate%20%241%20billion,America%2C%20told%20investors%20on%20Thursday
5. https://www.nbcnews.com/better/lifestyle/everything-you-need-know-about-buying-installing-ikea-closet-system-ncna1037216
6. https://www.msn.com/en-us/lifestyle/home-and-garden/why-is-the-infamous-ikea-pax-wardrobe-system-taking-over-tiktok/ar-AA1cmnpx
7. https://www.ikea.com/us/en/cat/pax-system-19086/
8. https://brickfact.com/blog/guidebooks/lego-pick-a-brick-everything-you-need-to-know

9. https://www.nike.com/id/nike-by-you, https://www.forbes.com/
   sites/shelleykohan/2021/12/20/customer-engagement-drives-
   nike-profits-up-16/?sh=4a7efdcb1452, and https://www.brushyour
   ideas.com/blog/inspiring-examples-brands-offering-product-
   customization/
10. https://www.subarusouthpoint.com/dealership/directions.htm
11. https://www.torquenews.com/1084/forester-only-subaru-score-
    high-jd-power-initial-quality-study
12. https://www.torquenews.com/1084/cr-s-6-best-suvs-under-30k-
    one-subaru-model-number-one-overall-pick
13. https://www.ray-ban.com/usa
14. https://configureid.com/2021/09/21/get-inspired-with-these-6-
    brands-winning-at-product-customization-examples/
15. https://www.comparably.com/brands/ray-ban
16. https://yoursustainableguide.com/is-forever-21-fast-fashion/ and
    https://www.news.com.au/finance/business/retail/fast-fashion-
    retailer-forever21-has-copped-criticism-for-a-controversial-post-
    on-instagram/news-story/057b2e6da117954e9ad37d2a49a1f387
17. https://medium.com/swlh/why-forever-21-failed-a85f64c4a7c4
18. https://www.zmescience.com/feature-post/culture/culture-
    society/nestle-company-pollution-children/#Baby_Formula_
    and_Boycott
19. https://www.ethicalconsumer.org/company-profile/nestle-
    sa#:~:text=Nestl%C3%A9%20was%20also%20marked%20
    down,alongside%20PepsiCo%20and%20Coca%2DCola.
20. https://www.theguardian.com/environment/2019/oct/29/the-
    fight-over-water-how-nestle-dries-up-us-creeks-to-sell-water-in-
    plastic-bottles
21. https://www.zmescience.com/feature-post/culture/culture-
    society/nestle-company-pollution-children/
22. https://palmoildetectives.com/2021/02/09/nestle/
23. https://waste-management-world.com/materials/the-top-
    plastic-polluters
24. https://www.tesla.com/modelx/design#overview
25. https://www.topspeed.com/what-makes-tesla-model-x-
    unreliable/
26. https://axleaddict.com/cars/Common-problems-with-the-
    Tesla-Model-X
27. https://www.castusglobal.com/insights/how-starbucks-missed-the-
    mark-in-australia#:~:text=Fundamentally%2C%20Starbucks%20
    struggled%20in%20Australia,to%20the%20local%20Australian%20
    tastes and https://www.youtube.com/watch?v=_FGUkxn5kZQ

28. Ibid.
29. https://www.forbes.com/sites/frederickallen/2011/11/07/the-three-principles-that-always-drove-apple/?sh=7ea3fbd914a3
30. https://www.choicehacking.com/2020/09/03/what-is-simplicity-theory-why-people-prefer-simple-experiences/
31. https://www.nytimes.com/2016/10/12/business/international/samsung-galaxy-note7-terminated.html
32. Ibid.
33. https://hbr.org/2016/10/why-samsungs-note-7-crisis-wont-hurt-its-brand-long-term
34. https://www.statista.com/statistics/249375/us-market-share-of-selected-automobile-manufacturers
35. https://www.investkorea.org/ik-en/cntnts/i-313/web.do
36. https://www.businesskorea.co.kr/news/articleView.html?idxno=115006 and https://www.telecomlead.com/smart-phone/south-korea-aims-to-capture-50-of-global-display-market-110466
37. Federica Laricchia. https://www.statista.com/statistics/1266988/global-leading-manufacturers-tv-market-share-sales-volume/
38. Choong Y. Lee, Daniel Froes Batata, and Ha Sook Kim; "A Comparative Study of Business Strategies Between Korea and Japan: A Case of Electronics Items Between Samsung and Sony," International Journal of Multidisciplinary Research 2, no. 3 (March 2012).
39. Ibid.
40. https://asia.nikkei.com/Business/Automobiles/Chinese-EVs-gain-in-Japanese-automakers-key-markets
41. https://richardkatz.substack.com/p/china-on-track-to-pass-japan-in-auto
42. Ibid. Note: Passenger cars only, no light trucks like SUVs or pick-ups; much of the decline in overall exports in 2020–2022 reflects the shortage of computer chips triggered by COVID-19.
43. Tim Hancock. https://www.bloomberg.com/news/articles/2023-01-26/how-china-is-quietly-dominating-the-global-car-market?embedded-checkout=true
44. https://www.scmp.com/business/china-business/article/3206875/chinas-car-exports-surpass-germanys-after-544-cent-surge-311-million-2022-narrowing-japans-lead?campaign=3206875&module=perpetual_scroll_0&pgtype=article
45. https://oilprice.com/Energy/Energy-General/Chinas-EV-Boom-Has-Sent-Its-Car-Exports-Soaring.html

46. https://www.cascade.app/studies/uber-strategy-study and https://medium.com/hackernoon/uber-s-marketing-strategy-in-7-steps-7638e6a88ac6
47. https://www.uber.com/blog/fill-your-suv-to-ride-free-on-your-birthday/ and https://medium.com/hackernoon/uber-s-marketing-strategy-in-7-steps-7638e6a88ac6
48. https://secondmeasure.com/datapoints/rideshare-industry-overview/
49. https://www.macrotrends.net/stocks/charts/LYFT/lyft/market-cap
50. Tensie Whelan, Ulrich Atz, Tracy Van Holt, and Casey Clark, "ESG and Financial Performance." chrome-extension://efaidnbmnnnibpcaj pcglclefindmkaj/https://www.stern.nyu.edu/sites/default/files/assets/documents/NYU-RAM_ESG-Paper_2021%20Rev_0.pdf
51. https://www.thecaq.org/sp-500-and-esg-reporting
52. The concept of results, which consists of output, outcome, and impact, refers to the OECD explanation.
53. https://www.indexindustry.org/insights/iias-members-highlight-the-rise-of-esg-indexes/
54. https://www.armanino.com/articles/esg-scores/
55. https://www.icaew.com/technical/financial-services/esg-assurance/what-is-esg-and-why-does-it-matter
56. https://quantive.com/resources/articles/what-is-esg
57. https://www.icaew.com/technical/financial-services/esg-assurance/what-is-esg-and-why-does-it-matter
58. https://www.mckinsey.com/capabilities/sustainability/our-insights/does-esg-really-matter-and-why

Chapter 4: The New Perspective of Cost

1. https://www.financecharts.com/screener/biggest
2. https://www.investopedia.com/articles/company-insights/091516/most-profitable-auto-companies-2016-tm-gm.asp
3. https://ijisrt.com/wp-content/uploads/2018/01/Toyota-Production-System-As-A-Benchmark-To-Improve-Business-Productivity.pdf
4. https://www.lean.org/the-lean-post/articles/profit-and-cost-at-toyota/

5. Ibid.
6. https://www.toyota-global.com/company/history_of_toyota/75years/text/taking_on_the_automotive_business/chapter2/section7/item1.html
7. Y. Monden and J. Lee, "How a Japanese Auto Maker Reduces Costs," *Management Accounting* 75, no. 2 (1993): 22–26; P. Horváth and J. Lamla, "Kaizen Costing," *Kostenrechnungspraxis* 40 (1996): 335–340.
8. Based on the idea of Taufik, deputy chairman of M Corp, Jakarta.
9. https://gdforum.sakura.ne.jp/ja/module/prsp/FGeese.htm
10. https://core.ac.uk/download/pdf/6987271.pdf
11. https://www.press.bmwgroup.com/global/article/detail/T0280837EN/20-%1fyears-%1fat-%1fthe-%1fcutting-%1fedge:-%1fbmwconnecteddrive?language=en#:~:text=It%20was%20back%20in%201998,visiting%20the%20BMW%20Connected Drive%20Store
12. https://papers.ssrn.com/sol3/papers.cfm?abstract_id=3576017
13. https://www.autoweek.com/news/green-cars/a36266393/tesla-made-more-money-selling-credits-and-bitcoin-than-cars/

Chapter 5: The New Perspective of Delivery

1. https://www.mckinsey.com/industries/technology-media-and-telecommunications/our-insights/ordering-in-the-rapid-evolution-of-food-delivery
2. https://www.royaleinternational.com/2022/03/top-10-common-causes-of-delayed-deliveries/
3. https://choco-up.com/blog/ecommerce-delivery and https://choco-up.com/blog/ecommerce-delivery
4. https://www.mckinsey.com/~/media/McKinsey/Industries/Retail/Our%20Insights/Future%20of%20retail%20operations%20Winning%20in%20a%20digital%20era/McK_Retail-Ops-2020_FullIssue-RGB-hyperlinks-011620.pdf
5. Ibid.
6. Ibid.
7. https://www.cnbc.com/2023/07/31/amazon-says-its-delivering-more-products-than-ever-in-one-day-or-less.html
8. https://www.ups.com/assets/resources/media/Saturday-Ground-Commercial-Infographic.pdf

9. https://www.supplychainbrain.com/articles/14912-impact-of-late-or-inaccurate-deliveries-can-be-disastrous-study-shows
10. https://www.hollingsworthllc.com/how-late-deliveries-impact-customer-retention/
11. https://en.wikipedia.org/wiki/DHL
12. https://www.maersk.com/about/our-history/the-founding-family
13. https://www.fastcompany.com/90847727/most-innovative-companies-logistics-2023
14. To understand further about mesh technology, please visit **https://about.ups.com/us/en/our-stories/innovation-driven/ups-s-vaccine-tracking-technology.html**
15. Ibid.
16. Alan Rushton, Phil Croucher, and Peter Baker, *The Handbook of Logistics and Distribution Management*, 5th ed. (The Chartered Institute of Logistics and Transport, 2014), pp. 83–84.
17. https://www.universalcargo.com/a-brief-history-of-logistics/
18. https://financesonline.com/the-role-of-technology-in-modern-fleet-management/
19. https://www.forbes.com/sites/theapothecary/2015/12/09/explaining-the-decline-fall-and-possible-rebirth-of-doctors-house-calls/?sh=df297f7384d5
20. https://investor.id/lifestyle/288433/penggunaan-telehealth-2021-naik-30, https://www.alodokter.com/about and https://mediaindonesia.com/humaniora/475399/alodokter-catat-pengguna-layanan-telemedisin-meningkat-30-di-2021
21. https://dailysocial.id/post/alodokter-perkenalkan-asisten-virtual-telekonsultasi-alni
22. Y. Chen, R.H.L. Chiang, and V. C. Storey, "Business Models for Ride-Hailing Services: A Comparative Analysis," *Journal of Service Management* 26, no. 5 (2015): 725–743.
23. https://www.smartcitiesdive.com/news/taxi-companies-ride-hailing-competitition/551449/
24. https://www.commercegate.com/the-rise-of-online-banking/
25. https://www.ad-ins.com/digital-banks-and-traditional-banks-their-differing-qualities/#:~:text=The%20most%20striking%20difference%20between,operate%20and%20provide%20their%20services
26. https://www.moodybank.com/news/post/digital-banks-vs-digital-banking-with-traditional-banks and https://www.tcafcu.org/wecanhelp/
27. https://link.springer.com/chapter/10.1007/3-211-32710-X_55
28. https://www.mcdonalds.com/us/en-us/mcdelivery.html

29. https://www.businessinsider.com/why-uber-launched-uber-eats-2016-3 and https://www.investopedia.com/articles/personal-finance/111015/story-uber.asp
30. https://sarimelatikencana.co.id/summary-brand.php?id=3
31. https://www.dhl.com/global-en/home/press/press-archive/2018/dhl-introduces-new-technologies-and-delivery-solutions-in-us-to-meet-evolving-demands-of-the-urban-consumer.html and https://supplychaindigital.com/technology/dhl-piloting-range-new-tech-meet-evolving-customer-demands, and https://supplychaindigital.com/technology/dhl-piloting-range-new-tech-meet-evolving-customer-demands
32. https://sell.amazon.com/blog/amazon-fba-for-beginners
33. https://golocad.com/shipping/economy-shipping/
34. Ibid.
35. https://goshippo.com/blog/ups-ground-shipping-for-e-commerce-business-what-you-need-to-know#:~:text=What%20is%20UPS%C2%AE%20Ground,truck%20rather%20than%20by%20airplane
36. https://www.bringg.com/blog/dispatching/scheduled-delivery/
37. https://www.fedex.com/en-us/delivery-manager.html#how
38. https://www.bringg.com/blog/delivery/the-on-demand-delivery-experience/
39. Ibid.
40. https://www.aboutamazon.com/news/amazon-prime/amazon-same-day-delivery
41. https://www.bringg.com/blog/logistics/green-logistics/
42. Ibid.
43. https://headsup-dc.org/adapting-to-extreme-climate-change-poses-a-challenge-to-many-farmers/
44. https://2sistersstorteboom.com/about-us/storteboom/ and https://doi.org/10.1109/icpre55555.2022.9960450
45. https://www.dhl.com/discover/en-us/about-dhl/dhl-stories/your-path-to-greener-credentials
46. Ibid.
47. https://aklogisticsandsupplychain.com/2020/03/02/1pl-2pl-3pl-4pl-5pl-6pl-the-advancement-of-party-logistics/
48. https://supplychaintechnews.com/index.php/technology/benefits-of-real-time-big-data-analytics-for-supply-chain-management-in-2023
49. https://biofriendlyplanet.com/green-logistics-strategies-for-eco-friendly-shipping/

Chapter 6: The New Perspective of Service

1. https://industryforum.co.uk/wp-content/uploads/sites/6/2015/07/QCD.pdf
2. https://ligsuniversity.com/blog/introduction-to-service-marketing#:~:text=There%20are%20four%20characteristics%20of,Kotler%20and%20Keller%2C%202007
3. https://www.researchgate.net/publication/225083670_A_Conceptual_Model_of_Service_Quality_and_its_Implication_for_Future_Research_SERVQUAL
4. https://en.wikipedia.org/wiki/Service_blueprint
5. https://www.singaporeair.com/saar5/pdf/Investor-Relations/Financial-Results/News-Release/nr-q4fy2223.pdf
6. https://hbr.org/1997/01/the-four-faces-of-mass-customization
7. https://journals.sagepub.com/doi/10.1177/1094670515591316
8. https://www.staward.org/past-winners/njn8kpcckm7tdulhfuregut19pv2tg

Chapter 7: Creativity and Innovation in the New Operational Excellence

1. https://news.samsung.com/global/samsung-spotlights-sustainability-efforts-at-galaxy-of-impact
2. https://news.samsung.com/global/bespoke-home-life-3-creating-more-sustainable-product-lifecycles-for-bespoke-appliances-their-users-and-the-planet
3. https://news.samsung.com/global/sustainable-practices-samsungs-eco-friendly-efforts-towards-a-better-tomorrow
4. https://news.samsung.com/global/samsung-electronics-announces-new-environmental-strategy
5. https://www.bcg.com/publications/2022/innovation-in-climate-and-sustainability-will-lead-to-green-growth
6. https://www.forbes.com/sites/johnkoetsier/2023/01/14/samsung-beats-ibm-apple-intel-google-for-2022-patent-crown-56-of-us-patents-go-to-foreign-firms/?sh=5fa7dd0e1891

7. https://www.wipo.int/edocs/pubdocs/en/wipo_pub_2000_2022/kr.pdf
8. https://www.bloomberg.com/news/articles/2021-02-03/south-korea-leads-world-in-innovation-u-s-drops-out-of-top-10#xj4y7vzkg
9. https://www.statista.com/statistics/1314374/south-korea-samsung-groups-revenue-as-a-share-of-gdp/
10. https://www.statista.com/statistics/1323082/south-korea-revenue-of-major-chaebols-as-percentage-of-gdp/
11. https://www.koreaobserver.net/2014/03/fans-brave-cold-weather-to-watch-k-pop.html
12. Euny Hong, *The Birth of Korean Cool: How One Nation Is Conquering the World Through Pop Culture* (Picador, 1994).
13. https://annyeongoppa.com/2019/11/18/your-guide-to-complete-hallyu-experience-in-south-korea/
14. https://martinroll.com/resources/articles/asia/korean-wave-hallyu-the-rise-of-koreas-cultural-economy-pop-culture/
15. Joseph S. Nye, *Soft Power: The Means to Success in World Politics* (PublicAffairs Books, 2005).
16. https://koreajoongangdaily.joins.com/2023/03/12/opinion/columns/Kpop-Kculture-Hallyu/20230312200322387.html
17. Sunmi Son and Thongdee Kijboonchoo, "The Impact of Korean Wave on the Purchase Intention of Korean Cosmetics of Thai People in Bangkok and Chonburi, Thailand," *PSAKU International Journal of Interdisciplinary Research* 5, no. 2 (July–December 2016). https://ssrn.com/abstract=3042116
18. https://www.lg.com/global/green-product-strategy
19. https://www.hyundai.news/eu/focus-topics/sustainability/sustainable-solutions.html
20. https://www.forbes.com/sites/ginaheeb/2021/03/11/coupang-the-amazon-of-south-korea-just-became-the-largest-foreign-ipo-on-wall-street-since-alibaba-heres-what-you-need-to-know/?sh=68c1d6e2b0a6
21. https://www.aboutcoupang.com/English/news/news-details/2022/Rocket-Delivery-Building-the-future-of-sustainable-commerce/default.aspx
22. https://www.iea.org/articles/the-potential-of-behavioural-interventions-for-optimising-energy-use-at-home
23. https://www.adb.org/publications/creative-productivity-index-analysing-creativity-and-innovation-asia
24. https://www.acledabank.com.kh/kh/eng/ff_overview
25. https://www.acledabank.com.kh/kh/eng/md_ln20230914

26. https://clevertap.com/blog/how-airasia-and-muuv-labs-personalize-in-real-time/
27. https://newsroom.airasia.com/news/successful-digital-transformation-underpins-airasias-sustainability-achievements#gsc.tab=0
28. https://jollibeegroup.com/news/jollibee-set-on-capturing-local-european-market-expands-customer-base-beyond-filipinos/
29. https://jollibeegroup.com/news/jollibee-group-reinforces-environmental-sustainability-across-its-supply-chain/
30. https://www.brandinginasia.com/thailand-joins-japan-in-the-top-10-creative-countries-ranking-according-to-gunn-report/
31. https://campaignbrief.com/ogilvy-thailand-ranks-1-in-asia-in-the-campaign-brief-asia-2023-creative-rankings-see-the-full-ranking-of-asias-197-hottest-creative-agencies/
32. https://www.thaiunion.com/en/about/company/award-and-recognition
33. https://www.thaiunion.com/en/blog/sustainability/546/tracing-traceability
34. Philip Kotler, Hermawan Kartajaya, Hooi Den Huan, and Jacky Mussry, *Entrepreneurial Marketing: Beyond Professionalism to Creativity, Leadership, and Sustainability* (Wiley, 2023).
35. https://blog.smu.edu.sg/academic/schools-libraries/smulkcsb/is-asia-creatively-challenged/

Chapter 8: Entrepreneurship and Leadership in the New Operational Excellence

1. https://www.worldbank.org/en/news/press-release/2023/05/03/ajay-banga-selected-14th-president-of-the-world-bank
2. https://www.forbes.com/sites/ronakdesai/2018/04/25/a-growing-number-of-indian-americans-are-leading-americas-best-business-schools/?sh=7892f5ca6f63 and https://www.siliconindia.com/news/business/8-indian-deans-at-worlds-top-bschools-nid-135460-cid-3.html
3. https://hbr.org/2014/03/are-ceos-really-indias-leading-export
4. https://www.hindustantimes.com/books/excerpt-the-made-in-india-manager-by-r-gopalakrishnan-and-ranjan-banerjee/story-btrwQGKtaKd8wykWLu5HxN.html

5. https://www.hindustantimes.com/trending/elon-musk-finds-list-of-indian-origin-ceos-of-global-companies-impressive-101693135595788.html; https://www.hindustantimes.com/world-news/list-of-highest-paid-ceos-in-the-united-states-who-are-of-indian-origin-101689905035265.html; and https://www.investopedia.com/10-top-indian-ceos-7487331

6. https://www.worldometers.info/world-population/population-by-country/ and https://www.statista.com/statistics/262879/countries-with-the-largest-population/

7. https://www.morganstanley.com/ideas/investment-opportunities-in-india

8. https://www.worldbank.org/en/country/india/overview

9. https://www.ey.com/en_in/tax/economy-watch/india-towards-becoming-the-third-largest-economy-in-the-world

10. https://hbr.org/2023/09/is-india-the-worlds-next-great-economic-power

11. R. Gopalakrishnan and Ranjan Banerjee, *The Made-in-India Manager* (Hachette UK, 2018) and https://timesofindia.indiatimes.com/blogs/voices/the-secret-sauce-behind-the-rise-of-indian-origin-ceos/

12. https://indianexpress.com/article/education/engineers-day-2023-iits-history-rankings-iitmadras-delhi-bombay-guwahati-kanpur-roorkee-kharagpur

13. https://indianexpress.com/article/education/engineers-day-2023-iits-history-rankings-iitmadras-delhi-bombay-guwahati-kanpur-roorkee-kharagpur-8940285/

14. https://www.vedantu.com/jee-advanced/iit-colleges-in-india

15. https://www.universityworldnews.com/post.php?story=20220827085440234

16. https://restofworld.org/2023/iit-graduates-dominate-tech/

17. https://tracxn.com/d/startups-by-alumni/iit-delhi-alumni/CuSC0Y1sZZgTP7oTm-11xLAyGbQ_7R570kBADv5-PSk

18. https://restofworld.org/2023/iit-graduates-dominate-tech/

19. https://www.infosys.com/about.html

20. https://www.infosys.com/investors/reports-filings/annual-report/annual-reports/ar-2022-23.html

21. https://www.indiatimes.com/worth/news/infosys-only-indian-company-in-time-100-best-companies-2023-list-615066.html

22. https://www.infosys.com/services/engineering-services/service-offerings/sustainability-practice.html

23. https://www.infosys.com/newsroom/press-releases/2023/recognized-worlds-most-ethical-companies.html

24. https://www.infosys.com/services/engineering-services/service-offerings/sustainability-practice.html
25. Philip Kotler, Hermawan Kartajaya, Hooi Den Huan, and Jacky Mussry, *Entrepreneurial Marketing: Beyond Professionalism to Creativity, Leadership, and Sustainability* (Wiley, 2023).
26. Katarzyna Piwowar-Sulej and Qaisar Iqbal, "Leadership Styles and Sustainable Performance: A Systematic Literature Review," *Journal of Cleaner Production* 382 (2023).
27. Philip Kotler, Hermawan Kartajaya, Hooi Den Huan, and Jacky Mussry, *Entrepreneurial Marketing: Beyond Professionalism to Creativity, Leadership, and Sustainability* (Wiley, 2023).
28. https://hbr.org/2011/11/why-don't-we-try-to-be-indias-most-respected-company
29. https://www.vinamilk.com.vn/en/development-history
30. https://www.vinamilk.com.vn/en/sustainable-development
31. https://www.vinamilk.com.vn/bao-cao-thuong-nien/bao-cao/2022/download-file/Vinamilk%20Annual%20Report%202022.pdf
32. https://www.acesawards.com/stories/sustainability/viet-nam-dairy-products-jsc-vinamilk/
33. https://www.hshgroup.com/en/about/corporate-profile
34. https://www.hshgroup.com/-/media/Files/HSH/Sustainability-Reports/2022/2022-CRS-initiatives-at-a-glance-EN_online
35. https://www.hshgroup.com/en/sustainable-luxury/sustainability-reports
36. https://www.kornferry.com/insights/this-week-in-leadership/leadership-shortage-hr-survey
37. https://www.strategy-business.com/article/00178

Chapter 9: Productivity and Improvement in the New Operational Excellence

1. https://hbr.org/2011/06/how-toyota-pulls-improvement-f
2. D. R. Kiran, *Work Organization and Methods Engineering for Productivity* (Butterworth-Heinemann, 2020).
3. https://www.toyotauk.com/about-toyota/history-of-toyota

4. https://www.toyota-global.com/company/history_of_
   toyota/75years/data/overall_chronological_table/1941.html
5. https://www.britannica.com/topic/Toyota-Motor-Corporation
6. https://fortune.com/company/toyota-motor/global500/
7. https://www.reuters.com/article/idUST138986/ and https://www
   .toyota-global.com/company/history_of_toyota/75years/data/
   overall_chronological_table/2001.html
8. https://www.toyota.co.id/en/sustainability/environment-
   initiatives
9. https://pressroom.toyota.com/10-ways-toyotas-environmental-
   impact-is-driving-sustainability-forward/
10. Ibid.
11. https://www.toyota.com/electrified-vehicles/
12. https://history.state.gov/milestones/1945-1952/japan-
    reconstruction
13. https://www.usnews.com/opinion/blogs/world-report/2014/
    06/06/the-lessons-from-us-aid-after-world-war-ii
14. https://leanfrontiers.com/the-history-of-twi-training-
    within-industry/
15. https://econreview.berkeley.edu/the-japanese-economic-miracle/
16. https://www.britannica.com/money/topic/economy-of-Japan
17. Kiran, *Work Organization and Methods Engineering for Productivity.*
18. R. Clark, *The Japanese Company* (Yale University Press, 1979).
19. Donald W. Katzner, "Explaining the Japanese Economic Miracle," *Japan and the World Economy* 13, no. 3 (August 2001): 303–319.
20. https://kadence.com/why-gen-z-values-sustainability-tips-for-
    marketing-to-the-eco-conscious-generation/
21. https://www.weforum.org/agenda/2022/03/generation-z-
    sustainability-lifestyle-buying-decisions/
22. https://insight.kellogg.northwestern.edu/article/the-case-for-
    investing-in-green-companies
23. https://money.usnews.com/investing/stock-market-news/
    slideshows/best-green-stocks-to-buy
24. https://www.ft.com/partnercontent/fujitsu-reimagine/the-rise-
    of-sustainable-productivity.html
25. https://deming.org/explore/pdsa/
26. https://asq.org/about-asq/honorary-members/deming
27. https://www.telenor.com/about/our-companies/asia/
    grameenphone-bangladesh/
28. https://www.oecd.org/derec/adb/Bangladesh-Grameenphone-
    Project.pdf

29. https://www.gobicashmere.com/us/blogs/culture/exploring-the-wonders-of-gobi-cashmere-a-behind-the-scenes/
30. https://www.gobicashmere.com/us/blogs/home/gobi-cashmeres-commitment-to-sustainable-luxury/
31. https://www.dentiste-oralcare.com/brand/
32. https://www.dilmah.com.au/dilmah-tea-company/dilmah-company-profile.html
33. https://www.dilmahtea.com/sustainability/environmental/research-and-development.html
34. https://www.forbes.com/sites/forbesbusinesscouncil/2023/07/25/innovation-or-improvement-the-most-important-philosophical-distinction-in-business/?sh=4d5d83aa6362 and https://www.ihi.org/communities/blogs/whats-the-difference-between-innovation-and-improvement

Chapter 10: Professionalism and Management in the New Operational Excellence

1. https://www.channelnewsasia.com/commentary/lee-kuan-yew-100-birth-anniversary-founding-prime-minister-nation-building-3767001
2. https://www.gfmag.com/global-data/economic-data/richest-countries-in-the-world
3. https://databankfiles.worldbank.org/public/ddpext_download/hci/HCI_2pager_SGP.pdf
4. https://country.eiu.com/article.aspx?articleid=252864608&Country=Singapore&topic=Business&subtopic=Business+environment&subsubtopic=Rankings+overview
5. https://www3.weforum.org/docs/WEF_GCR_Report_2011-12.pdf
6. Collated by Centennial Asia Advisors using CEIC database and various sources, 2012 figures.
7. https://www.emeraldgrouppublishing.com/archived/learning/management_thinking/articles/singapore_airline.htm%3FPHPSESSID%3Dracer3edvfkmf6gql7bcto2p56%26%26nolog%3D85620

8. J. Wirtz, L. Heracleous, and N. Pangarkar, *Managing HR for Service Excellence and Cost Effectiveness at Singapore Airlines* (Gabler EBooks, 2007). https://doi.org/10.1007/978-3-8349-9544-5_18

9. https://jochenwirtz.com/wp-content/uploads/2021/04/Case-Singapore-Airlines-by-Jochen-Wirtz_2016.pdf

10. https://jochenwirtz.com/wp-content/uploads/2021/04/Case-Singapore-Airlines-by-Jochen-Wirtz_2016.pdf

11. https://www.changiairport.com/corporate/about-us/our-belief.html#qualityservicemanagement

12. https://www.researchgate.net/publication/347714549_The_Success_behind_the_World's_Best_Airport_The_Rise_of_the_Changi

13. https://lpi.worldbank.org/sites/default/files/2023-04/LPI_2023_report_with_layout.pdf

14. https://www.haulio.io/blog/singapores-maritime-success-how-will-digitalisation-game-change-port-logistics-future/

15. https://sjsutst.polsl.pl/archives/2020/vol106/107_SJSUTST106_2020_Mindur.htm

16. https://dr.ntu.edu.sg/bitstream/10356/100669/2/ABCC-2001-003.pdf

17. https://www.prosperity.com/globe/singapore

18. https://www.mof.gov.sg/images/librariesprovider2/infographics/2022/opportunities-for-all.png

19. https://www.skillsfuture.gov.sg/AboutSkillsFuture

20. https://www.mof.gov.sg/singapore-public-sector-outcomes-review/citizens/opportunities-for-all-at-every-stage-of-life/quality-jobs

21. https://www.mof.gov.sg/images/librariesprovider2/infographics/2022/Quality-and-Sustainable-Living.png

22. Ibid.

23. https://www.mof.gov.sg/singapore-public-sector-outcomes-review/businesses/strong-and-resilient-economy/economy-and-labour-market

24. Ibid.

25. https://tablebuilder.singstat.gov.sg/table/CT/17806

26. Thum Ping Tjin, "Explainer: Inequality in Singapore," New Naratif (New Naratif, April 28, 2023).

27. https://www.adb.org/sites/default/files/publication/863591/sin-ado-april-2023.pdf

Chapter 11: The Yin-Yang Advantage

1. https://spice.fsi.stanford.edu/docs/introduction_to_the_cultural_revolution
2. https://spice.fsi.stanford.edu/docs/introduction_to_the_cultural_revolution
3. https://www.imf.org/external/pubs/ft/issues8/index.htm
4. https://www.wipo.int/edocs/pubdocs/en/wipo_pub_2000_2022/cn.pdf
5. Ibid.
6. https://power.lowyinstitute.org/countries/china/
7. Ibid.
8. https://documents1.worldbank.org/curated/en/839401593007627879/pdf/Chinas-Productivity-Slowdown-and-Future-Growth-Potential.pdf
9. https://www.csis.org/analysis/made-china-2025
10. World Bank, "China's Productivity Slowdown and Future Growth Potential," Policy Research Working Paper (2020).
11. William Yat Wai Lo, "The Concept of Greater China in Higher Education: Adoptions, Dynamics and Implications," *Comparative Education* 52, no. 1 (2016): 26–43.
12. Harry Harding, "The Concept of 'Greater China': Themes, Variations, and Reservations," *The China Quarterly* 136 (December 1993): 660–686.
13. https://eh.net/encyclopedia/economic-history-of-hong-kong/
14. https://www.imf.org/external/pubs/ft/fandd/1997/09/pdf/husain.pdf
15. https://www.imf.org/external/pubs/ft/fandd/1997/09/pdf/husain.pdf
16. Hong Kong, China. *Annual Digest of Statistics*. (1997). https://www.imf.org/external/pubs/ft/fandd/1997/09/pdf/husain.pdf
17. https://www.britannica.com/place/Macau-administrative-region-China#ref93744
18. https://www.imf.org/external/pubs/ft/fandd/1997/09/pdf/husain.pdf
19. Other sectors include insurance; bank and securities; transport, storage, and communications; hotel and restaurant; wholesale and retail; construction; industrial production; and other services. https://www.sciencedirect.com/science/article/pii/S0264275117308995#fn0005
20. Terance J. Rephan, Margaret Dalton, Anthony Stair, and Andrew Isserman, "Casino Gambling as an Economic Development Strategy," *Tourism Economics* 3, no. 2 (1997).

21. **https://www.sciencedirect.com/science/article/pii/ S0264275117308995#fn0005**
22. William R. Eadington, "The Economics of Casino Gambling," *Journal of Economic Perspectives* 13, no. 3 (1999): 173–192.
23. Ibid.
24. **https://milkeninstitute.org/sites/default/files/reports-pdf/ Recapturing-the-Taiwan-Miracle.pdf**
25. Suzanne Berger and Richard K. Lester, *Global Taiwan: Building Competitive Strengths in a New International Economy* (Routledge, 2005); Chao-Cheng Mai and Chien-Sheng Shih, *Taiwan's Economic Success Since 1980* (Edward Elgar Publishing, 2001).
26. Thomas B. Gold, *State and Society in the Taiwan Miracle* (Routledge, 1985).
27. **https://focus.cbbc.org/the-rise-and-rise-of-tencent/**
28. Tencent's official site. **https://www.tencent.com/en-us/index.shtml**
29. **https://www.dealstreetasia.com/stories/tencents-pony-ma-asian-tech-spaces-new-warren-buffett-84993**
30. Marc Gunther, "Why Warren Buffett Is Investing in Electric Car Company BYD," Fortune (April 13, 2009). **https://web.archive.org/web/ 20090427114106/** and **https://money.cnn.com/2009/04/13/technology/ gunther_electric.fortune/**
31. **https://asia.nikkei.com/Business/Automobiles/China-s-BYD-breaks-into-world-s-top-10-automakers-with-EV-push**
32. CNN News. **http://www.rationalwalk.com/?p=1376**
33. **https://wenku.baidu.com/view/f02878da50e2524de5187e32.html?_ wkts_=1695964143565&needWelcomeRecommand=1**
34. Jane P. Wu and Ya-Ting Kuo, "Successful Entrepreneurship and Innovative Strategies in China: The Experience of BYD," *International Journal of Business & Technology Leadership* (2012).
35. **https://hbr.org/2021/04/how-xiaomi-became-an-internet-of-things-powerhouse**
36. Yan-Hong Liu and Xiao-Wen Jie, "Exploring Haidilao Service Creativity: The Perspective of Maslow's Hierarchy of Needs," *Proceedings of the 2017 2nd International Conference on Humanities and Social Science*, Shenzhen, China (Atlantis Press, 2017), pp. 534–538.
37. **https://www.forbes.com/sites/kylewong/2018/11/29/what-brands-can-learn-about-customer-experience-from-hot-pot-chain-hai-di-lao/?sh=6516086bbc47**
38. **https://www.cfr.org/backgrounder/china-climate-change-policies-environmental-degradation#:~:text=China%20is%20 the%20world's%20top,and%20invest%20in%20renewable%20 energy**

39. https://www.globalcarbonproject.org/
40. https://www.weforum.org/agenda/2018/04/china-is-going-green-here-s-how
41. https://www.mckinsey.com/cn/our-insights/our-insights/seven-segments-shaping-chinas-consumption-landscape
42. https://www.adb.org/sites/default/files/publication/543276/eawp-017-population-aging-economic-consequences-prc.pdf
43. https://www.worldbank.org/content/dam/Worldbank/document/China-2030-complete.pdf

Epilogue

1. IFRS is an abbreviation for International Financial Reporting Standards. As an organization, the IFRS Foundation is a nonprofit and public interest organization established to develop high-quality, understandable, enforceable, and globally accepted accounting and sustainability disclosure standards. Please refer further to **www.ifrs.org**.

Appendix A: The Omnihouse Model

1. The content of Appendix A was written based partly on the Prologue and Chapter 1 of the book *Entrepreneurial Marketing: Beyond Professionalism to Creativity, Leadership, and Sustainability* (Wiley, 2023), written by Philip Kotler, Hermawan Kartajaya, Hooi Den Huan, and Jacky Mussry.

Appendix B: Inner Development Goals

1. https://www.sdgfund.org/mdgs-sdgs
2. https://static1.squarespace.com/static/600d80b3387b98582a60354a/t/6272f730e54fa847d7db62f5/1651701552398/IDG%E2%80%93Who+We+Are+220426.pdf
3. https://www.innerdevelopmentgoals.org/
4. https://static1.squarespace.com/static/600d80b3387b98582a60354a/t/61aa2f96dfd3fb39c4fc4283/1638543258249/211201_IDG_Report_Full.pdf

Appendix C: Humane Entrepreneurship

1. Zong-Tae Bae, Myung-Soo Kang, Ki-Chan Kim, and Ji-Hoon Park, "Humane Entrepreneurship: Theoretical Foundations and Conceptual Development," *The Journal of Small Business Innovation* 20 (2018): 11–21.
2. B. Talim, *In a Meaningful Change in Small and Medium Scale Enterprise: Human Entrepreneurship Approach* (International Council for Small Business, 2019).
3. H. Kartajaya, "Humane Entrepreneurship." International MSMEs Day 2018, Jakarta Indonesia (June 2018).

Appendix D: Marketing ZEN

1. https://www.mktgzen.com/en/what-is-marketingzen
2. https://www.linkedin.com/pulse/let-me-introduce-you-power-marketing-zen-shinji-tanaka/
3. https://www.amazon.co.jp/-/en/%E5%AE%8D%E6%88%B8%E5%B9%B9%E5%A4%AE-ebook/dp/B0BY199NBB/ref=sr_1_1?crid=39LE2U0MMI9LU&keywords=The+Power+of+Marketing+ZEN&qid=1697909107&s=english-books&sprefix=the+power+of+marketing+zen+%2Cenglish-books%2C266&sr=1-1-catcorr

About the Authors

Philip Kotler is professor emeritus of marketing at the Kellogg School of Management, Northwestern University, where he held the S.C. Johnson & Son Distinguished Professor of International Marketing. He is one of the world's leading authorities on marketing, widely regarded as the "father of modern marketing," recipient of numerous awards and honorary degrees from schools around the world, and voted as the Number 1 Guru in Management in the list of Top 30 Gurus of Management (2022). The *Wall Street Journal* ranks him among the top six most influential business thinkers. He holds an MA from the University of Chicago and a PhD from MIT, both in economics. Philip has an incredible international presence—his books have been translated into more than 25 languages, and he regularly speaks on the international circuit.

Hermawan Kartajaya is the founder and chairman of M Corp and was named by the United Kingdom's Chartered Institute of Marketing on the list of 50 Gurus Who Have Shaped the Future of Marketing. He received the Distinguished Global Leadership Award from the Pan-Pacific Business Association at the University of Nebraska–Lincoln. He is also the chairman of the Asia Committee for Small Business and a cofounder of the Asia Marketing Federation. He was the president of the World Marketing Association (2002–2006). Hermawan has been the thought leader and coauthor of 13 trade books with Philip Kotler since 1998.

Jacky Mussry is the deputy chairman at M Corp and chief executive officer at MarkPlus Institute, where he helps many companies design corporate and marketing strategies and their training programs. He is also lecturing at several prominent universities in Indonesia, in addition to being active as a writer and speaker. He obtained his master's degree in marketing management and a doctorate in strategic management from the Faculty of Economics and Business, University of Indonesia.

Index